The Modern Presidency

Second Edition

James P. Pfiffner
GEORGE MASON UNIVERSITY

ST. MARTIN'S PRESS
NEW YORK

For E. John Pfiffner, godfather, uncle, artist, friend
and for Morgan Meehan Pfiffner, my son

Sponsoring editor: Beth A. Gillett
Manager, Publishing services: Emily Berleth
Senior editor, Publishing services: Douglas Bell
Project management: York Production Services, Inc.
Senior production supervisor: Dennis J. Para
Photo research: Joyce Deyo
Cover design: Evelyn Horovicz
Cover art: Ralph Mercer

Library on Congress Catalog Card Number: 97-80009

Manufactured in the United States of America

3 2 1 0 9 8
f e d c b a

For information, write:

St. Martin's Press, Inc.
175 Fifth Avenue
New York, NY 10010

ISBN: 0-312-17804-2 (paperback)
0-312-21015-9 (hardcover)

Acknowledgments
Table 8–2: Presidential Reputation. (Schlesinger Poll, 1962, 1996) The *New York Times*, July 29, 1962, pp. 12ff, and December 15, 1996, pp. 46–51. Copyright © 1962, 1996, by The New York Times Company. Reprinted by permission. (Maranell Accomplishment Poll 1970) *Social Science Quarterly*, September 1970, p. 418. (U.S. Historical Society Poll 1977), from pp. 338–339 in *The American President*, 4th ed., by Robert E. DiCierico. Copyright © 1995. Adapted by permission of Prentice-Hall, Inc., Upper Saddle River, NJ. (*Chicago Tribune* Poll 1982) from *U.S. News & World Report*, January 25, 1982, p. 29. Copyright © 1982 U.S. News & World Report. (Murray Poll 1982) from *Journal of American History*, December 1983 and Arthur B. Murphy, "Evaluating Presidents of the United States" from pp. 437–448 in *The American Presidency* by David C. Kozak and Kenneth N. Ciboski. Copyright © 1985 by David C. Kozak and Kenneth N. Ciboski. Reprinted with permission of Nelson-Hall Publishers.

Contents

Preface

In 1933, Franklin Roosevelt had only a few aides to help him draft and shepherd into law his famous "100 Days" legislative agenda. In 1997 there were more than 400 people in the White House Office, 1,800 in the Executive Office of the President (which includes the White House Office), and a total of more than 3,500 serving the president and the White House more broadly. In the 1930s, there were fewer than 150 presidential appointees to manage the executive branch. In 1992 there were more than 600, and many more if part-timers were included. In the 1930s and 1940s, the aides to the president were most often generalists. In the 1990s, the presidency comprised a congeries of complex bureaucracies filled with specialists.

This book was written to try to explain how we got here from there. As an introduction to the presidency, it does not attempt to describe or explain all aspects of the office. Rather, its purpose is to focus on the transformation of the presidency from a small group of advisors to a large collection of bureaucracies supporting the president. Thus, the emphasis is not so much on the president as a person but on all of the supporting people and institutions; what some have called the "presidential branch," to distinguish it from the rest of the executive branch over which the president presides.

In analyzing the transformation of the modern presidency, the book considers the changes in the nomination/election process as the citizenry has become more involved through primary elections. The president's relationship to the public has also been transformed through sophisticated presidential use of modern communications technology. The techniques and institutions of White House communications are analyzed.

The book is based on the premise that advisors, organization, and institutions make a difference. If the presidency is well organized, the president is more likely to be successful. Poor administration can lead to blunders or disaster. Separate chapters are devoted to organizing the White House staff and choosing whether to appoint a chief of staff or operate on a more collegial basis. The book traces the institutionalization of White House functions in the Executive Office of the President and explains the gradual replacement of Cabinet secretaries by White House staffers as the primary advisors to the president.

The president still must deal with Congress, which has sufficient power to frustrate presidential intentions, particularly during periods of divided government (when the two branches are controlled by different political parties). Two chapters deal with presidential relations with Congress and examine more and less effective ways to promote the president's agenda in the domestic and national security arenas.

Finally, the problems of abuse of power and presidential reputation are considered. The modern presidency has seen disturbing instances of overreaching by presidents and examples of changing presidential reputation.

This book has benefited from the generosity of others. I would like to thank Don Reisman, who originally proposed the idea to me, for his enthusiasm and encouragement. Thanks also to Ron Geisler, executive clerk to the president since 1981, and his staff for helping me to understand the operation of the presidency, particularly the appointments process. My colleagues Paul Baker and Jane Long were generous in their research support. Louise White, chair of the department of public and international affairs at George Mason University, helped me considerably with my teaching schedule.

For encouragement and help in writing the second edition of *The Modern Presidency,* I would like to thank Beth Gillett of St. Martin's Press. Several scholars reviewed the draft of the second edition and made helpful comments: Cary R. Covington, University of Iowa; Kenneth R. Greene, Fairleigh Dickinson University; William D. Pederson, Louisiana State University at Shreveport; and Shirley Anne Warshaw, Gettysburg College. Ms. Deborah A. Stone copyedited the manuscript with professional skill. For helpful criticisms of the first edition, I would like to thank several colleagues: James Carter, Robert Cleary, Robert Dudley, and Katie Dunn Tenpas, as well as Martin Rooney, an insightful undergraduate student who caught some errors that all of the professionals missed. Tim Saunders succeeded his former boss, Ron Geisler, as Executive Clerk to the President and generously continued to provide me with authoritative data on the presidency and the White House. I am grateful to Thomas Mann, Director of Governmental Studies at the Brookings Institution, who found an office for me as a Guest Scholar while I was on leave from George Mason. Brookings was a congenial place for me to work on the second edition; and my colleagues there provided helpful advice and intellectual stimulation: Sarah Binder, Chris Foreman, Jacob Hacker, Stephen Hess, Pietro Nivola, Bob Katzman, John Kingdon, Allen Schick, Kent Weaver, Joe White, Margaret Weir, as well as Tom Mann. Fellow Guest Scholars Bruce Oppenheimer and John E. Owens spent some time helping me understand the dynamics of Congress, which I appreciate. Susan Stewart provided professional administrative support, and Judy Light created a warm atmosphere that makes Brookings the wonderful home for scholars that it is.

Finally, I would like to express my appreciation for the love and support from my wife, Deb, throughout the writing of this book and for the past eighteen years. I am also grateful for the careful attention of our children, Megan Cyr, Katherine Courtney, and Morgan Meehan, who made sure that I did not become too lonely when I was writing in my office.

James P. Pfiffner

About the Author

James P. Pfiffner is professor of government and public policy at George Mason University and teaches courses in doctoral, masters, and undergraduate programs. He has also taught at the University of California, Riverside, and California State University, Fullerton. He was a Research Fellow and has been a Guest Scholar at the Brookings Institution. He received his Ph.D. in political science at the University of Wisconsin, Madison, in 1975.

His research specialties are the presidency, American national government, and public management. His seven books on the presidency include *The Strategic Presidency: Hitting the Ground Running; The President, the Budget, and Congress: Impoundment and the 1974 Budget Act;* and *The Managerial Presidency* (edited).

He has been on project staffs of the National Commission on the Public Service (the Volcker Commission), the Center for Strategic and International Studies, and the National Academy of Sciences; he is a member of the National Academy of Public Administration. He has lectured widely in the United States and Europe on American Government and regularly briefs visiting foreign officials on the structures and processes of the presidency and the U.S. political system.

He received the Distinguished Faculty Award at George Mason University in 1990, and in 1970 he was awarded the Army Commendation Medal for Valor in Vietnam and Cambodia.

President William Jefferson Clinton delivers his second inaugural address after being sworn in for his second term by Supreme Court Chief Justice William Rehnquist on January 20, 1997. (AP/Wide World Photos/Wilfredo Lee)

One

THE PRESIDENCY: ORIGINS AND POWERS

The American presidency has undergone an amazing transformation in the last half of the twentieth century. Presidency scholars distinguish between the "traditional presidency," from 1788 to 1933, and the "modern presidency," from 1933 to the present.[1] The metamorphosis began with the presidency of Franklin Roosevelt and his presiding over major historical developments in the United States and the rest of the world through four elections.[2] The Roosevelt era marked the transformation of the presidency from a small, personalized office to a collection of specialized bureaucracies with hundreds of professional staffers. This book will examine the major elements of the modern presidency with special attention to the causes and consequences of the transformation from the traditional to the modern presidency.

Three broad themes will be explored. Chapters 1 and 2 will examine the changing relationship between the president and the American people. The presidency is now much more closely linked to the people through their right to vote in primary elections. But even more striking is the familiarity people feel with the chief executive because they see the president on television virtually every day of the year. Chapters 3, 4, and 5 will trace the growth of the presidency, its institutionalization, and its increasing control of the executive branch. Finally, Chapters 6, 7, and 8 will explore the limits on presidential power inherent in the separation of powers system and how the balance between the two branches of government has shifted over the course of the modern presidency.

---

[1]See Fred I. Greenstein, "Nine Presidents in Search of a Modern Presidency," in Greenstein, ed., *Leadership in the Modern Presidency* (Cambridge, MA: Harvard University Press, 1988), pp. 296–352. See also John Hart, *The Presidential Branch* (New York: Pergamon Press, 1987); Malcolm Shaw, ed., *The Modern Presidency: From Roosevelt to Reagan* (New York: Harper & Row, 1987). Some scholars have also argued that we have entered an era of the "postmodern presidency." See, for example, Richard Rose, *The Postmodern President,* 2d ed. (Chatham, NJ: Chatham House, 1991); and Ryan Barrileaux, *The Post-Modern Presidency: The Office After Ronald Reagan* (New York: Praeger, 1988).

[2]Fred I. Greenstein, "Change and Continuity in the Modern Presidency," *The New American Political System* (Washington, DC: American Enterprise Institute, 1978), pp. 451–481.

Franklin Roosevelt's twelve years in office saw the Great Depression challenge the newly industrialized nation and threaten the viability of a capitalist economy that had become one of the most powerful in the world. After weathering the depression, the U.S. economy was jolted into high production by the demands to mobilize for World War II. When the war ended, the United States assumed world economic leadership, helped design Japan's postwar recovery, and with the Marshall Plan, invested huge amounts of capital to rebuild Europe. The United States came out of the war as leader of the victorious allies and the sole possessor of the awful power of the atomic bomb.

The experience of the Great Depression led the U.S. public to demand a more positive governmental approach to the economy, and the Employment Act of 1946 embodied those expectations. The country modified the laissez-faire doctrine of minimal entanglement of government policy with the economy and determined to smooth out the economic cycles of boom and bust. The National Security Act of 1947 created a unified Department of Defense, a Joint Chiefs of Staff, and the Central Intelligence Agency. The national security policy institutions that would deal with the coming Cold War, as well as several hot wars, were in place by 1950. The domination of the world by the two superpowers and the aspirations of the emerging lesser-developed nations transformed international relations. At the same time, communications technology made possible instantaneous worldwide communication and provided the ability to reach mass audiences through radio and television.

These historic changes in international relations and technology were reflected in the office of the presidency. Just as the world would never be the same after the Great Depression, World War II, and the advent of modern communications, neither would the presidency. As the office adapted to the new realities of the mid-twentieth century, the capacity of the presidency to lead a much larger national government had to be enhanced. But the changes of the 1930s and 1940s merely laid the groundwork for the full development of the modern presidency. Since then the institutional capacity of the office has been transformed beyond the dreams of Franklin Roosevelt.

The Framers' deliberations over the nature of the presidency demonstrated their desire not only to avoid the dangers of executive tyranny (such as King George III) but also to moderate the potential for legislative extremism (such as inflating the money supply). They created an executive office that balanced legislative power but that was, because of the electoral college, removed from the people. One of the primary dynamics of American history over two centuries has been the creation of more direct links between the president and the public, beginning with the transformation of the presidential selection process.

The nominating system has been changed from a process dominated by political parties to one driven by primary elections. The proliferation of primaries led to the development of candidate-centered election organizations that raise their own money and conduct their own campaigns. Political parties, which used to dominate presidential politics, are now clearly subordinate to presidents and presidential candidates. But the rise of the candidate-centered organization and the relative decline of political parties has made the process of governing much more difficult. Presidents must knit together their own governing coalitions rather than depend on traditional party coalitions.[3] Presidential elections have been democratized over the past two centuries, with a much broader definition of citizenship than the Framers envisioned. But presidential election outcomes are still subject to the constitutional constraints of the electoral college. Modern presidents have also made deliberate use of modern communications technology to appeal directly to voters and to circumvent the traditional intervening filters of reporters and opinion leaders. The democratization of the presidency and the development of White House capacity to exploit the new communications technologies will be explored in Chapter 2.

As the size and complexity of the government grew, so did the dependence of the president on a more professional White House staff. The White House staff has done more than grow in size from a few informal, generalist aides to FDR to the highly specialized and bureaucratized White House Office of more than 500 staffers of the 1990s. The White House staff now has the capacity, in terms of expertise and power, to initiate policy in all areas of presidential concern. It even has the capacity to carry out presidential priorities, which has been valuable at times but also can lead to trouble for the president.

The transformation of the White House can be illustrated by comparing the contemporary White House bureaucracy with FDR's White House. According to Joseph Alsop:

> There literally was no White House staff of the modern type, with policy-making functions. Two extremely pleasant, unassuming, and efficient men, Steve Early and Marvin McIntyre, handled the president's day-to-day schedule and routine, the donkey-work of his press relations, and such like. There was a secretarial camarilla of highly competent and dedicated ladies who were led by "Missy" LeHand. . . . There were also lesser figures to handle travel arrangements, the enormous flow of correspondence, and the like. But that was that; and national policy was strictly a problem for the president, his advisors of the moment (who had constant access to the president's office but no office of their own in the White House), and his chosen chiefs of departments and agencies.[4]

The growth in White House staff since FDR has been both a boon and a bane to presidents. Presidents now have the ability to do things in the White House that used to be done in other agencies in the executive branch (e.g., foreign

---

[3]See Lester G. Seligman and Cary R. Covington, *The Coalitional Presidency* (Chicago: Dorsey Press, 1989).

[4]Joseph Alsop, *FDR: 1882–1945, a Centenary Remembrance* (New York: Washington Square Press, 1982), pp. 92–93.

policy, trade policy, legal advice) or by political parties (e.g., personnel recruitment or public liaison).

The White House staff is now so large that it needs a formal, hierarchical organization. The argument of Chapter 3 is that ever since the growth of the White House staff under Richard Nixon, the president has needed a chief of staff to organize the White House. But the corollary to that lesson is that a chief of staff who attempts to control too much (e.g., Sherman Adams, H. R. Haldeman, Donald Regan, or John Sununu) will lead to major problems, if not disaster.

While the large White House staff gives presidents a depth of policy and political advice that was not available before, it does not guarantee the quality of that advice. A large staff also creates the danger that White House aides will go off on their own, doing what they imagine is in the president's best interest. Without careful monitoring, this extended White House staff can lead to disaster as it did in the Watergate and Iran–Contra affairs.

The increase in governmental programs and the large number of agencies created during the New Deal resulted in a fragmented system that FDR tried to rein in through the proposals of the Brownlow Committee for more presidential power. The long-term result of the Brownlow proposals was an increasingly centralized capacity to control the executive branch from the White House; a trend that increased in momentum after 1960.

The offices and procedures that presidents created in the 1950s and 1960s soon became institutionalized. Elements of this include an elaborate and more centralized national security apparatus, an enhanced office of communications, a large legal counsel's office, a professionalized Office of Presidential Personnel, a legislative liaison capacity, and others. This growth in capacity has occurred because presidents do not want to depend on the rest of the executive branch for advice. They want immediate responses from people they trust implicitly, and they want the capacity available in the White House, not in cabinet departments.

But this capacity has set the presidency apart from the rest of the executive branch, over which the president presides as chief executive officer. Scholar Nelson Polsby argues that the single most important development during the modern presidency has been "the transformation of the American presidency from a position of leadership of the executive branch to the centerpiece of what can now sensibly be called a separate and distinct branch of government—the presidential branch."[5] In this new manifestation of the presidency it "sits *across* the table from the executive branch at budgetary hearings, and . . . imperfectly attempts to coordinate both the executive and legislative branches in its own behalf."[6]

This "presidential branch" includes the White House Office and the Exec-

---

[5]Nelson Polsby, "Congress, National Security, and the Rise of the Presidential Branch," in Howard Shuman and Walter Thomas, eds., *The Constitution and National Security* (Washington, DC: NDU Press, 1990), p. 202.

[6]Nelson Polsby, "Some Landmarks in Modern Presidential-Congressional Relations," in Anthony King, *Both Ends of the Avenue* (Washington, DC: American Enterprise Institute Press, 1983), p. 20.

utive Office of the President (EOP). Chapter 4 examines these units in general and traces the development of several subunits in the EOP. The original purpose of these offices in the presidency was to coordinate executive branch policy and provide expert advice to the president. But as the offices became institutionalized, presidents came to depend on them as tools to control the expanding executive branch. Once an office was created to perform certain important functions, the performance of those functions persisted across presidential administrations. Regardless of changes in name, the offices have grown in staff resources and importance, and it is argued that contemporary presidents are not free *not* to have these functions performed. They are essential to the operation of the contemporary presidency. This increased EOP capacity has given presidents the opportunity to shape the national agenda and initiate policies as never before, but it has also created a large bureaucracy that must be policed so that it is doing what the president wants and no more.

The cabinet, from Washington's time on, has traditionally been the primary advisory body to the president. Chapter 5 analyzes the president's cabinet and how its influence has declined in recent decades. While different presidents have used their cabinets to a greater or lesser extent, all presidents have called cabinet meetings to ask advice and to communicate with their top appointees. Cabinet secretaries, being the top-line officers of the government, are legally in charge of their departments and have broad leeway in carrying out the priorities of their presidents' administrations. But in the 1960s and 1970s, presidents began to centralize policy control in the White House and relegated cabinet secretaries to a distinctly subordinate role as compared with the previous 150 years of the Republic. While the relationship of some cabinet secretaries to their presidents has enabled them to maintain their traditional relative independence, most cabinet secretaries now must accept the fact that they will enjoy little access to the president and that White House staffers will probably have more influence over policy in their areas of jurisdiction than they have.

The cabinet as a deliberative body has lost its role as primary adviser to the president, but cabinet secretaries still play important roles in the presidency. Each administration also depends on the quality of the hundreds of presidential appointees in the subcabinet. Chapter 5 examines the recruitment of these appointees and their often uneasy relationship with the career civil servants who implement the laws and carry out the president's directives.

To deal with the economic crisis of the Great Depression, Franklin Roosevelt used his first 100 days in office to push through Congress a series of laws that began the New Deal. This presidential leadership and congressional cooperation in major policy changes was unprecedented in scope and volume. The president would henceforth be the country's chief legislator. In contrast to the traditional presidency, each president now has an annual legislative agenda and a professional legislative liaison team in the White House. Chapter 6 examines how this operation grew from a one-person specialty in the late 1940s to a fully professionalized office in recent decades, and more generally examines the relationship between the president and Congress. While the president can take some actions independently, most of the major policy initiatives of any administration require congressional action. After examining the constitutional and political fundamentals of this relationship, the chapter looks at what presidents can do to maximize their chances of winning congressional approval of their legislative proposals. Most of the time during the second half of the twentieth century interbranch relations endured the frustrations of divided government; that is, when one political party holds the presidency and the other controls one or both houses of Congress. The conclusion of the chapter is that, despite presidential domination of the executive branch, and often of the national agenda, Congress still plays a major balancing constitutional role.

The constitutional designation of the president as commander in chief of the armed forces has made the president the primary national leader in national security policy throughout the history of the Republic. The president's national security role was enhanced by the Cold War and the National Security Council (NSC) staff in the White House. The role of Congress, never preeminent in foreign policy, was further reduced by the president's new capacity. The president's power, however, was balanced by the congressional authority to declare war.

Chapter 7 examines the war power in the modern presidency and the shift of power toward the president, to the point where President Bush argued that he did not need congressional approval to initiate war in the Persian Gulf. In addition to increasing claims to constitutional powers, the presidency has had, beginning in the 1960s, the capacity in the White House NSC staff to coordinate and dominate national security policymaking, sometimes to the partial exclusion of the State and Defense Departments. The domination of the war power by the president, however, has not precluded active congressional intervention in other areas of defense and foreign policy.

In Chapter 8, the book turns to the potential for corruption and abuse of power in the White House. The Framers were acutely aware of the dangers of the corrupting temptations of power; they believed Lord Acton's axiom that power corrupts. Since those holding governmental power are not angels, the Framers designed a government in which each branch would have the motive and necessary means to resist any undue concentration of power in another branch. There have been instances of corruption at high levels in the U.S. government, but this chapter examines the two most dangerous scandals: the Watergate incidents that led to President Nixon's resignation and the Iran–Contra affair of the Reagan administration. The results of each of these scandals were mitigated by the countervailing actions of the Congress in its investigations of the executive branch.

The negative consequences of these incidents on the reputations of the two presidents involved leads into a discussion of the public approval and historical reputations of the modern presidents. In some cases, contemporary public approval and historical reputation are in general agreement. In other cases, presidential reputations undergo reevaluation several decades after their terms in office. The historical reputations of Presidents Truman and Eisenhower have each improved markedly in recent decades. The reasons for these vagaries of presidential reputation are explored.

The book ends with the observation that, encouraged by the overpromising of presidential candidates, voters have come to hold high expectations of how effective presidents can be in solving very complex social and economic problems facing the country. When these high expectations are not met, as they seldom are, citizens can easily become cynical. If citizens would have more realistic expectations and presidential candidates would moderate their promises, we might have a better appreciation of the possibilities of presidential leadership in a limited government of separated powers.

ORIGINS OF THE PRESIDENCY

The Framers' ideas about executive power were heavily influenced by the colonial experience and their familiarity with European history. The lessons they drew from this experience led them to distrust executive power, at least when it was unchecked. They suspected that any chief executive, if unfettered, would likely degenerate into tyranny.

The experience under King George III and his colonial governors was not a happy one for the colonists, who finally revolted against British control. Many of the royal governors abused their powers and gave short shrift to the colonial assemblies who represented the new settlers. The British monarch did not endear himself to the colonists when he imposed oppressive taxes, one of which led to the Boston Tea Party. The Declaration of Independence declared: "The history of the present King of Great Britain is a history of repeated injuries and usurpations, all having in direct object the establishment of an absolute Tyranny over these States."

This experience might have led the Framers to create a Constitution that severely restrained executive power and gave most governmental powers to a legislative body. The reason that this did not happen was their experience during the Articles of Confederation period. Neither the performance of the Continental Congress nor of the state assemblies was entirely satisfactory in the judgment of the Framers.

Because of the fear of tyranny, most states had dominant legislatures and weak executives who were chosen by the legislatures for one-year terms and who were often constrained by an executive council. This led to inefficient state governments that occasionally abused their powers and threatened property rights or inflated the money supply.

But perhaps more important in the Framers' minds was the immediate experience with the weak central government under the Articles of Confederation. The national government was run by the Continental Congress but had no independent executive. Each state had between three and five delegates to the one-house legislature, who could exercise one vote per state. The powers of the central government were restricted to those that were clearly national, including the authority to conduct war, make foreign policy, negotiate treaties, create a postal service, and regulate money. But the ability to make foreign policy was put at risk when Great Britain threatened to negotiate the end of the Revolutionary War with each state, independently, rather than with the central government.

The power to regulate money was limited by the central government's inability to impose taxes on the states; it could merely assess charges against the states but could not force payment. The national debt was increasing and the economy was doing poorly, but the states often refused to recognize each other's currency and imposed tariffs on goods coming into one state from the others. These were serious problems that the central government did not have the authority or power to solve. Contributing to all of these difficulties was the lack of an independent executive to take vigorous action to address any of the problems.

Thus, when delegates from five states met in Annapolis to deal with the problem of trade among the states they decided to propose a broader convention, and the Continental Congress decided to call a convention in May 1787 in Philadelphia. When the Framers met in the Constitutional Convention in May 1787 they brought with them a shared ambivalence about executive power, but most were convinced that the governing structure of the states had to have a stronger executive than either the separate states or the central government had up to that point. Some Framers were suspicious of an executive with too much power, and all were leery of popular opinion in the states, which was still very hostile to executive power because of the colonial experience. They knew they wanted an executive office that would provide more coherent leadership than they had under the Articles of Confederation, but they did not want to create an executive that would degenerate into a tyranny.

The initial Virginia Plan that was favored by the large states provided for an executive, but not a strong one. The executive could be one or several persons and would be chosen by the legislature. James Madison had come to favor a stronger executive to offset potential abuse by a legislature. According to Madison, "the legislative department is everywhere extending the sphere of its activity and drawing all powers into its impetuous vortex. . . . Executive powers had been usurped."[7] Alexander Hamilton even favored an elected president who would be a virtual monarch with lifetime tenure and the title of "His Excellency."

The level of power of a chief executive would depend on several factors, including: the number (single or plural), how chosen (by the legislature or pop-

---

[7] *Federalist* No. 48.

ular election), length of term, reeligibility for office, and of course the formal powers granted to the office by the Constitution. James Wilson of Pennsylvania favored a strong executive for reasons of efficiency and effectiveness: "a single magistrate" would provide the "most energy, dispatch, and responsibility to the office."[8] But the first reaction of the convention to his proposal was not enthusiasm but a "considerable pause." George Mason, however, feared that if a single person were given the executive power he would abuse it. "If strong and extensive powers are vested in the Executive, and that Executive consists only of one person; the Government will of course degenerate into a Monarchy."[9] Edmund Randolf of Virginia saw Wilson's plan as "the Foetus of Monarchy."[10] But after a heated debate, a single executive was decided upon on August 6.[11]

One way to make the chief executive strong and independent of the legislature would be to mandate selection by popular vote. The Framers, however, were distrustful of anything so democratic as having the people (as limited as was the electorate at that time, excluding women, blacks, and the propertyless) choose the chief executive. They felt that such important decisions should be limited to men of character and good breeding. George Mason expressed their suspicion of democracy: "It would be as natural to refer the choice of a proper characteristic for chief magistrate to the people as it would be to refer a trial of colours to a blind man."[12]

The most likely means of choosing the chief executive for most of the summer of 1787 was by the legislature and, when the convention took up the selection question, a vote on August 24 settled on legislative selection of the executive. But the Great Compromise between the large states and the small states had weakened the support for a legislatively selected executive enough to allow for a different method of choice. Under the terms of the compromise the legislature would be separated into two houses, one based on population (House of Representatives), and one with equal representation from each state (the Senate). When the large states had to accept the Senate as a balance to their power in the House they lost their enthusiasm for choosing the executive by the legislature. But when the Convention decided on August 24 upon a joint ballot of all members of the legislature to select the executive, the small states realized that the large states would still have the dominant influence, and their support for legislative selection was weakened. This paved the way for the final compromise that determined the mechanism for presidential selection.

---

[8]Max Farrand, *Records of the Federal Constitution,* Vol. 1 (New Haven, CT: Yale University Press, 1911), p. 65.

[9]Farrand, *Records,* Vol. 1, p. 66.

[10]Farrand, *Records,* Vol. 1, p. 88.

[11]Corwin, *The President,* p. 11.

[12]Farrand, *Records,* Vol. 2, p. 31.

On August 31 the Committee on Unfinished Business took up the issue of selection of the executive. In their deliberations the Congress lost the power to choose the executive, and the Senate also lost the ability to appoint federal judges and ambassadors. The committee settled on a compromise formula for choosing the chief executive: selection by electors who would be selected in each state. The number of electors from each state would be equal to the combined number of representatives and senators of the state. In order to preclude cabals and conspiracies, the electors would not meet together but separately in their states. After voting, the results would be forwarded to the Congress for counting. In order to prevent undue influence of the incumbent government, no member of the national government could be an elector.

To be declared the winner a candidate would have to receive a majority of the votes. Lacking a majority, selection of the president would be made by the House of Representatives voting by state among the top five vote winners (changed to three by the Twelfth Amendment). The Framers expected that the electors would be men of character and good judgment and would not be swayed by popular passions among the people. Nevertheless, many expected that most elections would fail to provide a majority of the electors for one candidate and the president would thus be chosen by the House. George Mason estimated that this would happen nineteen times out of twenty.

The deliberations about the office of the presidency were facilitated by the assumption on the part of all that George Washington, the "citizen king," would be elected as the first president of the Republic. The Framers were thus willing to give the presidency powers that they might have hesitated to grant to the office if they did not know who would be its first occupant.

The electoral college mechanism for choosing the president was a masterpiece of political improvisation and compromise rather than a formula based on any coherent political theory. For those who favored state control or democracy, the plan provided that state legislatures could decide how the electors would be chosen. (Most began with state legislative selection and soon changed to voting by citizens in the states.) The small states were guaranteed at least three votes, but the large states would have more because of their larger delegations to the House. For those who distrusted too much democracy, the electors would be men of good judgment and character. But most importantly for the immediate compromise, all assumed that George Washington would be the first president.

In conclusion, it is important to remember that it was not predetermined or implied in the political theory of the Framers that the president would be chosen by the people. If the convention decision of late August held, the Congress would have chosen the president, considerably weakening the office. The term of office or eligibility for reelection was not settled until the end of the convention. The options considered by the Framers included terms of office of two, three, seven, ten, fifteen, and twenty years, as well as the life term favored by Hamilton, and there were more than sixty votes taken on this issue.[13] If Congress had ended up with the power to select the president, the term of office would likely have been longer. But once it was clear that Congress would not control selection, the Framers settled on a four-year term with eligibility for reelection. The current arrangements for selecting the president have taken on an aura of fixedness that was not at all certain until the closing days of the Constitutional Convention.

In the vision of the Framers, the link between the president and the citizenry was attenuated and indirect. Electors could be chosen by state legislatures or by the limited holders of the franchise. And the House would decide if the electors did not produce a majority. The House was the only unit chosen directly by voters. Senators were to be selected by state legislatures, and judges appointed for life terms by the president.

This outline is a far cry from the twentieth-century vision of democracy in the United States. The franchise has been extended to include African Americans (Fifteenth Amendment) and women (Nineteenth Amendment), and property and literacy tests for voting have been prohibited. Senators are now popularly elected (Seventeenth Amendment), and all states have decided to have presidential electors selected in popular elections. The formal and legal links of the president to the people have been supplemented by even more far-reaching changes in presidential behavior, as we will see in the next chapter.

POWERS OF THE PRESIDENT

Article II of the Constitution is brief and vague when compared with the many enumerated powers granted to Congress in Article I. The presidential Article begins: "The executive Power shall be vested in a President of the United States of America." But it is not clear whether the "executive Power" is a separate grant of power or merely a designation of the president as head of the executive branch. The president derives much of his power from the execution of the laws (Section 3: "he shall take Care that the Laws be faithfully executed"), since the implementation of most laws necessarily entails a certain amount of discretion.

The commander-in-chief power is a broad grant of power and enables the president to direct the armed forces of the United States at his or her discretion. This power is affected by the power of Congress to declare war, provide for armies and navies, and set rules for their operation. The war power in important cases is, in effect, exercised by the president, as described in Chapter 5. The president has exclusive power to receive ambassadors, which implies the discretion to recognize foreign nations. But his power to appoint ambassadors to those nations is shared by the Senate, which has to confirm those

[13]Thomas E. Cronin, "Presidential Term, Tenure and Reeligibility," in Cronin, ed., *Inventing the American Presidency* (Lawrence: University of Kansas Press, 1989), p. 65.

nominations. The president has the power to negotiate treaties, but the Senate also shares this power by its power to ratify (by a two-thirds majority) or reject them.

The president has the authority to appoint officers of the United States, though the Senate shares the power by its confirmation duty. This power to name the political appointees who head all of the agencies of the executive branch is a significant one, allowing the president to effectively control the executive branch when he chooses, though the power levers of Congress are also significant. The appointment of judges, modified by the Senate's confirmation power, is a powerful tool. The power to appoint judges with lifetime tenure, given the low probability of the Senate to reject judicial appointments, allows the president to cast a long shadow over the interpretation of the laws. The president is also given the judicial power of granting pardons, reprieves, and amnesties. This pardon power is seldom used outside of attempting to right individual wrongs in the judicial system, though it can have a significant political impact, as when President Ford pardoned Richard Nixon for his Watergate actions, when Jimmy Carter granted amnesty to draft resisters of the Vietnam era, or when George Bush pardoned five participants in the Iran–Contra affair.

The president also has the legislative power to veto legislation, though a veto can be overridden by a two-thirds majority of each house. The president can recommend legislation to Congress, give state of the union addresses, and call Congress into special session. But these minimal formal legislative powers have been enhanced by historical development and political circumstance so that the modern president is considered the "chief legislator," a development analyzed in Chapter 5.

Presidential scholar Richard Neustadt[14] has observed that the separation of powers system is not so much a clear division of powers among the branches as it is a system of separate institutions sharing power. Thus, most of the powers granted in the Constitution are not given exclusively to one branch, but are divided among the branches and maintained in a shifting balance, depending on the political and historical circumstances. The congressional power of the purse (to appropriate money) can be affected by a presidential veto and by the power of the executive to actually spend the money (i.e., make contracts and write checks). The congressional war power is affected by the president's commander-in-chief power to deploy troops and order them into hostilities. Each branch's interpretation of its constitutional powers can be affected by the judicial power to interpret the law and the implied power of judicial review, i.e., to declare actions of the other two branches unconstitutional.

Thus, the Framers designed a system of shared powers within a system that is purposefully biased against change. With each branch jealously guarding its prerogatives and powers (ambition must be made to counteract ambition), no

[14]See Richard Neustadt, *Presidential Power and the Modern Presidents* (New York: Free Press, 1990).

one branch can move too far on its own. Thus, an overwhelming consensus must be achieved before both Congress and the president (with the acquiescence of the judiciary) can move together to make major changes in policy or direction of the country. This delicate balance of "parchment barriers" has held up amazingly well over the two centuries of U.S. history. The relative strength of the branches has shifted over the years, sometimes significantly, but the same questions of where the balance ought to lie are debated today in as strikingly similar terms as the debates of the constitutional era.

The real power of the presidency, however, is not so much a matter of formal constitutional powers, though these provide the framework within which presidents operate. The real power of presidents has been affected by the legitimacy provided by the shift to popular voting for president (despite the technical reality of the Electoral College). But historical circumstance and presidential personality have provided the opportunity for presidents to become powerful and have an impact on the history of the country. Those presidents who have been considered powerful and often great have governed the country during times of crisis or major historical change; for example, Washington, Lincoln, Wilson, and Franklin Roosevelt. Some presidents, by force of their personality and political will, have had important impacts on the direction of the country; for example, Andrew Jackson, Theodore Roosevelt, and Ronald Reagan. In addition, the apparatus of the institutional presidency, described in subsequent chapters, gives modern presidents added levers of control.

CONCLUSION

But the reality of the presidency is that, in itself, it is not a powerful office. Because of the power of Congress, presidents who want major change must use the "bully pulpit" to build coalitions of support for their policies. Richard Neustadt characterized presidential power as "the power to persuade." That is, presidents cannot command obedience to their wishes but must persuade others that their own best interests lie with presidential preferences. This basic reality has become reinforced in the modern presidency by the fragmentation of governmental power. Richard Darman, who worked in the White House during the Reagan presidency and was George Bush's director of the Office of Management and Budget observed:

> I think if we're speaking of "running the government," there's a somewhat simple-minded conception of how power works in the American political system that presumes that presidents have great power. In my opinion, none of the above have great power. Power is highly fragmented, much more than in just the civics text version of separation of powers. Power is dispersed and the effective people are people who can build coalitions where the coalitions represent a critical mass that can move the system.

TOLES © 1993 The Buffalo News. Reprinted with permission of UNIVERSAL PRESS SYNDICATE. All rights reserved.

> But single individuals, whether presidents or anybody else in the system—staff or whatever—simply do not have anything remotely like the power that is presumed to reside in their offices.[15]

It is this fragmentation of power that has prompted modern presidents to use all the tools at their disposal (some legitimate, some not) to centralize power and control in the White House. Yet this centralization of control in the presidency, which is a major theme of this book, has not led to the clear domination of the political system by the president. The countervailing powers of Congress and the pluralistic political system prevent presidents from exercising complete control over the government. The Framers' design still works.

15"Darman Reflects on the Reagan Era," *Washington Post* (April 1987). For Richard Neustadt's analysis, see *Presidential Power and the Modern Presidents* (New York: Free Press, 1990).

Two

THE PRESIDENT AND THE PUBLIC

The relationship between the president and the American public has changed dramatically since the time of the Framers. The Constitution created a republican government; citizens would not govern themselves directly, but rather they would elect representatives to exercise governing power. The Framers were careful not to make links to the people too direct because they were afraid of mob rule and tyranny of the majority. Thus, members of the House of Representatives were the only directly elected public officials in the national government. Judges were appointed for life terms; senators were selected by state legislators; and the president was chosen by an electoral college.

Senators are now directly elected by the people of the states (Seventeenth Amendment), and the electors of the president are also selected by voters in the states. This chapter will trace the democratization of the presidency in the United States in two major areas. First, the changes in nomination and election processes will be examined. The development of political parties early in the eighteenth century gave citizen partisans a greater say in who would be nominated for the presidency. The development of primary elections in the twentieth century, especially the proliferation of primaries after 1968, brought the nomination process under much closer control by rank-and-file voters and took control away from political party elites.

This democratizing trend also weakened political parties and gave way to the growth of a much more personal (rather than party) candidate. Prospective presidential candidates now had to raise their own money and put together their own campaign organizations. Appeals had to be made to the public for support rather than to a small group of party leaders. This increased the importance of television as a medium of political appeal, further weakening the strength of political parties.

These changes in nominating and electing procedures had important impacts on the conduct of the presidency. Presidents could no longer count on automatic and sustained support from their partisans in Congress or from the coalitions that traditionally supported their political parties.[1] They felt the need

[1]See Lester G. Seligman and Cary R. Covington, *The Coalitional Presidency* (Chicago: Dorsey Press, 1989).

to carry into the White House some of the strategies used in their campaigns for nomination and election. The White House thus has developed the institutionalized capacity to reach out to the American public in unprecedented ways and to use sophisticated modern communications technologies.

This chapter will trace these developments by examining first the nomination process and how it changed from the congressional "King Caucus" in the early nineteenth century to the party convention–dominated process over the next century, and finally to the primary-dominated process of the late twentieth century. The emphasis will be on the recent developments of the modern era.

Presidential elections will then be examined with the emphasis on how presidents have come to be seen as the one national leader elected by all of the people, that is, a national voting constituency. The perception of the legitimacy of the presidency residing in popular selection will be contrasted with the constitutional reality of the electoral college. Few citizens are aware of the electoral college provisions of the Constitution, but the possibility for a runner-up in the popular vote becoming president still exists.

Finally, this chapter will take up the effect of these democratizing developments on the conduct of the presidency. The weakening of political parties, combined with advances in modern communications technology, has led presidents to fight for their policy agendas much more by direct appeals to the public rather than by the more traditional tactics of bargaining among Washington elites. The tactic of direct appeal for popular support has been termed "going public" by presidential scholars, and this more active presidential outreach to the public will be examined.

As with other functions of the modern presidency the carrying out of these appeals to the public has been established in the White House and institutionalized in the Office of Communications. Along with communications technology the science of public opinion polling has also had a great impact on the presidency, with White House staffers devoting many hours to obtaining favorable media coverage for the president and to keeping public approval ratings high. The positive and negative aspects of the sometimes obsessive concern with public opinion ratings will be considered at the end of the chapter.

NOMINATING THE PRESIDENT

The Framers provided no formal system for deciding the finalists from whom the electors would choose when they cast their ballots for president. All expected that Washington would be elected first, and they did not foresee the emergence of political parties. They must have assumed that since electors would be men of affairs, they would be familiar with those most qualified to be president and the field would soon be narrowed to a manageable number of candidates.

Opposing political factions, however, soon developed into incipient parties, and Congress split along partisan lines, with the Federalists being opposed by the Republicans. In 1796, the Federalist John Adams was elected president but his supporters among the electors could not agree on his running mate, so his opponent for the presidency, Thomas Jefferson, was the runner-up in electoral votes and thus became vice president.

In 1800, the members of each of the parties in Congress met in caucus to decide who would be the presidential candidate representing their party. Though congressional caucuses were never formalized as nominating mechanisms, they continued to select presidential nominees for the first two decades of the nineteenth century. But as the Federalist party declined and political power began to be decentralized the caucuses began to lose power and legitimacy. In addition, "King Caucus," as it was disparagingly known, was finally discredited by the 1824 election in which Andrew Jackson received the most popular votes, but since he did not receive a majority of the electoral votes, the selection of president was left up to the House of Representatives. When Speaker of the House Henry Clay threw his support behind John Quincy Adams, who had come in second, Adams was elected president and appointed Clay secretary of state.

With the congressional caucus discredited and state-based electors too dispersed to coalesce effectively around a single candidate, the developing political parties began to organize nominating conventions. Beginning in the 1830s, national nominating conventions began to develop as an increasingly formalized mechanism for nominating the person to run for president from each of the parties. Each state's delegation was based on the number of electors to which it was entitled, but the delegates from each state were chosen by the political party leaders in the states with little participation from voters. The convention system developed throughout the nineteenth century as party leaders met to formulate a coherent platform for their candidate to run on and to strike bargains among the various factions of the party.

But the domination of the conventions by the political bosses in the various states led to criticisms that the citizenry was being relegated in selecting the president from among the two candidates chosen by the party bosses and did not have a chance to participate in selecting the candidates. As early as 1878, a petition of nine million signatures declared that "The convention is a small body. Its members vote secretly, and are not held accountable for what they do. . . ."[2] The petition went on to demand that Congress create primary elections in which voters could choose the nominees of their parties.

This pressure for reform was intensified by the progressive movement at the end of the century. By 1912, primaries were being held in twelve states, with 33 percent of Democratic and 42 percent of Republican delegates chosen by primary. The number of states holding primaries remained between twelve and twenty for the next half century, and the number of delegates chosen by the primary method was generally between 35 and 45 percent for the two parties.[3]

---

[2]Quoted in Nicholas von Hoffman, "Conventional History," *The New Republic* (August 26, 1988), p. 26.

[3]Stephen J. Wayne, *The Road to the White House: 1996* (New York: St. Martin's Press, 1996), p. 11.

But primaries in this period never caught on as the most important path to the nomination for the major presidential candidates. The initial enthusiasm for primaries fell off after World War I, in part because they were expensive and turnout by voters was relatively low. But more importantly they were a direct threat to party leaders, who could not control their outcomes. Leading contenders for presidential nominations could ignore them and depend on their reputations with the party leaders to ensure their nomination at the national conventions. Only those candidates who were long shots found the primaries essential to demonstrate that they could win votes. Front-runners felt no need to risk running in them, and only underdogs depended on primaries alone.

In 1952, for example, Senator Estes Kefauver won twelve of thirteen primaries he entered, but Adlai Stevenson, who chose not to run in the primaries, was nominated by the Democratic party. Dwight Eisenhower entered primaries the same year, not because he was an underdog, but to demonstrate that as a popular general who had never been a partisan politician he could also win votes. In 1960, John Kennedy entered the West Virginia primary and was able to defeat Hubert Humphrey, demonstrating that a Catholic could win in a Protestant state. Humphrey summed up the professional politician's attitude toward primaries in 1960: ". . . any man who goes into a primary isn't *fit* to be president. You have to be crazy to go into a primary. A primary, now, is worse than the torture of the rack. It's all right to enter a primary by accident or because you don't know any better, but by forethought. . . ."[4]

But all of this changed after 1968. Forty states had instituted primary elections by 1996, and a much larger percentage of the delegates to the national conventions were determined by primary election: 67 percent of the Democrats and 90 percent of the Republicans by 1996.[5] This revolution in the nomination process came about as a result of a series of reforms that changed the Democratic party and swept Republicans along with them.

The opening shot was the traumatic Democratic convention in Chicago in 1968. The Democratic party was so torn apart by the war in Vietnam that Lyndon Johnson chose not to run for reelection after Eugene McCarthy won 42 percent of the vote in the New Hampshire primary against Johnson's 49 percent write-in vote. Vice President Hubert Humphrey was the party establishment pick to succeed Johnson, but McCarthy and George McGovern were challenging Humphrey from the left in the primaries. Humphrey chose not to run in the primaries, but with the support of the party regulars was able to control the convention and beat back the antiwar insurgents to win the nomination.

Hostility toward the war, along with the frustration of not being able to break the control of the party regulars, incited the Democratic insurgents to de-

---

[4]Quoted by Theodore H. White, *The Making of the President, 1960* (New York: Atheneum House, 1961), p. 104.

[5]Wayne, *The Road to the White House*, p. 11.

mand a reexamination of the nomination process. Senator George McGovern was named to head the commission that came up with a number of proposals to reform the process. The reforms that were proposed and adopted by the Democrats included: the elimination of party leaders being included ex officio as convention delegates; the requirement of written notice of times and places of caucus meetings; and the establishment of quotas for women, young people (under thirty), and African Americans. This was a triumph of the amateurs over the party professionals. Later reform commissions would modify some of these requirements, loosening the quotas and allowing more elected officials as automatic delegates, but the thrust of the reforms transformed the nominating system. Party caucuses had to be open to any member of the party who wanted to participate in them, so the party professionals would no longer be able to dominate the selection process.

The effect of these reforms can be seen in the changed characteristics of the candidates to national party conventions over the years. In 1968, the percentage of women delegates was 13 percent for the Democrats and 16 percent for Republicans. By 1996, the numbers had changed to 57 percent and 39 percent, respectively. In 1968 only 5 percent of the Democratic delegates were African Americans. By 1996, their representation had increased to 21 percent in the Democratic convention and 2 percent in the Republican convention.[6]

As a result of these reforms, many more states replaced caucus conventions with primary elections as a means of choosing delegates to the national party conventions. Since state legislatures decide on state elections, the Republican party had no choice but to go along with changes in state laws that were often taken by Democratic controlled legislatures.

With forty states choosing convention delegates through primary elections rather than caucuses, the nomination system was transformed. Party professionals no longer dominated the selection process. The process was much more open to "outsiders," and the Democrats chose two non-regular party candidates in 1972 and 1976: George McGovern and Jimmy Carter.

The domination of the nominating process by primary elections rather than by party professionals in caucuses and conventions has magnified the importance of early contests, particularly the New Hampshire primary. By state law it must be the first in the nation. When other states moved up their election, New Hampshire moved theirs up even earlier. The reason for its importance is that it is the first electoral contest that candidates face. The earlier Iowa caucuses occasionally play an important role, as they did for Jimmy Carter in 1976 and Gary Hart in 1984, but the New Hampshire contest is the make or break test for many candidacies.[7]

---

[6]Stephen J. Wayne, *The Road to the White House, 1996,* p. 117.

[7]Between 1952 and 1988 no candidate won the presidency without first winning the New Hampshire primary. In 1992 Bill Clinton came in second to Paul Tsongas, but turned the defeat into a boost for his candidacy by arguing that he did much better than expected.

The crucial difference is not only who wins or comes in second or third, but also who performs better than or worse than expected by the media commentators who establish and magnify the conventional wisdom. This was the case when antiwar candidate Eugene McCarthy received 41.9 percent of the vote in 1968: a result that helped convince Lyndon Johnson to withdraw from the race. Many people remember that McCarthy won the primary, but in fact President Johnson received 49.6 percent as a write-in candidate. In 1979, Senator Edward Kennedy challenged President Carter and showed that Carter was vulnerable; Reagan beat Carter in the general election. In 1992, conservative Patrick Buchanan challenged incumbent George Bush and won 36 percent of the Republican votes. The challenge highlighted Bush's vulnerability, and he went on to lose to Bill Clinton in the general election.

The irony is that New Hampshire has about 850,000 eligible voters in a nation of 189 million voters. New Hampshire is not representative of the rest of the nation, with very few African Americans or other minorities and a political culture that is noticeably more conservative than most of the nation. Yet the news coverage of the early contests is so crucial to candidate visibility that it can ignite the candidacy of a long shot or ruin the hopes of a "front-runner." A New Hampshire victory can create momentum that will carry a candidate into the multiple primaries over the next several weeks and build a momentum that is hard to stop.

The preeminent position of New Hampshire as the presidential primary bellwether may have been undercut in 1996. Conservative fundamentalist Pat Buchanan actually beat front-runner Robert Dole 27.2 percent to 26.2 percent, even though Buchanan had little chance to win the nomination and Dole easily outdistanced him in subsequent primaries.

But more importantly, independent actions by a number of states had the result of "frontloading" the primary selection process even further. As states rescheduled their primaries earlier in the season, more delegates became committed earlier. California, the biggest delegate prize, had moved its primary date from June up to March 26 with the hope of playing a decisive role in determining the nominee. But by the previous week in 1996 more than 50 percent of the delegates had been chosen, and Dole was the all but certain winner. After March 26 two-thirds of the convention delegates had been chosen within the previous 44 days.[8] In 1980 and 1984, Reagan was chosen in May and his Democratic opponents in June. In 1988 and 1992, George Bush had been chosen as nominee at the end of April and his Democratic opponents not until June. But in 1996 both candidates had been determined before the end of March.

This increasing frontloading of primaries is seen by many as a problem for several reasons. Frontloading favors those candidates who are already well known and who can raise the most money early in order to saturate the air waves with their ads early in the process. (Though in 1996 Senator Phil Gramm, who had raised $24 million and Steven Forbes who invested $30 million of his own money, proved that money cannot buy the nomination.) With so many delegates committed by

[8] Wayne, *The Road to the White House, 1996,* p. 106.

mid-March, there is less chance for dark horse candidates to attract contributions and press attention.

Thus, there have been several proposals to reform the process by spreading primary elections more evenly over the spring months. This would allow voters more time to evaluate candidates and use their performance in victory and defeat to help them choose the strongest candidates. One possibility would be a "time zone primary" spread over four months in which the time zone to vote first would be rotated each election. But the odds are against reform, in part because elections are governed by state law, and a way would have to be found to allow the political parties to coerce the states into complying with a new schedule. In addition, there is the danger that unintended consequences would upset the electoral strategies of both parties, which are formulated around the present system.

The broader implications of the proliferation of primaries were the weakening of the party system and the rise of the "personal candidate." The road to the White House was no longer exclusively through the political party but included appealing to voters across the nation in primary elections. Those who wanted to win the nomination would now raise their own money and spend many months or years campaigning in the early primary states. Jimmy Carter had spent months in Iowa before most of the electorate knew who he was.

Candidates no longer depend on the political party for funds or expertise in campaigning. They recruit (or are recruited by) professional campaign consultants, who help them devise a strategy and raise campaign money by direct mail to qualify for federal matching funds. The national political party apparatus is now the tool of the winning candidate rather than an independent center of power with which the candidate must cooperate.

While the present primary system is more democratic in the sense that more people get to participate in the selection of the party nominee, critics of the present nominating system argue that the primaries have contributed to the decline of political parties. The important role that parties traditionally play, acting as intermediaries between the voters and the government and presenting coherent alternative governing choices, is now played by the media. Political scientists also argue that, once a president has been elected, the weakening of party ties has meant that members of the president's party in Congress have less incentive to be allies and form a governing coalition, making governing more difficult. Critics of the new primary system also argue that the judgment of party professionals is valuable and is not weighed heavily enough. They argue that party professionals are more likely to be able to judge which nominee will appeal to the general electorate. The primary process, in their opinion, is too prone to produce candidates further toward the extremes in both parties than the centrist candidates who most often win elections.[9]

---

[9]For opinion data showing that convention delegates tend to be further toward the wings of their party than party identifiers in general, see Martin Plissner and Warren J. Mitofsky, "The Making of the Delegates 1968–88," in Stephen J. Wayne and Clyde Wilcox, *The Quest for National Office* (New York: St. Martin's Press, 1992), pp. 154–160.

PRESIDENTIAL ELECTIONS

It was the intention of the Framers that the electors would be people of public affairs who would exercise independent judgment in deciding for whom to cast their ballots for president. Electors would probably be personally familiar with most candidates and would be able to judge the character of the nominees as well as their stands on policy issues. But with the development of political parties and the growth of the country, the procedures for elections began to change.

During the first half of the nineteenth century, property qualifications for voting were gradually eliminated, resulting in virtually universal white-male suffrage. States also exercised their right to determine how electors would be chosen, and by 1832 all states provided for choosing electors by votes of citizens rather than by selection by state legislatures. States also adopted the "unit rule" by which all of the electoral votes from each state would be cast for whichever candidate won a plurality of the popular vote. This winner-take-all practice increased the stakes for any candidate who has a chance to come in first in voting in any given state. This practice helps the large states in particular, where the most electoral votes are at stake. But there is a compensating bias in favor of very small states, all of which have a minimum of three electoral votes.

The constitutional electoral arrangement as designed by the Framers allows for the possibility that a candidate who does not receive the most popular votes (those cast by individual citizens on election day) will end up winning the presidency. This can happen in three different ways:

1. The possibility of several "faithless electors";
2. If no candidate wins a majority in the electoral college, the House of Representatives selects the winner (who does not have to be the winner in the popular election); or
3. A candidate may win a majority of electoral votes without winning the majority of the popular votes.

The problem of the "faithless elector" has not been a serious problem so far. Virtually all electors consider themselves morally bound to cast their ballots for the candidate to whom they are pledged, and there have been fewer than ten faithless electors in our history. Many states have passed laws that are intended to bind electors to vote for their declared candidates, but the constitutionality of such laws has not been tested and would be in serious doubt. But the possibility of faithless electors making the difference in a close election is a very remote possibility.

The second condition is a real possibility; the Constitution provides that if no candidate wins a majority of electoral votes, the president is determined by a vote in the House of Representatives. The House, with one vote per state delegation and provided two-thirds of the states are present, selects the president from the top five electoral vote winners (now the top three). The vote of a majority of all of the states is necessary to elect the president. The House has selected the president twice in our history. In 1800, all Republican electors cast their ballots for Thomas Jefferson and Aaron Burr, creating a tie with neither having a majority. Thus, the election was thrown into the House, despite the general understanding that Jefferson was the presidential candidate. The House was still controlled by the lame-duck Federalists who had been voted out of office but who would not be replaced until March 1801, giving the choice of president to the party that had lost the election. On the first ballot there were actually more votes of individual representatives for Burr than for Jefferson, but each state has only one vote, and eight states voted for Jefferson and only six for Burr. The vote in two state delegations was tied, giving Jefferson a plurality but not a majority of all the states. It was not until the thirty-sixth ballot that some Federalists were convinced to cast blank ballots, allowing Jefferson to be elected president and Burr vice president.[10]

This unexpected circumstance led Congress to pass the Twelfth Amendment to the Constitution providing for separate ballots for president and vice president and also providing that the House would select (by majority of all states, with one vote per state) from among the top three rather than the top five candidates if there were no majority in the electoral college voting. The vice president would be chosen by the Senate (by majority of all senators, one vote per senator) from the top two electoral vote-getters for vice president.

In 1824, the winner of the popular vote was Andrew Jackson, who won ninety-nine electoral votes (and a plurality of the popular votes cast) compared to eighty-four votes for John Quincy Adams, forty-one for William Crawford, and thirty-seven for Henry Clay. In accord with the Constitution and the Twelfth Amendment, the House decided among the top three candidates. Speaker of the House Henry Clay threw his support behind Adams, who was elected president, to the outrage of Jackson. Adams subsequently appointed Clay to be secretary of state, in what many assumed to be a prearranged deal.

The next election in which the winner of the popular votes was not chosen president was the 1876 contest in which Democrat Samuel J. Tilden received 250,000 more popular votes than Republican Rutherford B. Hayes. Tilden had 184 electoral votes to Hayes's 165, with 185 needed for a majority, and it was recognized that ballot fraud was engaged in by both political parties. A commission was established to examine the validity of the disputed electoral votes of several states, and it voted along strictly partisan lines to validate all of the Republican electoral votes. This gave Hayes the one-vote majority needed in the electoral college to win the presidency. Democrats agreed not to further challenge the presidential vote in exchange for an agreement by Hayes to end reconstruction and remove the carpetbag Republican governments from the southern states.[11] This delivery of political power in the South

[10]Wayne, *The Road to the White House, 1996,* p. 15.

[11]Norman J. Ornstein, "Three Disputed Elections," in Walter Berns, ed., *After the People Vote* (Washington, DC: American Enterprise Institute Press, 1992), pp. 40–43.

to the Democrats led to the disenfranchisement of African Americans in the South over the next several decades and the creation of the "solid south" for the Democratic party.[12]

The only election in which a candidate who did not win a plurality of the popular vote was directly elected president by the electoral college occurred in 1888. Democrat Grover Cleveland, the incumbent president, ran about one percentage point behind his Republican opponent, Benjamin Harrison. Harrison won slim majorities of the popular vote in Indiana and New York, allowing him to capture all of their electoral votes and a majority of all electoral votes to win the election despite coming in second in the popular vote count.[13] Cleveland won a plurality by about 95,000 popular votes but received only 168 electoral votes compared with Harrison's 233.

Admittedly these potential constitutional crises have not happened for a long time, and the odds are against them happening in any given presidential election. But the possibility exists that the winner of the popular vote might lose the presidency by losing the large states by narrow margins and winning the small states by large margins. With our contemporary sense of the legitimacy of the popular vote and the norm of one-person-one-vote, this could well create a constitutional crisis. Similarly, if the nominee of one party won a plurality of electoral votes yet lost the election in a House of Representatives controlled by the opposite party, many would question the legitimacy of the decision, despite its clear constitutionality.

While these circumstances might seem remote, we have had some close calls. In 1948 Harry S Truman received 2 million more votes (of 49 million cast) than Republican challenger Thomas Dewey. But if 12,487 votes in Ohio and California had switched, the election would have been thrown into the House, and if 29,294 had switched in California, Ohio, and Illinois, Dewey would have won. In 1960, a shift of fewer than 9,000 votes in Illinois and Missouri (of 69 million cast) would have denied John Kennedy a majority of electoral votes, and a switch of 11,424 in five states would have given the election to Nixon. In 1968, a switch of 53,034 in three states (of 73 million votes) would have thrown the election into the House, which was controlled by Democrats. In 1976, a shift of 9,246 votes in Hawaii and Ohio (of 81 million cast) would have given the election to Gerald Ford, despite Carter's popular vote margin of more than 1.5 million votes.[14]

With numbers like this, some argue that the electoral college system is an accident waiting to happen. Because of this, there have been a number of reforms proposed to change the system. They include:

---

[12]See A. James Reichley, "The Electoral System," in Stephen J. Wayne and Clyde Wilcox, eds., *The Quest for National Office* (New York: St. Martin's Press, 1992), pp. 5–15.

[13]Ibid, p. 13.

[14]These data are from Neal R. Peirce and Lawrence D. Longley, *The People's President* (New Haven, CT: Yale University Press, 1981), pp. 257–258.

- *The automatic plan:* would eliminate the problem of the faithless elector by casting each state's electoral votes automatically for the winner of the popular election, leaving no discretion for individual electors.
- *The district plan:* would give one electoral vote for each congressional district won and the two extra votes to the overall winner of the popular vote in each state.
- *The proportional plan:* would divide the electoral vote in proportion to the popular vote in each state.

These reform proposals, while making some improvements (though not all would consider them improvements) in the system, would not eliminate the major problem: the chance that the runner-up candidate could win the election. The following proposal would:

- *Direct popular election:* whoever received a plurality of the popular votes, as long as it constituted at least 40 percent of the votes, would be elected. If no candidate got 40 percent, there would be a runoff election between the top two contenders.

While these plans have all had political support over the years, and have been heavily represented among the more than 500 proposals introduced in Congress to amend the electoral college process, none of them has garnered enough political support in both Houses of Congress to set the amending process in motion. Some object to the direct-vote plan because they think that it will undermine the federal system, lead to the proliferation of parties, and permit candidates to campaign for regional rather than national support.

Those who prefer to leave the electoral system as it is often argue that the probability is very low that the runner-up in popular votes will be declared president and the possible costs of any significant change in the system are too high. They argue that direct election of the president would undermine the federal system by aggregating votes across state lines and allowing the possibility of a regional candidate to win. They also argue that a direct vote would undermine the two-party system by encouraging third parties to mount candidacies in the hopes of publicizing their causes. But proponents of a direct-vote system argue that the probability of a runner-up becoming president, even if very low, would result in a crisis of legitimacy for the electoral system, and that preventing this possibility is desirable. Proponents of the direct vote argue that federalism will be well enough protected by the Senate, the House, and the states, and a direct election of the president will not affect it negatively. They also argue that a direct vote would not encourage third (or multiple) parties any more than the present system does.[15]

---

[15]For analyses of this issue from different perspectives, see Judith A. Best, *The Case against Direct Election of the President* (Ithaca, NY: Cornell University Press, 1975); and Peirce and Longley, *The People's President*.

In addition to these principled arguments, in a given year either political party may feel that it has an advantage under the existing rules for elections and will resist any basic change in the system. In addition, Americans are loath to make basic constitutional changes, especially when the full consequences of the changes cannot be foreseen. This inertia has prevented many smaller changes in the system, which most people might feel desirable, from being implemented, and will probably prevail until the next close call or crisis, when the American political system will be moved to make some alterations.

Third-Party Presidential Candidates

As it now stands, the electoral system discourages third-party attempts to win the presidency. With votes aggregated by state, all but two of which (Maine and Nebraska use a district system) allocate their electoral votes by the unit rule (winner take all), potential third parties cannot hope to win any electoral votes unless they capture more votes in a state than either of the two major-party candidates. This is difficult to do. The most serious third-party attempt was made by Theodore Roosevelt, who ran again on the Progressive "Bull Moose" party ticket in 1912 and captured 27.4 percent of the popular vote and eighty-eight electoral votes to Woodrow Wilson's 41.9 percent of the vote and 435 electoral votes.[16] The Progressive Robert LaFollette, in 1924, won 16.6 percent of the popular vote and thirteen electoral votes. In 1948, the Democratic party was split when Strom Thurmond led southern Democrats, who opposed Harry Truman's stand on civil rights for African Americans, to form the Dixicrat party to win 2.4 percent of the popular vote and thirty-nine electoral votes. That same year Henry A. Wallace defected from the left of the Democratic party and ran as a socialist, winning 2.4 percent of the popular vote, but no electoral votes because his candidacy was not regionally based.

The next serious third-party attempt was made by segregationist George Wallace, governor of Alabama, who was able to capture 12.8 percent of the popular vote and forty-six electoral votes. Wallace's success in capturing so many electoral votes was due to the concentration of his racist and states' rights appeal in the South, allowing him to win several states. The next significant third-party candidate was John Anderson, a Republican member of Congress from Illinois, who in 1980 wanted to provide a moderate alternative to Ronald Reagan. He ran as an independent, but had to mount ten lawsuits to get his name on the ballot in various states; he was successful in all ten suits and got his name on all fifty state ballots.[17] Anderson's support was national, rather than regional, and he won 6.6 percent of the popular vote, but no electoral votes.

The final vote for third-party candidates is usually below their early support because of the "wasted vote" argument. If it seems certain that they will not capture the presidency, and that a vote for them will not affect the out-

---

[16]Data in Peirce and Longley, *The People's President,* p. 243.

[17]Author's interview with John Anderson, Arlington, VA (August 14, 1992).

come, their supporters cast their ballots for their second choice, one of the two major candidates, who have a better chance of winning. Thus, Wallace's final popular vote of 13.4 percent was significantly less than his peak of support in the polls of 21 percent in September 1968. In June 1980, John Anderson reached a high point of 24 percent in the polls, but captured only one-fourth of that in the general election.[18]

In the spring and summer of 1992 it seemed a third-party candidate had a serious chance to win a significant number of votes; some thought he even had a chance to win the presidency. In February 1992, Texas billionaire Ross Perot announced on a TV talk show that he would run for president if his name was placed on the ballot in all fifty states. Among voters, disaffection with the two major parties was running high, and there was a feeling in the country that "politics as usual" was not solving the major problems facing the nation: a huge national debt and deficits above $300 billion, a sluggish economy with high unemployment, a decaying infrastructure, and a growing underclass. When Perot set up a telephone headquarters he received 6,000 calls of support the first day, and a spontaneous outpouring of support encouraged his candidacy.[19] He promised to confront the budget deficits and end the partisan fighting between the president and Congress.

His candidacy was taken seriously because of his widespread national support and because he could match the spending of the Democrats and Republicans—even outspend them—because of his personal wealth. He promised a "first class" campaign and said he was willing to spend $100 or $200 million on it. In June 1992, he had hired campaign professionals Ed Rollins, who had run Reagan's 1984 reelection campaign, and Hamilton Jordan, who had engineered Jimmy Carter's out-of-nowhere campaign in 1976. He was ahead of both President Bush and probable Democratic challenger Bill Clinton with 36 percent support in national polls.[20]

In July, however, Perot dropped out of the race only to reenter the contest later in the fall. The final vote count gave Perot 19 percent of the popular vote, making him the most serious third-party candidate since Theodore Roosevelt. Because his appeal was national rather than regional, however, Perot did not win any electoral votes with his almost one-fifth of the popular vote. The Perot candidacy—especially the suddenness of his appearance as a serious presidential candidate—demonstrates the weakness of political parties and the vulnerability of the political system to antigovernment and antiestablishment appeals.

The Perot candidacy was reminiscent of the 1923 draft movement enjoyed by Henry Ford. He had the broad-based support of those who felt that he would bring businesslike efficiency to the government. Ford formally pulled out after he won the Michigan primary in 1924. There is an enduring streak in

---

[18]Rhodes Cook, "Perot Positioned to Defy a Past Seemingly Carved in Stone," *Congressional Quarterly Weekly Report* (June 13, 1992), pp. 1721–1729.

[19]Laurence I. Barrett, "Perot Takes a Walk," *Time Magazine* (July 27, 1992), pp. 32–33.

[20]Barrett, "Perot Takes a Walk," pp. 32–33.

American political culture that yearns for a nonpolitician to take over the government and run it on a businesslike basis, someone who would eschew the petty politics of traditional politicians. The problem is that our government of separated powers and the U.S. electoral system are not like businesses. The more serious a candidate becomes, the more bargaining and coalition-building is necessary; and things begin to look like politics as usual.

After his surprisingly strong showing in the 1992 elections, Ross Perot did his best to remain in the public eye. In the fall of 1993 he campaigned against ratification of the NAFTA Treaty but came out second in a debate with Vice President Gore on the topic. Perot decided to institutionalize his political movement, United We Stand America, by establishing "Reform Party" in 1995. Over the next year his supporters succeeded in qualifying the party for the ballot in all fifty states.

Perot proclaimed that "this is not about me" and said, "We're trying to create a situation where if George Washington the Second comes along, he could get on the ballot without going through the Republican Party or Democratic Party meat grinders, the character assassinations, the fund raising. . . ."[21] But few nationally known political figures showed any interest in seeking the new party's nomination, and the closest the Reform Party could come to George Washington the second was Ross Perot. In the Reform Party's "electronic" convention in August, 5 percent of Reform Party members cast ballots, and nominated Perot over his rival, former Colorado Governor Richard Lamm, who complained that he could not get a list of party members for a mailing or even a ballot a week before the voting.[22]

After criticizing public financing of presidential elections and spending more than $60 million of his own money in 1992, Perot decided to accept $29 million in public funds for his 1996 race.[23] Despite Perot's trenchant criticism of the abuses of campaign financing and other problems with the two party system, he was not able to capture the imagination of most voters. Four years after his first presidential campaign he still was unwilling to be specific about the type of campaign finance system he would support or where the budget would have to be cut to bring it into balance.

In the fall election he won 8 percent of the vote (and no electoral votes), respectable for a third-party attempt, but nowhere near the 19 percent he shocked the country with in 1992. The disaffection with the two parties was still there, but his Reform Party turned out to be more of a personal vehicle than a genuine third force in American politics. In 1997, organizational meetings of the new party made it clear that Perot loyalists were still in control of the Reform Party.

---

[21]Sam Howe Verhovek, "Perot as a Political Presence: 1992 All Over Again?" *New York Times* (January 23, 1996), p. A10.

[22]"The Spoiler Returns," *New York Times* editorial (August 20, 1996), p. A18.

[23]Deborah Kalb, "Perot Gets Reform Party Nod," *Congressional Quarterly Weekly Report* (August 24, 1996), p. 2396.

The General Election

Once candidates have run the gauntlet of the primary elections and have been nominated by the national party conventions, they must face the general electorate in campaigning for the presidency. But the characteristics of the general electorate—all voters who will vote in the presidential election—are not the same as the people who vote in primary elections. The American electorate tends to fall into the center of the political spectrum. Most voters do not consider themselves strong Republicans or Democrats, but have a preference for one or the other party, and an increasing number of voters consider themselves independents, with no, or very weak, preferences between the two major parties.

Thus, the candidates that the two parties choose as their standard-bearers are most often in the middle of the political spectrum, and tend to move more toward the middle (ideologically) after the primaries and as the general election approaches. This is a rational strategy for presidential candidates hoping to capture a majority of the votes in most recent elections.

In 1960, Richard Nixon, the sitting vice president, won the Republican nomination, and John F. Kennedy, a young senator from Massachusetts, was the challenger for the Democrats. Nixon emphasized the experience in foreign affairs he had gained in the Eisenhower administration, and Kennedy promised to "get the country moving again" after the Eisenhower years. Kennedy emphasized a strong defense and argued that there was a "missile gap," with the Soviet Union enjoying a distinct advantage (this later turned out not to be true). Both candidates were fiscal conservatives, but Kennedy was clearly more liberal on civil rights and other domestic issues. The campaign was about competence and character, and there was not a sharp ideological difference between the two candidates. This was reflected in the outcome of the election, one of the closest in our history, with Kennedy winning by 114,673, merely .3 percent of the popular vote.[24]

In 1968, Hubert Humphrey was the sitting vice president, and while he might have wanted to distance himself from his administration's policy in Vietnam, Lyndon Johnson would not allow it. Richard Nixon had come back again to capture the Republican nomination, and he said he had a plan to end the war. Even though there were differences about domestic priorities between the old-time liberal Humphrey and the fiscally conservative Nixon, the campaign brought them both to the center of the political spectrum. The result was another close election, with Nixon winning 43.2 percent of the vote against Hubert Humphrey's 42.7 percent (third-party candidate, George Wallace, took most of the rest of the votes).

In 1976, Jimmy Carter ran against the incumbent Gerald Ford, who had replaced Spiro Agnew as Nixon's vice president, and against the Nixon adminis-

---

[24]For vote totals, see Wayne, *The Road to the White House, 1996,* Appendix A, p. 320.

tration and Watergate. Carter projected competence, being a businessman, nuclear engineer, and former naval officer, and he promised honesty in government. There were differences in political values between Carter and Ford, but their fiscal conservativism put both of them close to the middle of the American political spectrum. Again, it was a close election, with Carter receiving 50.1 percent of the vote to Ford's 48.0 percent.

With this rational tendency for political parties to put up presidential candidates who are in the middle of the political spectrum, how can we explain the Republicans' choice of Barry Goldwater in 1964 and the Democrats' choice of George McGovern in 1972? Goldwater was clearly on the right wing of the Republican party in the 1960s. He was much more "hawkish" on Vietnam than was Lyndon Johnson, who was running as the "peace" candidate in the campaign. Goldwater promised "a choice, not an echo," emphasizing that he was not a clone of the Democratic candidate and that there was a clear ideological difference between him and the Democratic nominee. Johnson placed himself in the middle of the political spectrum and won a resounding victory in 1964, becoming president in his own right (61.0 percent to 38.5 percent).

George McGovern challenged Richard Nixon in 1972 from the left wing of the Democratic party. The former World War II bomber pilot had built his national reputation as an antiwar candidate, and he was more liberal on economic and social issues than most voters. The electorate clearly recognized this and gave Richard Nixon an overwhelming victory in the 1972 elections (60.7 percent to 37.5 percent).

How can we explain this seeming irrationality on the part of the two political parties? Goldwater was decisively to the right of the political spectrum and McGovern was clearly on the left; each lost in a landslide. Why didn't the Republicans in 1964 and the Democrats in 1972 nominate more-viable candidates?

The explanation lies in the differing levels of political activism of the general electorate and those who participate in the nomination process. The people who determine the outcome of nominations tend to be political activists who are firmly committed to political ideals. In the Democratic party, these people are most often on the left of the spectrum; in the Republican party, on the right.[25] Goldwater and McGovern were able to activate and energize the "true believers" on their respective ends of the political spectrum to capture the nomination of their parties. The truly committed backers of such candidates are very effective in helping them win nominations. They go to caucus meetings to select national-convention delegates committed to their candidate, or they work to get out the vote for primary elections. Thus, in the fight for the nomination, they have certain advantages over their more moderate opponents.

But once the nominations are over, and the candidates must appeal to the

[25]See Plissner and Mitofsky, "The Making of the Delegates 1968–1988," pp. 154–160.

general electorate, the strategic situation is different. Most voters are not firmly committed to one end of the political spectrum. In addition, many more voters turn out to vote in the general election than in primary elections. As a result, if the winners of nominations do not move quickly toward the middle of the political spectrum, they will likely lose the election. The problem is that candidates who are very liberal or conservative may not want to move to the middle of the spectrum, or might not be able to convince voters that they are indeed moderate, after the nomination campaign.

The 1980 election contest between moderate Jimmy Carter and conservative Ronald Reagan might have turned out differently, but Reagan was able to change his image with the voters and appear much more mainstream than he had in his earlier campaigns. In addition, Carter was saddled with the hostage situation in Iran and had dropped in voter estimation. Reagan won convincingly with 50.7 percent to Carter's 41.0 percent of the vote, with independent John Anderson winning most of the rest of the votes. In 1988 both George Bush and Michael Dukakis held very similar policy views, and Dukakis declared that the campaign was about competence rather than ideology. But in the campaign Bush was able to tar Dukakis with the label of "liberal" and was able to win the election quite soundly, 53.4 percent to 45.6 percent.

In 1992, Bill Clinton carefully presented himself as a moderate Democrat after winning the nomination. After the Republican convention had made appeals to the conservative wing of the Republican party, President Bush distanced himself from the tone of the convention and moved toward the center of the political spectrum. But with an ailing economy and no obvious foreign threat to highlight Bush's foreign-policy experience, Clinton was able to win 43 percent of the popular vote to Bush's 38 percent, with Perot winning 19 percent.

In 1996 President Clinton benefitted from the bimodal nature of the primary electorate. As sitting president he began reelection planning early and preempted challengers from the left of the Democratic Party (especially Jesse Jackson) by adroit political maneuvering and raising huge sums for his campaign war chest. Thus, as the first Democratic president to run for reelection without a challenger in the primaries since 1964, he was able to position himself in the middle of the political spectrum, since the liberal wing of the party had no alternative candidate to vote for in the primaries. In addition, Clinton used the millions he and the Democratic Party raised to begin running TV ads in the summer of 1995; the ads were designed to establish Clinton's image as a moderate who would appeal to the broad middle of the American electorate.

Bob Dole was not so lucky. Even though he was the front-runner and had raised the most money, he had to run to his right so as not to alienate the conservative wing of the Republican Party, particularly the well-financed and effectively organized Christian Coalition. Conservative Republican voters did have alternative candidates on Dole's right, particularly Pat Buchanan, who had beat Dole in the New Hampshire primary. Thus, Dole had to run to his right in the primaries and then scramble back to the center once he had the nomination sewed up. The outcome of the 1996 race did not hinge on the ideological differences between Dole and Clinton, both of whom were in the middle of the spectrum. But the above calculations were important in the ways the two candidates presented themselves to voters early in the election year.

President Clinton won reelections in 1996 because of a number of factors, none of which was evident immediately after the huge Republican victories in the 1994 congressional elections. In early 1995, President Clinton and the Democrats were discouraged after losing both Houses to the Republicans; the House was controlled by Republicans for the first time in forty years.

But Bill Clinton was fortunate because the Republicans overplayed their hand, thinking they had received a mandate to move the country in a sharply conservative direction. When they tried to implement their program by passing a budget that was balanced by cutting sharply a number of programs such as Medicare, environment, and education, President Clinton was able to present himself as the protector of programs that Americans liked, especially Medicare. Clinton's public approval ratings rose and stayed up, while Newt Gingrich and the Republicans were seen as too extreme. (See the case study in Chapter 6 for the details of this turnaround.)

Thus, Bill Clinton went into the 1996 election year much stronger politically than he had been after the 1994 elections. He was able to position himself in the middle of the political spectrum by arguing that he was in favor of family values and personal responsibility. He was also able to argue that he could moderate the extreme policies of the conservatives in Congress led by Newt Gingrich. Since the Cold War was over, Republicans did not enjoy their traditional advantage of being tough on national security issues, and Clinton's major foreign policy initiatives (free trade, intervention in Haiti, and peacekeeping in Bosnia) were successful, or at least not failures. Robert Dole also suffered from the age issue; at 74 he would have been the oldest president to take office had he been elected. In November Clinton won with 49.2 percent of the vote against Dole's 40.7 percent. Ross Perot captured 8.4 percent of the popular vote, less than half of his 19 percent in 1992.

Electoral Trends

The election of 1932 and the popularity of Franklin Roosevelt in the 1930s produced the "New Deal Coalition," which endured into the 1960s. This electoral coalition included the "solid south," blue-collar workers, Catholics, Jews, and others who favored the activist government programs of the New Deal. These political preferences translated into relatively stable party allegiances, with most voters identifying themselves with the Democratic party and a minority with the Republicans. A smaller group considered themselves "independents." Party identification was reasonably stable over people's lives and over the middle decades of the twentieth century. It was relatively easy to predict a person's vote by their party identification. The Democratic advantage did not mean that Democrats always won the presidency, because special circumstances or an attractive Republican candidate could cause Democrats to desert their party and independents to vote heavily for the Republican. One example of this was the popularity of General Eisenhower, who was elected to the presidency in 1952 and 1956.

But the stable party allegiances that characterized the 1930s, 1940s, and 1950s, began to break down in the 1960s. The beginning of the breakup of the Democrats' large margin of preference was marked by arch-conservative Barry Goldwater's unsuccessful presidential campaign in 1964. Even though Goldwater lost in a landslide, his conservativism appealed to the socially conservative and very patriotic South. The South had been solidly Democratic ever since the harsh Republican Reconstruction after the Civil War. The only way for a politician to have any hope of success was to be a member of the Democratic party. Thus, even though the South was very conservative, its political leaders were, predictably, Democrats. In addition, the African-American vote in the South had been solidly Democratic since the New Deal and the Democratic support of civil rights.

Goldwater in 1964, and succeeding conservative Republican presidential candidates, appealed to these traditional conservatives and began the breakup of the solid south. Social issues, such as skepticism about civil rights for African Americans, support of U.S. policy in Vietnam, law and order, and prayer in public schools, all appealed to conservative southern voters. In 1952, 85 percent of southern whites identified with the Democratic party; by 1992 40 percent did. In the 1994 congressional elections, for the first time since reconstruction, Republicans captured a majority of the southern vote. With this decline in Democrats in the south, the Republicans averaged 66 percent of the southern presidential vote from 1972 to 1988, with Democratic candidates not able to win even one southern state in 1984 or 1988.[26]

The breakup of the solid south was only one part of the revolution in electoral politics. Party identification across the country began to change also. The Democrats enjoyed a 47 percent to 27 percent edge in voter identification in 1952, with 22 percent calling themselves independent. Democratic voter identification rose to a high of 52 percent in the LBJ landslide of 1964, but then declined to 36 percent in 1988. The 1952 Republican total of 27 percent dipped to a low of 23 percent in 1972 (in spite of the Nixon landslide) and edged back up to 28 percent in 1988.[27]

But the basic realignment of the electorate that would have signaled an en-

[26]See Earl Black and Merle Black, *The Vital South* (Cambridge, MA: Harvard University Press, 1992), p. 295, and passim; Paul Frymer, "The 1994 Electoral Aftershock: Dealignment or Realignment in the South" in Philip Klinker, ed. *Midterm: The Elections of 1994 in Context* (Boulder, CO: Westview Press, 1996); Stephen J. Wayne, *The Road to the White House, 1996,* p. 84.

[27]See Joseph A. Pika, Zelman Mosley, and Richard A. Watson, *The Presidential Contest* (Washington, DC: CQ Press, 1992), p. 125.

during Republican majority in partisan identification did not occur. The reason was that, in contrast to previous realigning elections (as in 1932), voters did not switch allegiances from one party to another. Instead, those defecting from Democratic ranks began to consider themselves independents rather than Republicans. Those who identified themselves as independent of either party rose from 22 percent in 1952 to 39 percent in 1995.[28] The decline in self-identification with either political party was accompanied by widespread disaffection with both parties. In the summer of 1992, one professional opinion poll indicated that 82 percent of Americans felt that "both political parties are pretty much out of touch with the American people."[29]

The decline in party identification, along with the proliferation of presidential primary elections after 1968, combined to make political party support much less important in presidential elections. Richard Nixon raised most of his own money rather than depend on the Republican party for fund-raising. In the 1968 and 1972 campaigns, he emphasized his own qualifications for office rather than his party allegiance. Neither George McGovern nor Jimmy Carter, though they were Democrats, were closely identified with Democratic party professionals.

In the 1970s and 1980s, the presidential candidate dominated the political party and named its national chairperson, rather than depend on the party organization for support in elections. In the 1990s, the party organizations became important as conduits for financial contributions for presidential candidates. This presidential control developed because candidates began to form their own organizations and raise their own money rather than depend on their political parties. Money became more important because expensive television time became essential in reaching voters in primary elections, and political party organizations took second place to TV coverage. Personal organizations in the primary states were put together by individual candidates rather than by party regulars.

Another indicator of party breakdown was the rise in split-ticket voting, with voters voting for a presidential candidate of one party and a congressional candidate of the other party. Ticket-splitting rose from about 12 percent of ballots in 1952 to an average of 25 percent from 1972 to 1988, to a high of 36 percent in 1992.[30]

Decreasing voter turnout for elections has accompanied the decline of political parties. In the 1950s and 1960s, turnout for presidential elections was about 60 percent of the eligible electorate, but in the 1970s it began to decline, and in the 1988 election it was only 50 percent. Part of the reason for the decline was the Twenty-sixth Amendment to the Constitution, which gave the right to vote to all citizens eighteen years old or older. Since young people vote at

---

[28]George Edwards and Stephen Wayne, *Presidential Leadership* (New York: St. Martin's Press, 1997), p. 61.

[29]Richard Morin and E. J. Dionne, Jr., "Majority of Voters Say Parties Have Lost Touch," *Washington Post* (July 8, 1992), pp. 1, 10.

[30]Peter F. Galderisi, et al., *Divided Government* (Lanham, MD: Rowman and Littlefield, 1996), p. 38.

significantly lower rates than older voters (33 percent for eighteen- to twenty-year-olds versus 68 percent for ages forty-five and above), part of the decline is due to their inclusion in the electorate.[31] But the decline goes beyond the age turnout differentials, and it probably reflects an alienation and disillusionment with politics that is widespread in the electorate. Turnout jumped to 55 percent in 1992, but dropped to 49 percent in 1996, the lowest showing since 1924.

These trends have had a profound effect on the American presidency. The personalization of the presidential campaign and its separation from political parties has made the process of governing much more difficult. Presidents have the party label when they run their campaigns, but not the party organization.[32] Weakening the ties of the president to the political party has made winning partisan support in Congress more difficult, because presidents now have shorter coattails and, thus, members of Congress have fewer reasons to feel indebted to the president of their own party. But divided government has even further weakened what was once seen as the common electoral stake in governing the country. The party breakdown also removes the president even farther from state and local parties and elected officials. The lack of mutual dependence of the president and Congress has made forging governing coalitions between the two branches even more difficult.

Political parties play important functions in a representative democracy. Their primary function is to aggregate interests and present relatively coherent choices to voters. Without these unifying organizations candidates would have to run on their own personalities and a series of shifting coalitions of narrow interests. Political parties are able to bring many different interests and issues under broader umbrellas of unifying political philosophy that lend coherence to political choice and allow the nation to move in one of two general directions. They also provide vehicles for citizen participation in electoral politics and government. They help moderate the appeals of narrow ideological groups.

Thus, the decline of political parties is of concern to those who worry about the governability of the country. Several proposals for constitutional amendments intended to move the United States toward a parliamentary system will be examined later in the book, but it is not at all clear that any structural fix would solve the problem.

GOING PUBLIC AND PUBLIC APPROVAL

The Framers were fearful of selecting the president by popular vote because of their fear that such an important and volatile source of power for the chief executive could lead to tyranny. Thus, the presidency began as an office quite

---

[31]Pika et al., *The Presidential Contest,* p. 122.

[32]Edwards and Wayne, *Presidential Leadership,* p. 268.

insulated from popular opinion. But presidents have always known that public opinion is an important source of their power. President Lincoln declared: "Public sentiment is everything. With public sentiment nothing can fail, without it nothing can succeed."[33] Theodore Roosevelt began the more active use of the "bully pulpit" of the presidency to build public support for his favorite issues. And Woodrow Wilson said of the president's power: "Let him once win the admiration and confidence of the country, and no other single force can withstand him, no combination of forces will easily overpower him. . . ."[34]

Contemporary presidents have the capacity to reach the public in ways that could not have been imagined by these earlier presidents, and they have consciously formed their strategies of governing to exploit that capacity. Throughout most of American history, presidential communication with the American public was indirect. Presidents would give speeches that would be heard by scores or hundreds of people, at most, and word of mouth would carry their ideas further. Reporters would copy their words, opinion leaders around the country would read them, and their reactions would become part of the public opinion about presidents.

At the end of the nineteenth and beginning of the twentieth century a professional Washington press corps developed to report the actions of a national government that was playing a greater role in the United States and the world. The advent of radio enabled the words of presidents to be heard directly by people throughout the nation, and Franklin Roosevelt effectively used the medium to address the nation in his famous "fireside chats." But FDR's main mechanism for reaching the public remained the Washington press corps. FDR held a total of 998 press conferences and averaged 6.9 per month, more than any other modern president.[35] He averaged no more than two "fireside chat" radio broadcasts per year.[36]

After FDR, the number of press conferences presidents held steadily declined, and John Kennedy began the modern era of presidential communications. The "Kennedy system" was marked by the introduction of live television coverage of press conferences.[37] Television coverage was so appealing to Kennedy because it allowed him to speak directly to the people without his words being selected and mediated by the Washington press corps. While this was resented by Washington print journalists, presidents now could communicate directly with the public and have greater control over the message that people received. Other elements of the "Kennedy system" included the grant-

---

[33]Quoted in Edwards and Wayne, *Presidential Leadership,* p. 90.

[34]Quoted in Paul Brace and Barbara Hinckley, *Follow the Leader* (New York: Basic Books, 1992), p. 18.

[35]Samuel Kernell, *Going Public* (Washington, DC: CQ Press, 1986), p. 69.

[36]Kernell, *Going Public,* p. 106.

[37]Kernell, *Going Public,* pp. 69–76.

ing of private interviews to favored reporters and special meetings with representatives of local newspapers to the exclusion of the national press.

The Kennedy strategy of "going public" marked a key turning point in presidents' efforts to control how they are perceived by the public. Political scientist Samuel Kernell argues that the national political system has been undergoing a subtle but basic shift from a system of "institutionalized pluralism" to one of "individualized pluralism." In the older system the political establishment was relatively stable and was dominated by the major power centers of Congress, the political parties, the national press, and the most important broad-interest groups (e.g., big business and big labor unions). A major part of presidential power was the president's personal reputation with this relatively stable constellation of power centers.

But the political landscape has changed in the later decades of the twentieth century. With the growth of the welfare state, national public policy affects many more individual citizens than it did in the past. Power in Congress has become more decentralized and individual members behave much more as entrepreneurs than as loyal party members. Political parties have declined as the major intermediaries between the public and the government. Presidential candidates are no longer dependent on their party but rather dominate it. All of these developments have been accelerated by breakthroughs in communications technology.[38]

As a result of these developments, especially party breakdown, presidents come to office without a ready-made coalition of a political party and the interest groups associated with it to support their agendas. They must try to cobble together more temporary coalitions of narrower interests for separate policy issues. In trying to put together these more temporary coalitions they have found that a major tool they can use is "going public"; trying to get groups outside of Washington to use their political power to put pressure on Washington power centers, primarily Congress, to support the president's policy proposals. Thus, presidents have become much more active in developing political support in constituencies outside of Washington as part of their overall governing strategies.

These far-reaching changes in the political environment have had a profound effect on the way presidents have conducted their relations with the American public, as presidents have sought to exploit new communications technology in their efforts to affect public opinion. While the number of press conferences has declined since FDR's time, the number of presidential addresses to the nation have increased. But more striking is the huge increase in the number of *minor* presidential addresses over the years. The average number of these minor public speeches has increased by a factor of five between the 1930s and the presidencies of Nixon, Carter, and Reagan.[39] The total number of public appearances by presidents and the amount of their political travel

[38]Kernell, *Going Public,* chap. 2.

[39]Kernell, *Going Public,* p. 92.

have also steadily increased.[40] President Bush averaged a record number of domestic trips in his first three years in office.[41]

The picture that emerges is that presidents are much more personally involved in selling their policies to the American public than were presidents at midcentury, and that the selling is more retail than wholesale. That is, they make more appearances and appeals to a large number of smaller groups than the governing strategies of the 1940s and 1950s dictated.

Recent advances in communications technology have enabled presidents to focus their appeals more narrowly and to bypass the mediating effects of the national press. Presidents have tried to bypass the national print media by granting special access to reporters from local newspapers. While President Reagan gave fewer press *conferences* than most of his predecessors, he granted 194 press *interviews* and 150 special White House *briefings* to the non-Washington press corps in his first three years in office.[42] Presidents would rather talk with local reporters than the much more aggressive and skeptical national press corps. Local press reporters are less likely to ask tough questions than the national press corps and are likely to focus on the local angle to any presidential activities. Presidents can thus tailor their messages to local media markets and speak to the special concerns of local regions, which can be more politically effective than broader-based appeals.

The same trend is evident in television. With the development of satellite technology to transmit programming directly to local TV stations throughout the country, there has been a surge in the White House catering to the locals. Between 1981 and 1984 the number of local TV news stations with bureaus in Washington increased from fifteen to fifty, and in the 1980s the White House made special efforts to cater to these local media outlets.[43]

In the 1992 presidential campaign, the appearances of candidates on talk shows with sympathetic hosts demonstrated the trend of appealing directly to voters. Even the presidential debates were affected when one debate format called for questions direct from an audience of "regular people," rather than the usual questioning by members of the national press corps.

Once in office, the Clinton administration continued to exploit opportunities for direct contact between the president and citizens through town meeting–type forums and links to local media. The Washington press corps was upset that Clinton seemed to try to go around them to local media outlets and that President Clinton did not even hold a formal press conference until March 23, 1993, and only two in his first 100 days in office. In a remark aimed at the national media, Clinton said, "You know why I can stiff you on the press con-

---

[40]Kernell, *Going Public,* pp. 93–98.

[41]Samuel Kernell, *Going Public,* 2nd ed. (Washington, DC: CQ Press, 1993), pp. xv, 105.

[42]Kernell, *Going Public,* p. 74.

[43]Kernell, *Going Public,* p. 74.

ferences? Because [talk show host] Larry King liberated me by giving me to the American people directly."[44] The Clinton administration also experimented with on-line computer access to subscribers to computer services. Computer users could access speech texts and other White House documents and even send e-mail (computer messages) directly to the White House through their computers.

Some scholars have argued that the line between campaigning and governing has become increasingly blurred. During his first term Bill Clinton retained some aspects of his campaign organization, experimenting with the central media control center like the "war room" rapid response team of the campaign. The reelection campaign began running TV ads for the president in mid-1995, eighteen months before the election. The high cost of this early start on the 1996 campaign was fueled by an aggressive fund-raising drive run from the White House that sometimes skirted the borders of propriety.

This campaigning approach continued into his second term as Clinton tried to develop public support for his initiatives. One White House official characterized Clinton's thinking: "Clinton has come to believe that if he keeps his approval ratings up and sells his message as he did during the campaign, there will be greater acceptability for his program. . . . The idea is that you have to sell it as if in a campaign."[45]

Presidents put a lot of effort into trying to control the image of their administrations in the media, and thereby affect public opinion. How successful are they? What are the limits of presidential control of public opinion?

Modern public polling techniques have become much more sophisticated in the second half of the twentieth century, and by examining these polls historically we can try to understand the waxing and waning popularity of presidents. President Franklin Roosevelt occasionally used polls to gauge public reaction to various public policy directions, and Lyndon Johnson was the first president to have a pollster on the White House staff.[46] In the early 1970s news organizations relied on private polling organizations, but by the end of the 1970s every major news organization had its own professional public opinion survey operation. Polling became pervasive in American politics and, in the Carter administration, polling became a permanent part of the White House staff.[47]

Administration sensitivity to public opinion polls is another way in which governing has come to seem like an extension of the presidential campaign. Instead of relying on the "mandate" established in the presidential election, the

[44]Sidney Blumenthal, "The Syndicated Presidency," *New Yorker* (April 5, 1993), p. 42.

[45]Allison Mitchell, "Clinton Seems to Keep Running Though the Race Is Run and Won," *New York Times* (February 12, 1997), pp. A1, A20.

[46]*Congressional Quarterly Guide to the Presidency* (Washington, DC: CQ Press, 1989), p. 751.

[47]*Congressional Quarterly Guide to the Presidency*, p. 751.

FIGURE 2-1
Presidential Approval Ratings—Annual Averages

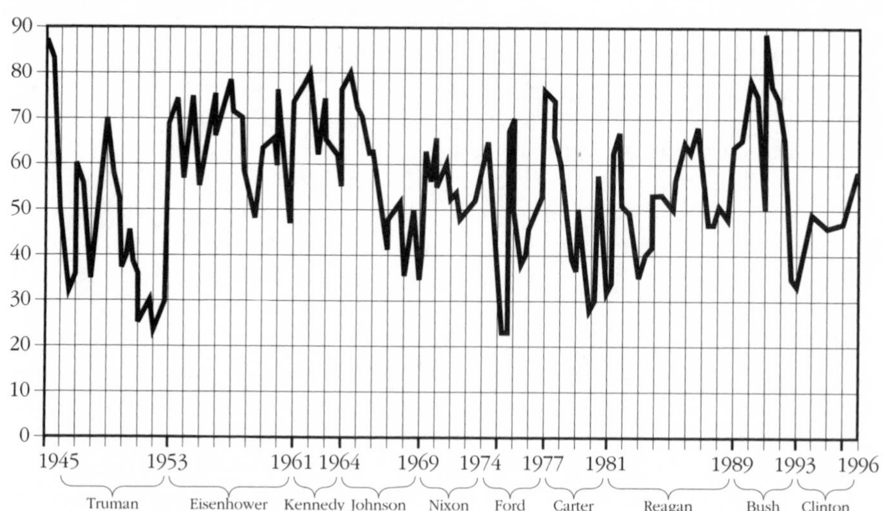

Source: Adapted from the Gallup Poll web site and the *Washington Post* (August 17, 1992), p. A11. Copyright © 1992 The Washington Post. Reprinted with permission.

White House is sensitive to and attempts to affect an ongoing "mandate" as polls are taken throughout a presidential administration and used to defend administration policy. Presidents, however, are not easily able to control their public-approval ratings.

While some presidents seem more popular than others, we can detect certain regularities in the pattern of public approval of presidents over the cycle of their terms. In comparing the public approval of presidents, the summary measure used is the question that has been asked of the public over the past five decades: "Do you approve of the job President ______ is doing as president?" A wide variety of different questions are asked on specific public-policy issues, but this is the question that is weighed most heavily by presidents and used by scholars for comparative purposes. (See Figure 2–1.)

The most certain prediction that we can make about presidential approval ratings is that a president's popularity is likely to decline during the first term. Presidents begin their terms in office with a "honeymoon" of public support and goodwill. Candidates who have been successful in winning election usually increase their level of public support between the time of election and inauguration. From Eisenhower through Clinton (with the exceptions of Reagan and Bush), every newly inaugurated president's approval rating was ten percentage points or more greater than his election margin.[48]

---

[48]Edwards and Wayne, *Presidential Leadership,* p. 104.

What accounts for this immediate jump in popularity between election and inauguration? Part of it is the halo effect of formally becoming president. Past presidents have taken on mythic stature in the United States. The new president just might be the one to take a place among the pantheon of the great presidents: Washington, Jefferson, Lincoln, and Franklin Roosevelt. The irony here is that the largest public approval of presidential job performance is often given before the president has had any chance to perform on the job.[49] But this makes sense because everyone can hope that the new president will pursue policies they approve of. Campaign promises are often vague, and presented as all gain and no pain. That is, everyone can win and there are no losers. There is also the dynamic of high expectations stemming from campaign rhetoric and stirring inaugural addresses. The former merely political candidate takes on the legitimacy of the office of the president, and opinion leaders and the media refrain from criticizing the new president.[50]

But this postinaugural glow is an artificially high level of support, and soon reality and the inevitable decline in public approval begins. The initial approval rating is artificially high because it is usually much higher than the percentage of the electorate who voted for the candidate. But it is also high because the new president has not made any of the hard policy tradeoffs that any presidential agenda necessarily entails. Whenever a policy choice is made some will be disappointed that their option was not chosen. As more choices are made these disappointments accumulate, and the president's approval ratings slip.

The honeymoon with the public may last several months or half a year, but after the sixth month in office the polls begin to slide and usually decline through the third year of the term before turning up as the election approaches.[51] If the president is reelected, there is no honeymoon with public opinion comparable to the first term.[52] Of course, presidential approval ratings fluctuate during any term depending on the particular president or external events. One of the most important determinants of presidential popularity is the state of the economy, especially inflation and unemployment. Presidents have very little short-term control over these factors. All presidents want a healthy economy, and they do what they can to strengthen economic performance. The problem is that even if most economists agree on the right prescription, presidents can affect economic performance only marginally. Increasingly, the world economy is a major determinant of U.S. economic performance. It is a truism of American politics that presidents are blamed or given credit for the state of the economy regardless of the fact that they are seldom responsible for the country's economic performance.

The other major predictable factors in presidential polls are dramatic in-

---

[49]Brace and Hinkley, *Follow the Leader,* p. 170.

[50]See Richard A. Brody, *Assessing the President* (Stanford, CA: Stanford University Press, 1991), p. 29.

[51]Brace and Hinkley, *Follow the Leader.*

[52]Brody, *Assessing the President,* p. 32.

ternational events that involve the United States. These events sometimes produce a "rally effect" in public opinion because the public "rallies around the flag" to support the president as the representative of the United States in a hostile and unpredictable world. The irony of these events is that the rally effect of a jump in approval of the president can occur whether or not the president has acted successfully in an international crisis. For example, Eisenhower's approval rating rose after a U.S. spy plane was downed over the Soviet Union; John Kennedy's approval rose after the Bay of Pigs failure; Jimmy Carter's polls increased after the Iranians took over the U.S. embassy in Tehran and after the Soviet invasion of Afghanistan.[53]

Of course, when presidents act successfully in international crises, as in the Persian Gulf war of 1991, their popularity increases dramatically. If a dramatic international event involving U.S. security is accompanied by an effective speech by the president, the effect of the rally is increased. But even though the effect of these events is fairly predictable, it must be stressed that the duration of the public-approval effect is short-lived (usually one to four months), and the effect only occurs if the event is dramatic and involves U.S. security.[54] The transience of rally-based popularity was demonstrated dramatically when George Bush's high approval rating of 91 percent immediately after the Persian Gulf war was followed by the largest steady drop of popularity in polling history, followed by his defeat in the 1992 election.

While the technology and increasing sophistication of public opinion polling allows the president to gauge and thus be responsive to the wishes of the citizenry, there are dangers in relying too heavily on reacting to the latest opinion polls. If presidents become obsessed with the latest poll numbers they may be tempted to act with a short-term perspective on what will favorably affect their polls rather than on what is in the best interests of the country. They may follow the short-term demands of public opinion rather than take a long-term perspective on what is best for the nation. The real task of leadership is to educate the public about the long-term best interests of the nation, and then lead the nation in that direction, even if it means short-term sacrifice.

CONCLUSION

Short-term "pandering" to the public opinion of the moment is the classic problem with democracies, whether in campaigning or once in office. The technology of polling has made the gauging of opinion more immediate and ac-

[53]See Brace and Hinkley, *Follow the Leader*, p. 27 and chap. 5. See also Brody, *Assessing the President*, chap. 3. George Edwards argues that many rally events do not produce substantial increases in approval ratings in *The Public Presidency* (New York: St. Martin's Press, 1983), pp. 242–247.

[54]Brace and Hinkley, *Follow the Leader*, p. 167.

urate. True leadership, however, will be measured in the long run rather than by short-term popularity. As will be argued in the last chapter, longterm presidential reputation does not necessarily correspond with popularity while in office. The most striking example of a discrepancy between the two is the presidency of Harry Truman. Truman's poll ratings were among the lowest of modern presidents, yet he is ranked highest by historians among the post–World War II presidents. Part of his historic reputation may even be due to his dismissive attitude toward presidential approval ratings. "I wonder how far Moses would have gone if he'd taken a poll in Egypt? . . . It isn't polls or public opinion of the moment that counts. It is right and wrong leadership. . . ."[55]

[55]Brace and Hinkley, *Follow the Leader,* p. 19.

Three

THE WHITE HOUSE STAFF AND ORGANIZATION

One of the defining characteristics of the modern presidency is a large an differentiated White House staff system at the service of the president. is not merely a group of people serving the president but a collection o bureaucracies: the White House Office, the Executive Office of the President, an several military units, as well as the Secret Service, which is technically in the Tre sury Department. This chapter will trace the increasing size and complexity of th White House staff in the modern presidency. The role of staffers as advisers to th president and occasional implementers of policy will be examined. The chapte will argue that the White House needs the firm control of a chief of staff, but th too domineering an approach to the job will result in trouble.

In the nineteenth century, presidents had personal aides and servants. I the early part of the century, these were usually clerical helpers and most o ten relatives and junior aides who were paid from the president's own pock etbook. At the turn of the century, the functions of these people began to in clude liaison with Congress and other political power centers. But president still relied primarily on their cabinets and nongovernmental advisors for con sultation and advice. President Hoover caused a bit of a stir when he double the White House staff from two to four assistants.

The dramatic shift came with Franklin Roosevelt and the birth of the mod ern presidency. Under Roosevelt, the scope of governmental activity was in creased greatly in the effort to fight the Great Depression. Scores of new agen cies were created by Congress to administer the various New Deal program enacted to counteract the effects of the Great Depression. By the mid-1930s th executive branch had more than 100 agencies.

Roosevelt decided that he needed more managerial tools to fight the frag mentation of the executive branch and to rein in the "alphabet" agencies of th New Deal. In 1936, he assigned the task of planning a strategy for manageria control to a committee of three public-administration scholars headed by Loui Brownlow. In 1937, the Committee on Administrative Management (the Brown low Committee), with careful guidance from FDR, announced that "The presi dent needs help." With the principle that the president should be the center o control in the executive branch, its ambitious recommendations proposed mor legal power for the president, centralized control of staff agencies (personnel and budget), tighter fiscal controls, extension of the merit system, bringing independent commissions into the purview of the major executive-branch departments, and professional staff help for the president.

These far-reaching proposals were seen as a power grab by Congress, which had just rejected Roosevelt's proposal to "pack" the Supreme Court by increasing its size. The set of recommendations was thus rejected and the legislation was defeated in Congress. Finally, in 1939, two of the proposals were approved by Congress: reorganization power for the president, subject to a legislative veto, and the provision of six administrative assistants who would be officially part of the White House but not subject to Senate confirmation. FDR quickly used his new reorganization power to create the Executive Office of the President (EOP), through Executive Order 8248, and recruited his six top aides over the next several years.

While these two expansions of presidential power were not major changes, the Brownlow Committee Report was to have major repercussions over the years. The report articulated the justification for an active White House staff to serve the president and thus laid the foundation for the growth in numbers and power of the White House staff in the modern presidency.

In describing the role envisioned for presidential aides, the report declared:

> These aides would have no power to make decisions or issue instructions in their own right. They would not be interposed between the president and the heads of his departments. They would not be assistant presidents in any sense. . . . They would remain in the background, issue no orders, make no decisions, emit no public statements. . . . they would not attempt to exercise power on their own account. They should be possessed of high competence, great physical vigor, and a passion for anonymity.[1]

Despite the fact that these precepts have gone by the wayside and the White House staff now includes hundreds of people, the norms articulated by Brownlow still define the ideal for White House aides.

As the White House staff has grown from the relatively small staff of Franklin Roosevelt to more than five hundred in the 1990s, presidents have had to confront the problem of how to manage the increasing numbers of people. Presidents have taken different approaches to the problem of organization, with some choosing a relatively unstructured, collegial White House organization. Others have chosen a more structured, hierarchical approach with a chief of staff to oversee the White House. This chapter will examine the contrasting approaches taken by the modern presidents to White House organization.

---

[1]President's Committee on Administrative Management. Reorganization of the Executive Departments (Washington, DC: Government Printing Office, 1937) 75th Congress, 1st Sess., Senate, Document No. 8, p. 5.

ROOSEVELT AND TRUMAN: LAYING THE FOUNDATIONS

Franklin Roosevelt's administration began the transformation to the modern presidency in terms of the size and scope of government and the institutionalization of the presidency. Under FDR, the White House staff took on new roles and functions that have been continued and expanded to meet more recent challenges. The initial impetus for this transformation and broadening of the functions of the White House staff included the same two factors that caused the expansion of the role of the federal government in the 1930s and 1940s: the Great Depression and World War II. Under FDR, the federal government came to have more than 150 agencies with almost fifty reporting directly to the president.

Just as FDR laid the groundwork for the institutional presidency with the creation of the EOP, he also initiated the use of an extensive set of White House aides to help him personally with his conduct of the newly enlarged presidency. FDR made a careful distinction between the institutional staff of the presidency in the EOP and his *personal* staffers, who were to concern themselves intimately with his own daily work.[2] In ensuing decades, this distinction was to become blurred.

Though the number of aides was small compared to recent presidents, with three or four top-level assistants and a total White House staff, including clerical, of less than fifty, the aides acted as an extension of FDR's personal will. He used the high-level personal staffers as ". . . chore-boys, trouble shooters, checker-uppers, intelligence operatives, and as magnets for ideas, gripes, gossip in the administration, on the Hill, and with groups outside government."[3] The expanded staff was necessary not only because of the increased size of the government, but because of the activist policy role that FDR played as president. But in contrast to more recent presidents, FDR kept his staffers on a very short leash.

Franklin Roosevelt conducted his White House so as to maximize his flexibility and sources of information. He gave his personal staff broad assignments but doled out jobs on an ad hoc basis. He did not want his staffers to go into business for themselves so he gave them conflicting assignments to keep them off balance. He even used people from outside the government to check up on or duplicate his staffers' work.[4] FDR was legendary for his manipulation of his staffers. He thrived on conflict in his personal entourage and used it consciously to his advantage. This was frustrating to his subordinates but useful to Roosevelt. It generated creative conflict and ideas. It kept his channels of information open and kept powerful staffers in check. Roosevelt presided over

---

[2]Richard Neustadt, "Roosevelt's Approach to Staffing the White House," Attachment A to "Memo on Staffing the President-Elect" (October 30, 1960), pp. 1–2.

[3]Neustadt, "Roosevelt's Approach to Staffing the White House," p. 4.

[4]Neustadt, "Roosevelt's Approach to Staffing the White House," p. 5.

his own morning staff meetings, and no one short of the president coordinated or integrated the White House staff's work.[5]

Though FDR had a press secretary (Stephen Early), an appointments secretary (Marvin McIntyre), and a special counsel (Samuel Rosenman) for legal and other advice, most of his top staffers were generalists with shifting assignments. Unlike future presidents, he had no specific person to deal with Congress, to recruit political appointees, or to act as liaison with the cabinet or the rest of the executive branch. Roosevelt did all of these things himself and gave specific assignments to different staffers at different times.

FDR's need to dominate his staff and his insistence on personal loyalty was tinged by a "thin streak of sadism," according to Robert Sherwood.[6] But Roosevelt felt that his assertion of control was necessary to keep his staffers from going into business for themselves. When James Rowe once insisted that he knew the best way to engineer a personnel shift in the government, he said: "Mr. President, you should do it my way and not yours." In putting Rowe in his place, FDR made clear the basic relationship between staffers and the president: "I do not have to do it your way and I will tell you the reason why. The reason is that, although they may have made a mistake, the people of the United States have elected me president, not you."[7] But FDR had a need for loyal staffers, as he commented to a skeptical observer on the role of his intimate, Harry Hopkins, who lived in the White House. FDR said that, if you are president, "you'll be looking at that door over there and knowing that practically everybody who walks through it wants something out of you. You'll learn what a lonely job this is, and you'll discover the need for somebody like Harry Hopkins, who asks nothing except to serve you."[8]

When Harry S Truman succeeded to the presidency upon FDR's death in April 1945, the war was all but over, though Truman was still to make the fateful decision to drop atomic bombs on Japanese cities. Truman's challenge was to reorient the country from war to peace, guide the economy through demobilization, and to consolidate the Democratic agenda of the New Deal. Truman did not immediately fire FDR's cabinet and White House staff but gradually began to adjust the White House to his own presidential style.

Truman, unlike FDR, was uncomfortable with personal conflict and did not give out overlapping assignments or encourage conflict among his staffers. His White House was more orderly and formal. He held daily staff meetings with his top dozen aides at precisely 9:30 AM, received regular national security briefings, and held weekly meetings with the congressional leadership and Demo-

---

[5]Neustadt, "Roosevelt's Approach to Staffing the White House," p. 4.

[6]Robert E. Sherwood, *Roosevelt and Hopkins* (New York: Harper, 1948), p. 537. Quoted in Richard Tanner Johnson, *Managing the White House* (New York: Harper & Row, 1974), p. 20.

[7]Quoted in Patrick Anderson, *The Presidents' Men* (New York: Doubleday, 1969), p. 79.

[8]Michael Medved, *The Shadow Presidents* (New York: Times Books, 1979), p. 198.

cratic party leaders. There was never any formal organization chart of the White House, and only the president ever gave any senior White House staffer a direct order, as future chiefs of staff would.[9]

Truman, reflecting in part his path to the presidency but also his own insecurity, was not as sure of himself as FDR. Truman saw himself as a man of modest intelligence but with the willingness to make tough decisions without agonizing deliberation (as in the decision to use the atomic bomb). This led Truman to delegate much more responsibility than had FDR, an option made more workable with a more fixed and formal White House organization. But the final responsibility and authority rested with him as was signified by the famous sign resting on his desk in the Oval Office, "THE BUCK STOPS HERE."

The Truman White House began the trend toward functional specialization that has come to characterize the modern presidency. In addition to the press secretary and appointments secretary that FDR had, Truman gave more fixed assignments to individual staffers. As the White House staff began to increase in size, primary aides began to recruit their own staffs and the first layering of the White House staff began.[10]

Truman hired two staffers of special importance to his presidency. The first was John R. Steelman, who was given the title of assistant to the president. Steelman had special responsibility for labor relations, which plagued the federal government after the tight economic controls of World War II. But his broader responsibility was for the coordination of domestic policy agencies. He often performed the role of future chiefs of staff by negotiating and settling disputes among cabinet secretaries that were not of sufficient importance to involve the president directly.

The most eminent aide to Truman was Clark Clifford, who took on Rosenman's title of special counsel. When someone asked the question what does the special counsel do, Clifford's answer was, "Whatever the president wanted."[11] Clifford's role represented the modern practice of having policy advocates, as opposed to merely coordinators or troubleshooters, in the White House. Clifford saw himself as an advocate for the liberal part of the Democratic agenda, "fighting for the mind of the president."[12] Clifford and his allies were arrayed against the conservatives in the White House, including John Steelman. While Clifford was a major factor in Truman's domestic policy, he was crucial to Truman's foreign policy, where he acted as Truman's personal adviser and as a counterweight to Secretary of State Dean Acheson and Secretary of Defense James Forestall.

Truman asserted an important principle about the role of White House

---

[9]Clark Clifford, *Counsel to the President* (New York: Random House, 1991), p. 77.

[10]See the discussion in Stephen Hess, *Organizing the Presidency,* 2nd ed. (Washington, DC: Brookings Institution, 1988), pp. 40–54.

[11]Clifford, *Counsel to the President,* p. 75.

[12]Quoted in Hess, *Organizing the Presidency,* p. 44.

staffers in the modern presidency in an Oval Office meeting in May 1948. At that meeting, Secretary of State George Marshall and State Department officials were discussing with Truman whether the United States should recognize the newly declared state of Israel. Secretary Marshall objected to the presence of Clifford, because he felt that Clifford was merely a political advisor and that his presence was inappropriate at a meeting about serious matters of state. When Marshall angrily objected to Clifford's presence, Truman replied, "Well, General, he's here because I asked him to be here."[13] Marshall was implying more than a difference in expertise; he was also noting the difference between his statutory office and Clifford's merely advisory capacity. The point of Truman's reply is a dual one: presidents can choose to invest their trust in their personal staffers, but the power of those staffers is derivative and entirely dependent on the president's continuing confidence.[14]

EISENHOWER INSTITUTIONALIZES THE WHITE HOUSE

While FDR began the modern staffing system in the White House and Truman organized it more explicitly, it was under Eisenhower that the White House staff became institutionalized. Before he became president, Dwight Eisenhower had the advantage of having been an executive for many years, directing U.S. forces during World War II, and coordinating the allied effort to victory in the war. During his career he had given considerable thought to leadership in organizations, and came to the presidency with firm ideas about how the White House should be organized. He was of the strong opinion that White House organization needed improving.

> For years I had been in frequent contact with the executive office of the White House, and I had certain ideas about the system, or lack of system under which it operated. With my training in problems involving organization it was inconceivable to me that the work of the White House could not be better systemized than had been the case in the years I observed it.[15]

Eisenhower stressed the importance of organization: "Organization cannot make a genius out of an incompetent. . . . On the other hand, disorganization can scarcely fail to result in inefficiency and can easily lead to disaster."[16] Thus,

---

[13]Clark Clifford, *Counsel to the President* (New York: Random House, 1991) p. 12.

[14]See Samuel Kernell, "The Creed and Reality of Modern White House Management," in Samuel Kernell and Samuel Popkin, eds., *Chief of Staff* (Berkeley: University of California Press, 1986), pp. 193–232.

[15]Dwight D. Eisenhower, *Mandate for Change* (Garden City, NY: Doubleday, 1963), p. 87.

[16]Eisenhower, *Mandate for Change,* p. 114.

Eisenhower organized his White House much more formally than either Truman or Roosevelt.

For his immediate staffers he chose people who were familiar to him from his campaign and his military years, but in general they were more professional in their backgrounds than were the staffers of Truman or FDR.[17] He also gave them much more specialized assignments than existed previously in the White House. Eisenhower kept the previous existing positions of press secretary, appointments secretary, and special counsel (though it was more exclusively focused on legal matters than before). But Eisenhower added a number of other positions and organizational systems in the White House. Truman had used one person to coordinate congressional liaison, but Eisenhower elevated the position and created a special office for the function.

With Eisenhower's appreciation for the need to coordinate activities in a large organization, he set up two secretariats for coordination: the secretary to the cabinet and the staff secretary. The cabinet secretary, Maxwell Rabb, and his assistants ensured that cabinet meeting agendas were in the participants' hands in time, that all cabinet papers were in order, and that follow-up to cabinet meetings and decisions was carried out. The staff secretary, Paul Carroll (later Andrew Goodpaster), acted as the coordinator and clearing house for all papers and issues that came up to the president. If staff work was incomplete, or if someone who should have seen some papers had not seen them, it was the staff secretary's responsibility to get the job done. In Eisenhower's words, the function of the staff secretary was: "I look to my staff to keep such things straightened out. I should not have to be my own sergeant major. . . ."[18]

Eisenhower also upgraded the importance of the National Security Council staff, which had been headed by an executive secretary. He created the title of Special Assistant to the President for National Security Affairs and appointed Robert Cutler to the position. The special assistant would be responsible for the agenda of the council, briefing the president, and coordinating national security issues for the president.

Perhaps the most important and lasting contribution of Eisenhower to the organization of the presidency was the office of chief of staff, whose function was to oversee and coordinate the much enlarged and more complex staff for the president. The combination of the powers of the office and the personality of its first occupant, Sherman Adams, made it the most powerful position (short of the president) in the government. Adams's official title was Assistant to the President, but his function was chief of staff. "I think of Adams as my chief of staff, but I don't call him that because the politicians think it sounds too military," admitted Eisenhower.[19]

Adams saw his job as making sure that staff work was complete and that

---

[17]See Stephen Hess, *Organizing the Presidency,* p. 64.

[18]Quoted by Fred Greenstein, *The Hidden-Hand Presidency* (New York: Basic Books, 1982), p. 142.

[19]Medved, *The Shadow Presidents,* p. 243.

any issues brought to the president were ripe for presidential involvement. According to Eisenhower: "A man like that is valuable because of the unnecessary detail he keeps away from the president. A president who doesn't know how to decentralize will be weighed down with details and won't have time to deal with the big issues."[20] Adams spent a considerable amount of time forcing reluctant cabinet secretaries to settle their disputes and turf battles short of the president. "Either you make up your minds or else tell me and I will do it. We must not bother the president with this. He is trying to keep the world from war."[21] As Adams explained his role, "Eisenhower simply expected me to manage a staff that would boil down, simplify, and expedite the urgent business . . . and keep as much work of secondary importance off his desk as possible."[22]

Much of Adams's power stemmed from his control of access to the president. Given Eisenhower's preference to be spared details, his absence from the White House much of the time, and his conscious decision to stay behind the scenes, Adams's position became that much more powerful. Despite organization charts and official policy that gave direct access to the president to all cabinet officers and a number of White House staffers, the reality was that Adams usually had final say as to who would see the president and what papers would reach him.

But controlling access was only one of the important roles that Adams played for the president as chief of staff. He took the heat for the president for tough political decisions, such as firing people and negotiating political patronage. He acted as a buffer for the president and organized the White House and cabinet with an iron hand. After Eisenhower's first heart attack in 1955, Adams ran the executive branch virtually by himself.

Carrying out tough decisions and controlling access are all legitimate and often necessary roles for the chief of staff, but the way they are handled can make a large difference. They can be done in a heavy-handed manner or they can be accomplished with a firm hand, but without overt hostility. Cabinet members and staff may chafe under the decision in either case, but hostility and ill feeling will result if the bearer of the bad news is gratuitously rude also. Although Adams ran the White House the way Eisenhower wanted, his tight control and personal style contributed to his eventual undoing. One current joke had it that it would be unfortunate if Eisenhower died and Nixon became president, but a disaster if Adams died and Eisenhower was forced to be president.

Adams's downfall began in June 1958, when it became public that a textile manufacturer and old friend of Adams's, Bernard Goldfine, had on several occasions requested that Adams determine the status of charges against him with federal regulatory agencies. Adams made the calls for Goldfine from the White House to find out the status of the cases but did not suggest any change in agency actions. While the calls in themselves may have been free of im-

---

[20]Anderson, *The Presidents' Men*, p. 161.

[21]Medved, *The Shadow Presidents*, p. 245.

[22]Johnson, *Managing the White House*, p. 93.

proper intent, the very fact that an official of Adams's status, power, and proximity to the president was making the call cannot help but to be taken seriously by any agency in the government. Adams did not seem to be sensitive to the implications or appearance of his calls.

Adams became doubly vulnerable when it was disclosed in congressional hearings that he had accepted gifts from Goldfine, who had paid for hotel rooms for Adams and had given his wife a vicuña coat and an oriental rug.[23] Despite Adams's protestations that he had also given gifts to Goldfine in the context of their friendship, the combination of gifts to Adams with the inquiries from the White House appeared too much like official actions in exchange for gifts.

An additional important cause of Adams's downfall was his personal rudeness to colleagues and others he dealt with on an official basis. To Eisenhower, Adams's curtness was merely his way of communicating in the most efficient manner: "he never added a word to his 'yes' or 'no' if such an answer sufficed. It never occurred to him to say 'Hello.' . . . For Sherman Adams this was neither bad manners nor pretense; he was busy." While Adams's bruskness did not bother his boss, it often did bother his subordinates and others he dealt with. Adams's habitual harshness frequently reduced his secretaries to tears, and at one time he had five of them crying at the same time.[24] Adams treated members of the cabinet and Congress the same way, feeling no need for the usual amenities of human communication. This did not endear him to many, and when he was in trouble and needed friends to defend him, few were willing to come forth. Many in Congress and the executive branch felt that he was an arrogant, power-hungry tyrant who was getting his just deserts.

Even a personal plea and vote of confidence from Eisenhower could not save Adams. After Adams's congressional testimony, in which he argued that he had done nothing wrong, Eisenhower said: "I believe that the presentation made by Governor Adams to the Congressional Committee yesterday truthfully represents the pertinent facts. I personally like Governor Adams. I admire his abilities. I respect him because of his personal and official integrity. I need him."[25] But the plea was seen more as a weakness on Eisenhower's part than an effective defense of Adams. Finally, Adams was persuaded to resign.

KENNEDY AND THE COLLEGIAL MODEL

Although both were popular presidents, John Kennedy and Dwight Eisenhower provide stark contrasts in their personalities and dispositions for organizing the presidency. Kennedy was a young Democrat who took an activist view of the presidency and wanted to "get the country moving again." Eisen-

---

[23]See Medved, *The Shadow Presidents,* p. 253.

[24]Medved, *The Shadow Presidents,* p. 248.

[25]Medved, *The Shadow Presidents,* p. 254.

hower was an elderly statesman who chose to run as a Republican (he had a choice, Truman even offered to step down if Ike ran as a Democrat in 1948) who wanted to slow the changes the Democrats had begun with the New Deal. Eisenhower was an experienced organizational leader, while Kennedy had presided over small groups of staffers in the House and Senate.

These contrasts in background were reflected in the two presidents' approach to staffing and organizing the White House. Whereas Eisenhower wanted issues to be fully staffed out with most of the details settled at subordinate levels, Kennedy wanted issues raised to the presidential level early in the policy development process so he could make personal judgments on defining the alternatives. While Eisenhower wanted to save his energy for the most important decisions, Kennedy wanted to be at "the vital center of action in our whole scheme of government . . . the president [must] place himself in the very thick of the fight."[26] Eisenhower felt at home in large organizations and knew how to bend them to his will. Kennedy was slightly suspicious of the career bureaucracy and felt that established organizations would not be flexible enough for bold, new initiatives.

Thus, when Kennedy came to office he immediately abolished many of the committees and organizational systems that Eisenhower had instituted in the White House (though they would reappear in future administrations). The staff secretariat and the secretary to the cabinet were eliminated. The several committees and subcommittees of the National Security Council, including the Operations Coordinating Board, were abolished. Kennedy felt uncomfortable with committee systems, and preferred to work with small groups in short meetings that were tightly focused on the problem immediately at hand.

In contrast to Eisenhower's genius for organization and ability to design organizations that would mesh together total strangers and harness them to a common purpose, Kennedy thought in terms of individuals and was able to meld them together into a team through his personal charisma.[27] Eisenhower's staff was a competent, machine-like football team marching down the policy field. Kennedy's staff was a small, fluid basketball team trying to create fast breaks. Kennedy held few cabinet meetings and had no regular staff meetings, preferring to call ad hoc meetings to deal with specific situations.

Since Kennedy rejected much of the organizational apparatus of the Eisenhower White House, he saw no need for its major integrating mechanism, the office of chief of staff. He accepted the advice of his two transition advisers, Clark Clifford and Richard Neustadt, who argued in transition memos that a chief of staff would appear to wall the president off from the rest of the government and the people. Neustadt argued that Kennedy should be his own chief of staff and model his White House after Roosevelt's. Kennedy would be

---

[26]Arthur M. Schlesinger, Jr., *A Thousand Days* (Boston: Houghton Mifflin, 1965), p. 120.

[27]See Carl Brauer, "John F. Kennedy: The Endurance of Inspirational Leadership," in Fred I. Greenstein, *Leadership in the Modern Presidency* (Cambridge, MA: Harvard University Press, 1988); and Hess, *Organizing the Presidency,* chap. 6.

the hub of the wheel for his White House with a small circle of advisers reporting directly to him. He would be the giver of assignments and the integrator and receiver of all staff reports. No one person short of the president would coordinate the White House staff.[28]

The White House staff did, however, have a first among equals, though not in an organizational sense. Theodore Sorensen had been with Kennedy in the Senate and through the campaign and had been coauthor of Kennedy's best-selling book, *Profiles in Courage.* Sorensen served as Kennedy's major adviser and coordinator of legislative efforts and domestic policy, but did not give orders to other staffers, filter their work, or control access to Kennedy. With the memory of Sherman Adams fresh in his mind, Kennedy reminded Sorensen:

> Every man that's ever held a job like yours—Sherman Adams, Harry Hopkins, House, all the rest—has ended up in the shithouse. Congress was down on them or the president was hurt by them or somebody was mad at them. The best way to stay out of trouble is to stay out of sight.[29]

Although it is impossible for so important a presidential aide to remain anonymous, Sorensen took Kennedy's advice and turned down many invitations to give speeches. But Kennedy was not jealous of his staff's publicity in the way that Roosevelt and Johnson were. When McGeorge Bundy received positive press accounts describing his foreign policy duties, Kennedy commented in a humorous, though not sarcastic tone, "I will continue to have some residual functions."[30]

The powerful role of Kennedy's White House staff vis-à-vis the rest of the executive branch, and the beginning of the centralization of control of the government by the president, were shaped in important ways by the Bay of Pigs disaster. The plan to invade Cuba had been charted in the Eisenhower administration, and its major architects and proponents were CIA Director Allen Dulles and his assistant Richard Bissell. They assured Kennedy that social conditions on the island were ripe for overthrowing Fidel Castro, and Kennedy interpreted the military evaluation of the plan's feasibility as favorable. When the operation, with several key Kennedy changes, failed miserably and embarrassed the new president domestically and internationally, Kennedy drew profound lessons that altered his presidency and echoed in future presidencies.[31]

The Bay of Pigs fiasco reinforced Kennedy's suspicions of the career bureaucracies, and he resolved to appoint more of his own people to departments and agencies. He concluded that he had to rely more heavily on his own White

---

[28]For an analysis of the Clifford and Neustadt memos, see James P. Pfiffner, *The Strategic Presidency* (Chicago: Dorsey Press, 1988), pp. 23–25. Neustadt's memo is reprinted in Pfiffner, *The Managerial Presidency* (Pacific Grove, CA: Brooks/Cole, 1991).

[29]Medved, *The Shadow Presidents,* p. 273.

[30]Quoted in Johnson, *Managing the White House,* p. 132.

[31]See the discussion in Hess, *Organizing the Presidency,* pp. 74–87.

House advisers and create a stronger White House capacity to evaluate and oversee the bureaucracy. He would no longer allow the designers of plans to be their advocates also. He moved McGeorge Bundy's NSC office from the Old Executive Office Building to the west wing (where it has stayed ever since) and encouraged him to set up a "Little State Department" in the White House. He had the Situation Room built in the west wing basement so that it could serve as the command post in crisis situations; but perhaps more importantly, its officers would skim off the most important secret cables from the Departments of State and Defense and the CIA.[32]

Similar moves were implemented in dealing with economic policy, which had traditionally been dominated by the Treasury Department and the Bureau of the Budget (BOB). The Council of Economic Advisors that had been created in 1946 and had weathered a threat to its existence in the Eisenhower administration, was raised to a new level of importance under Kennedy. His respect for its chairman, scholar Walter Heller, prompted Kennedy to weigh his advice heavily and use the analyses of his relatively small staff, relegating to secondary importance the larger, more established professional staffs of Treasury and BOB.

Kennedy's impact on the presidency was to make it less formal in organizational terms. Yet the secular trend, independent of personality, of greater centralization and White House capacity was furthered during his years in the White House. Future presidents would reject his loose organizational approach but would further intensify his centralizing direction.

While Eisenhower had expanded the White House staff and organized it formally, the Kennedy administration increased the centralization of executive branch policy control in the White House by creating the nascent capacity to develop and formulate policy independent of the major departments and agencies of the executive branch. Kennedy also began to use his brother Robert and Theodore Sorensen as general advisors whose advice cut across all dimensions of policy, foreign and domestic. The changes in structure and decision-making style were evident in the administration's successful handling of the Cuban missile crisis in 1963.

LYNDON JOHNSON'S ONE-MAN SHOW

When Lyndon Johnson took over the presidency after the assassination of Kennedy, he stressed continuity with the Kennedy administration. He did not make any cabinet changes for thirteen months, and he kept on most of the Kennedy staff, at least for a while. While the Kennedy staff was waiting a decent interval before leaving, Johnson was beginning to build his own staff, in effect running two parallel staffs for the first year of his presidency.

---

[32]See Bradley Patterson, *The Ring of Power* (New York: Basic Books, 1988), pp. 119–121.

Johnson's personal style and psychological makeup determined his approach to his White House staff and organization. He was jealous of his staffers' publicity and deflated their egos whenever they received more attention than he approved of. According to a personal friend, "Lyndon has a clock inside him with an alarm that tells him at least once an hour to chew somebody out."[33] Johnson wanted all of the credit for his administration's accomplishments and demanded absolute loyalty from his subordinates. The volatility of Johnson's moods was reflected in the volatility of his staff. Because of his treatment of his staff, turnover was high, with only two of the twelve top staffers that he had in 1964 still with him in 1968.[34]

Johnson was unwilling to let any aide become too important or to act in authority over the rest of his staff. Thus, he never had a chief of staff. Johnson occasionally asked people to prepare organization charts of the White House staff, but no one was ever successful, because assignments were not fixed or constant, and any formulation would be out-of-date by the time it was printed. Bill Moyers commented on one such effort:

> [L]et me briefly say such an exercise is a gross misuse of a good man's time; nothing useful can come of it, since the White House reflects the personal needs of the president rather [sic] a structural design. If there is a design, it is radial—like the spokes of a wheel radiating out from the hub. Each person has a special relationship to the president and does what the president needs done; you can define very briefly what each man does, but it is impossible to catch the full scope of his duties. In his own mind the president knows what each man does; he doesn't need an organization chart to show him. In our minds, we know what the president expects of us; a chart is irrelevant.[35]

Bill Moyers played an important role for Johnson, both as friend and policy adviser. Moyers ran the 1964 campaign and became the coordinator for domestic policy and legislation in 1965. Moyers played the major role in creating and managing the fourteen task forces that formulated the ideas that were to make up the Great Society initiatives. When George Reedy left the administration in 1965, Moyers became press secretary and left the administration in late 1966.

The other person who played a major role on the domestic side of the Johnson presidency was Joseph Califano, who came to coordinate most of domestic policy, particularly as the war in Vietnam began to escalate and Moyers left. Just as McGeorge Bundy, and later Walt Rostow, coordinated and integrated national security policy, Califano used his position in the White House

---

[33]Quoted in Johnson, *Managing the White House,* p. 180.

[34]Johnson, *Managing the White House,* p. 179.

[35]Quoted in Emmette S. Redford and Richard T. McCulley, *White House Operations: The Johnson Presidency* (Austin, TX: University of Texas Press, 1986), p. 52.

to oversee the domestic side of the Johnson policy agenda. The role was to provide coordination of programs cutting across departmental boundaries (most did), to provide follow-through on presidential decisions, to spot crises, and to keep the president informed of developments in the executive branch.[36] On the domestic policy side, Califano occasionally had the duty of "knocking heads together" to settle cabinet disputes.[37] Califano's wide-ranging duties, however, did not approach the scope or authority that Sherman Adams had in the Eisenhower administration.

NIXON'S TIGHT HIERARCHY

When Richard Nixon returned to the White House after serving as Eisenhower's vice president and observing the Kennedy/Johnson years, he resolved that his administration would be more formally organized than the Democrats had been and closer in tone to Eisenhower's. Nixon began his term with intentions of delegating authority to his cabinet secretaries to select their own subordinates and to accomplish the goals of his administration. He would spend much of his time on international affairs; in domestic policy he would take only the big plays. In May 1968, Nixon declared:

> For one thing, I would disperse power, spread it among able people. Men operate best only if they are given the chance to operate at full capacity. I would operate differently from President Johnson. Instead of taking all power to myself, I'd select cabinet members who could do their jobs, and each of them would have the stature and the power to function effectively. Publicity would not center at the White House alone. Every key official would have the opportunity to be a big man in his field. On the other hand, when a president takes all the real power to himself, those around him become puppets. They shrivel up and become less and less creative. . . . your most creative people can't develop in a monolithic, centralized power set-up.[38]

Nixon's initial intentions were echoed by H. R. Haldeman: "Our job is not to do the work of government, but to get the work out to where it belongs—out to the departments."[39] Nixon's intentions were reflected in his selection of cabinet secretaries of stature and independent political standing and a White House staff that included the disparate viewpoints of liberal Patrick Moynihan and conservative Arthur Burns.

But disillusionment soon set in. Nixon found that the Democratically con-

---

[36]See Anderson, *The Presidents' Men,* p. 447.

[37]See the discussion in Anderson, *The Presidents' Men,* pp. 434–449.

[38]Quoted in Stephen Hess, *Organizing the Presidency* (Washington: Brookings, 1988), pp. 105–106.

[39]Quoted in William Safire, *Before the Fall* (New York: Doubleday, 1985), p. 116.

trolled Congress was not about to give him what he wanted, and he shifted to an administrative strategy to accomplish his goals. He would use all of the tools of the executive branch at his disposal. Nixon became convinced that a wide array of forces were intent on frustrating his aims. The Congress would not pass his proposals, the media were critically hostile, and the career bureaucracy would drag their collective feet and sabotage his policies. He even came to the conclusion that his own appointees in the executive departments had "gone native" and become more concerned with their own power and standing in their policy areas than in carrying out his priorities.

He decided to rein in the departments and agencies and created several mechanisms to facilitate White House control. Thus, instead of getting the work of the administration out to the departments and agencies, Nixon decided to bring the work of the departments and agencies into the White House, where he could carefully control policy development and oversee implementation.

Nixon's concept of the presidency was that the executive branch ought to be at his disposal. As John Ehrlichman put it: "There shouldn't be a lot of leeway in following the president's policies. It should be like a corporation, where the executive vice presidents (the cabinet officers) are tied closely to the chief executive, or to put it in extreme terms, when he says jump, they only ask how high."[40]

As Nixon became disillusioned with the executive branch he gave correspondingly greater power to his White House staff. The role of the staff came to be to buffer the president and to protect his time so that he could read, write, and ponder the big picture. In Nixon's words, "My disposition is to see that the president's time is not frittered away. I've found a way to do it. I'm a reader, not a buller."[41] Nixon's preference for time alone reinforced the tendency of the White House staff to guard access to him. The line between protecting the president's time and isolating the president became a fine one. According to Henry Kissinger, Nixon usually made decisions "in solitude on the basis of memoranda or with a few very intimate aides. He abhorred confronting colleagues with whom he disagreed . . . and he shunned persuading or inspiring his subordinates. He would decide from inside his self-imposed cocoon. . . . All this led to a vicious circle in which the president withdrew ever more into his isolation and pulled the central decisions increasingly into the White House."[42]

From the beginning Nixon had wanted a chief of staff to run his White House, and the role came naturally to H. R. Haldeman, a brilliant and hard-nosed organizer who had been with Nixon since his 1960 campaign for the presidency. To the rest of the executive branch and the outside world Nixon seemed isolated behind his "Berlin Wall" of Haldeman, Ehrlichman, and

---

[40]Quoted in Frederick C. Mosher, et. al., *Watergate: Implications for Responsible Government* (New York: Basic Books, 1974), p. 44.

[41]Quoted in Hess, *Organizing the Presidency,* p. 118.

[42]Quoted in Michael Genovese, *The Nixon Presidency* (New York: Greenwood Press, 1990).

Kissinger. According to one Nixon staffer, "The White House became an echo chamber that magnified the voice of the president but sacrificed true pitch."[43]

Haldeman was the linchpin in the White House staff system. He became the most powerful White House aide since Sherman Adams and ran the system with an iron hand. He clearly took precedence over the other staffers. "We all knew where we fit. There were five of us that were equal, but as [Bryce] Harlow said: there was a first among equals, and it was clearly me. Nobody questioned it. I never asserted it; I never argued it. I never had to."[44] According to Haldeman, "If I told someone to do something, he knew it wasn't me—he knew exactly what it was; it was an order from the president. They knew an appeal wouldn't get anywhere."[45]

His role, as he saw it, was to institute a "zero-defects system" in the staffing operation. He would ensure that all issues and options for the president were fully "staffed out" and that all bases had been touched. Access to the president by anyone except Kissinger was carefully controlled by Haldeman, and cabinet members frequently resented his gatekeeping. When cabinet secretaries actually did get in to see the president, Haldeman would be present to take notes, and the agenda for the meeting would often be presented to the president in such a way as to determine the outcome to the staff's satisfaction but not the visitor's.[46]

He controlled the paper flow and White House staffing. There was a follow-up system that would impose deadlines for staff projects. As the deadline approached, the staffer or his secretary would be reminded, and if the work was not ready or of unacceptable quality, increasingly heavy-handed reminders would hound the person until the work was completed to Haldeman's satisfaction.

The ostensible purpose of the tightly run system was to save the president from nonpresidential details so that he could concentrate on the big picture. The irony was that despite the time that Nixon reserved for thinking great thoughts, he was obsessed with details of the White House operation, both of substance and style. He was concerned with White House furniture, who had what photographs of former presidents in the Executive Office Building, and he wanted extensive memos to him on what wines would be served at White House functions. He had White House staffers log the comments visitors made on the paintings displayed in the west lobby and he kept careful inventory of small gifts (cuff links, ash trays, and copies of *Six Crises*) that were given out to visitors to the White House. There were many memoranda about the White House tennis courts.[47]

Although the Watergate scandals were not caused by the staffing system, both Watergate and the staff organization were reflections of Nixon's psychol-

[43]Hess, *Organizing the Presidency,* p. 119.

[44]Author's interview, Los Angeles, CA (May 25, 1983).

[45]Author's interview, Los Angeles, CA (May 25, 1983).

[46]See Johnson, *Managing the White House,* pp. 218–221.

[47]See the testimony of Alexander Butterfield before the House Impeachment Committee reprinted in Larry Berman, *The New American Presidency* (Boston: Little, Brown, 1987), pp. 264–272.

ogy and character. Despite the fact that Haldeman was close enough to the president to occasionally delay implementation of questionable off-the-cuff orders and demands by an irritated Nixon, there was never any question or doubt in the White House about covering up the initial Watergate break-in. The tone was set by Nixon, and the staff unquestioningly carried out his wishes. The problem was that Haldeman and the staff system he set up faithfully reflected and reinforced Nixon's dark side and need for isolation. Thus, the zero-defects system allowed the Watergate "horrors" and led to the resignations and convictions of top White House staffers and the unprecedented resignation of a U.S. president.

FORD'S AND CARTER'S LESSONS

When Richard Nixon's resignation elevated Gerald Ford to the presidency, as Henry Kissinger said, "The presidency was in a shambles."[48] Ford's challenge was to make a sharp break with the Watergate aspects of the Nixon presidency, but to maintain some continuity of leadership and policy. Ford chose to distance himself rhetorically and symbolically from Nixon, proclaiming that "Our long national nightmare is over," and being very visible and accessible.

Part of the Watergate baggage that Ford wanted to throw out was the tightly hierarchical White House organization symbolized by H. R. Haldeman. "A Watergate was made possible by a strong chief of staff and ambitious White House aides who were more powerful than members of the cabinet but who had little or no practical political experience or judgement. I wanted to reverse the trend and restore authority to my cabinet."[49] Ford resolved that there would be no powerful chief of staff, and his transition team of advisers concurred with his judgment, though it recommended a "staff coordinator." Ford got along for a while with nine of his top aides reporting directly to him, but after a month of staff squabbling and difficulties in coordination he brought the ambassador to NATO, Donald Rumsfeld, to fill the role.

Rumsfeld knew he had to bring order to the White House advising system and begin to assert control over access to the president, who was being overwhelmed by his too-open system. Rumsfeld also had to impose order on policy development. Ford had given his vice president, Nelson Rockefeller, jurisdiction over domestic policy and control over the domestic policy staff. One of Rumsfeld's roles was to say no to the vice president; a very delicate task, given his constitutional status and the turf ceded to him by the president. But someone had to make sure that the policies proposed by the administration were

[48]Quoted in Roger Porter, "Gerald R. Ford: A Healing Presidency," in Greenstein, *Leadership and the Modern Presidency,* p. 200.

[49]Quoted in Porter, "A Healing Presidency," p. 212.

consistent with Gerald Ford's conservative philosophy, and Ford did not want to say no to Rockefeller. Someone had to say no, and Rumsfeld was the one to do it.[50]

The order brought about by Rumsfeld convinced Ford that the role of firm coordinator was necessary, and when Ford replaced James Schlesinger at Defense with Rumsfeld, he gave the task to Richard Cheney, Rumsfeld's deputy. In admitting that the spokes-of-the-wheel approach would not work, Ford said:

> I believe a president has to have a chief of staff who is an expert manager and one who does not seek on his own a high identity—in fact, one who purposely avoids that. That individual has to coordinate everything that transpires in the west wing of the White House and the Oval Office. . . . If you don't have that kind of person, I don't think the president's job can be well done.[51]

Cheney's approach to the position, which was finally acknowledged to be the chief of staff and not the euphemism of staff coordinator, was to maintain very low visibility. He took seriously the prescription of the Brownlow Committee that White House aides should have a "passion for anonymity."

He made no public speeches and talked with reporters on the understanding that his name would not be used in the articles. "I had made a very determined decision to keep my head down, and I stuck to it. I thought I could get a hell of a lot more done if I was not a public figure."[52] His low visibility was a source of strength in his role. He did not have a policy agenda of his own, and he was a neutral broker among disparate advice going to the president. In his role, he was not heavy-handed as Sherman Adams and H. R. Haldeman had been in performing the same role. But his courteous and "nice guy" image did not prevent him from asserting a firm control over White House policy development and staff.

Cheney imposed order on policy development by guarding against "oh, by the way" decisions. The presidency is always subject to the wiles of cabinet officers and others who try to gain an advantage by getting the president alone in an unguarded minute to push their own policy preferences. If this is not caught and nipped in the bud, it can be very embarrassing to the president by prematurely committing him to a decision before it has been fully staffed out, and can lead to embarrassing reversals by the president. If an aide or cabinet member wanted to raise an issue with the president, Cheney would insist that it be vetted with all others who had a legitimate say in that policy area.

Cheney recognized the tenuousness of the delicate balance needed to

---

[50]See the remarks by Rumsfeld in Samuel Kernell and Samuel Popkin, *Chief of Staff* (Berkeley: University of California Press, 1986).

[51]Quoted in Porter, "A Healing Presidency," p. 212.

[52]Quoted in Medved, *The Shadow Presidents,* p. 340.

make his approach to the chief of staff position successful. "It's really a matter of trade-offs. . . . There is no question that to the extent that you involve a number of people in the consultative process before you make a decision, you raise the level of noise in the system. You enhance the possibility of premature disclosures and leaks. You also take more time, cut down in efficiency. On the other side, by encouraging different viewpoints you make sure that the president's got a wide variety of options so he won't be blindsided."[53]

The difference between Cheney's approach to the chief of staff position and that of Adams and Haldeman was that Cheney was courteous and solicitous, while they were brusque, harsh, and imperious. Cheney maintained a very low profile by design, while they received much press coverage because of their assistant president images. Cheney controlled access to the president, but they constricted the flow to a trickle that they personally controlled. Cheney did the "dirty deeds" that a chief of staff must do, but did not relish the task, while they seemed to revel in asserting their power. Cheney kept his channels to the Hill open, while they never made serious attempts to court Congress. Finally, Cheney worked for Gerald Ford, who consciously tried to be open, while they worked for presidents who, though very different people, each wanted to be buffered and protected from many of the pressures that focus on the presidency.

Jimmy Carter won a narrow victory over Gerald Ford in 1976, but came to office with the same predilections about Watergate and White House organization. He ran as an outsider, owing little to the Democratic party. He promised to clean up the "horrible bureaucratic mess" in Washington and never to lie to the American people. He promised cabinet government with access to the president and a White House staff that would not assert itself over cabinet secretaries.

Carter's approach to White House organization reflected his personality. In addition to thinking that Nixon's hierarchical White House, with a strong chief of staff, was a cause of Watergate, he felt that he was smart enough to be his own chief of staff. There was no doubt about his intelligence. He had been a nuclear engineer in the Navy and could comprehend a greater amount of written material than any of his staffers. But according to Jack Watson, Carter was more of a problem-solver than a politician, and in his in-depth grasp of policy problems did not understand that the best is the enemy of the good.[54] He also did not want to choose one from among his Georgia staffers to be in charge of the others.

But the problem of White House organization is more than a question of the intelligence of the president, it is also a matter of filtering information and regulating access. With eight top White House aides reporting directly to Carter

[53]Quoted in Medved, *The Shadow Presidents,* p. 339.

[54]Jack Watson's remarks at a conference on the "Origins, Development and Future of the American Presidency," at Gannon University, Erie, PA (April 25, 1987).

President and Mrs. Clinton, along with all of the living former U.S. presidents and their wives, at the funeral of former President Richard M. Nixon on April 27, 1994. *(Left to right)* Bill and Hillary Clinton, George and Barbara Bush, Ronald and Nancy Reagan, Jimmy and Rosalyn Carter, Gerald and Betty Ford. (Reuters/Gary A. Cameron/Archive Photos)

and no staff secretary or chief of staff to coordinate policy development, no one short of the president was in charge. As a result, Carter took up his time with policy details that might have been settled at lower levels and spent time settling White House staff and cabinet secretary disputes that no one else had the authority to settle, even if the issues were not of presidential importance. Another problem was that Carter was unwilling to choose priorities from among his many policy initiatives. Thus, the first year of his administration was rocky, with some victories and some defeats, but with no overall theme that he could use to unify his administration or project to the country.

With the seeming lack of vision haunting his presidency, and an oil shortage that created block-long lines of cars for gas in the summer of 1979, Carter went up to Camp David to reassess his presidency. After talking with many people from all walks of life and seeking advice on his administration, he gave a prime-time speech to the nation and argued that tough decisions had to be made on energy and other policy areas. The same week he also accepted the resignations of five of his cabinet secretaries and designated Hamilton Jordan as his chief of staff. The final recognition that a chief of staff was necessary to coordinate policy development and relations between the White House and the cabinet was a salutary one, but it was undercut by choosing Jordan. Jordan had been with Carter longest and was closest to him of all of the Georgians; but Jordan was a brilliant campaign strategist, not an organizational genius. But coordination did improve when Jordan left the White House to run the campaign and Jack Watson was named chief of staff and Alonzo McDonald was named staff director.

Scholars have speculated as to why Carter's White House staff, which was made up of highly intelligent individuals, did not gel into an effective White House team. One of the probable causes was that Carter was unwilling to leaven his Georgian staffers with more Washington insiders. Among his top White House staff, only Zbigniew Brzezinski was not from Georgia and, among the Georgians, only Stuart Eizenstat had previous Washington experience. Former Senator Walter Mondale was a close adviser to Carter personally, but as vice president could not be expected to hold the White House staff in line.[55]

What the Ford and Carter presidencies proved was that, with the growth of staff in the White House and the expanded functions it is expected to perform for presidents, the modern White House cannot function effectively without a chief of staff. This person does not have to fill the role as the strong chiefs of the Eisenhower and Nixon presidencies did, but must at least coordinate and take charge of the policy process and advice to the president. The two contrasting ways to fill the chief of staff role were exemplified by the Adams-Haldeman model of the strong chief contrasted with the facilitating model of Cheney-Watkins. The Reagan presidency was to exemplify the best and worst of the two approaches in its first and second terms.

REAGAN'S CONTRASTING TERMS

As it is with all presidents, the shape and role of the White House staff was a reflection of Ronald Reagan's personality. By all accounts, both friendly and critical, Reagan was extremely passive in his approach to the White House staff. He was not passive with respect to the major direction of his presidency or public policy; his was an active administration. But once the direction was set by Reagan, his aides formulated the policies and carried them out; Reagan was interested only in outcomes and did not want to be bothered with details.

Part of his passiveness was due to his uncritical trust in whatever people told him or what he read.[56] This passiveness made him dependent on his staff,

---

[55]See Q. Whitfield Ayres, "The Carter White House Staff," in M. Glen Abernathy, et. al., eds., *The Carter Years* (New York: St. Martin's Press, 1984), pp. 144–164.

[56]See Lou Cannon, *President Reagan: The Role of a Lifetime* (New York: Simon & Schuster, 1991), chap. 10 and p. 181.

who had to make sure he was not unduly influenced by the most recent person he saw.[57] Donald Regan recalled, "I cannot remember a single case in which he changed a time or cancelled an appointment or ever complained about an item on his schedule."[58]

Reagan's hands-off approach to his staff was based on a management philosophy that relied on delegation of authority. In his words: "Surround yourself with the best people you can find, delegate authority, and don't interfere as long as the policy you've decided upon is being carried out."[59] This approach occasionally frustrated administration officials because of Reagan's unwillingness to give them policy guidance. Donald Regan complained: "In the four years that I served as secretary of the treasury I never saw President Reagan alone and never discussed economic philosophy. . . . I had to figure these things out like any other American, by studying his speeches and reading the newspapers. . . . After I accepted the job, he simply hung up and vanished." Reagan "laid down no rules and articulated no missions" and thus conferred great "latitude on his subordinates."[60] To David Stockman, Reagan "seemed so serene and passive; . . . He gave no orders, no commands; asked for no information; expressed no urgency. . . . Since I *did* know what to do, I took his quiet message of confidence to be a mandate."[61] Stockman observed that, whenever there was an argument, Reagan would smile and say: "Okay, you fellas work it out."[62]

Reagan's passivity and penchant for delegation made his staff crucial to his presidency in a way that was not true of Franklin Roosevelt, John Kennedy, or George Bush. The unique division of labor in his first term worked in a particularly felicitous way for Reagan. The definition of staff roles began before the inauguration, immediately after the election, when the decisions were made about the structure and organization of the top staff. The outcome was driven by the widespread expectation that Edwin Meese, who had run the campaign, headed the transition, and had run Reagan's gubernatorial office in California, would naturally be named Reagan's White House chief of staff. But others around Reagan judged that Meese, though unquestionably loyal and ideologically dedicated, did not have the organizational talent or discipline to perform well as chief of staff.

Reagan must be given credit for accepting their advice that he needed a Washington insider for his chief of staff and saying no to the loyal Meese. Baker had supported George Bush for the presidential nomination in 1976 and 1980,

---

[57]Hedrick Smith, *The Power Game* (New York: Random House, 1988), p. 305.

[58]Donald Regan, *For the Record* (New York: Harcourt Brace Jovanovich, 1988), p. 272.

[59]Ann Reilly Dowd, "What Managers Can Learn from Manager Reagan," *Fortune* (September 15, 1986), p. 33.

[60]Regan, *For the Record,* pp. 142–143, 144.

[61]David Stockman, *The Triumph of Politics* (New York: Harper & Row, 1986), p. 76.

[62]Stockman, *The Triumph of Politics,* p. 109.

but he turned out to be the architect of the historic Reagan victories of the first year. In order to get Meese to go along with the plan, he had to be convinced that he would still play a major role in the administration. This task was accomplished by a memo initialed by both Baker and Meese that divided up the responsibilities of the two advisers. On the surface, the division was heavily slanted toward Meese, giving him jurisdiction over administration policy, both foreign and domestic. Meese was to have the title of "counselor to the president for policy," along with cabinet rank, and was to participate in all meetings of the full cabinet. He was in charge of "coordination and supervision" of the domestic policy staff and the National Security Council.[63] Thus, Meese was given a very wide range of responsibilities indeed. What was left for Baker?

Baker was to get the formal title of chief of staff and the traditional process and staffing powers of that position. He was given control over "coordination and supervision of White House staff functions," "hiring and firing authority over all elements of White House staff," "coordination and control of all in and out paper flow to the president and of presidential schedule and appointments," and he was to "preside over meetings of White House staff." Baker also claimed the traditional chief of staff office in the west wing. An addition, written in longhand, ensured that both Meese and Baker had the right to "attend any meeting which Pres. attends—w/his consent."[64]

On the surface Meese had a huge advantage, with cabinet participation and control of foreign and domestic policy; the memo was designed so that Baker received no substance and all process. But in the White House, process often determines policy outcomes, especially with as detached a president as Ronald Reagan, and thus Baker had the advantage over Meese in the administration's policy deliberations.

As chief of staff, Baker hired skilled Washington insiders to help him, and he orchestrated the administration's policy agenda for the first term. He did not seek complete control over access to the president, sharing it with Meese and Michael Deaver, and he exercised his power in a subtle rather than a heavy-handed way. With his reputation for pragmatism that invoked the suspicion of the ideological Reaganites, he was careful to keep open his lines of communication to the right wing of the Republican party, and he assiduously maintained his ties to members of Congress. He was accessible to and trusted by the press, and often received favorable news coverage, which he used to the administration's advantage. He thus was attentive to the major constituencies that Reagan would need to accomplish his agenda. Richard Darman was staff secretary and controlled paper flow to the Oval Office.

Michael Deaver, the third member of the troika, had been with Reagan for

---

[63]See Smith, *The Power Game,* pp. 314–315. The memo is reproduced in Bob Schieffer and Gary Paul Gates, *The Acting President* (New York: E.P. Dutton, 1989), p. 83.

[64]Memo dated November 13, 1980, reproduced in Schieffer and Gates, *The Acting President,* p. 83.

many years in California and was so close to the Reagans that they considered him almost a son. Deaver became deputy chief of staff, but he was not concerned as much with the substance of policy as with the staging of the president and his presentation to the public.[65] He concerned himself with everything that affected Ronald Reagan as a person: his comfort, his schedule, the backdrops for his political actions, etc. Perhaps most importantly, Deaver was the primary link to the east wing, that is, to Nancy Reagan. He would pass on her wishes, either explicitly or as his own ideas, to the west wing staffers. Baker appreciated the importance of Mrs. Reagan, and sensitively allied himself with her and accommodated her wishes.

Nancy Reagan was not interested or active in policy across-the-board, but she selectively inserted her views very effectively when she felt that the president's person or reputation was at stake. Several times this affected foreign policy and, quite often, staffing decisions. She played a role in the resignations of cabinet secretaries James Watt, Raymond Donavan, Edwin Meese, and a number of White House staffers, including Donald Regan.[66]

The White House was to change drastically in Reagan's second term, with large-scale changes of personnel at the top. Despite the 1986 tax reform, Reagan's second term brought no sweeping victories comparable to the economic agenda of 1981, and the administration slid into the disaster of the Iran–Contra scandal. The second term troubles were due, in no small part, to the change in chiefs of staff. Treasury Secretary Donald Regan and Chief of Staff James Baker decided to exchange jobs, and characteristically, Regan, Baker, Deaver, and Nancy Reagan had agreed on the switch before it was presented to Reagan. Characteristically, Reagan agreed to the staff decision with no questions.

When Regan came in to run the White House he had several personal priorities. He wanted to do away with the collegial staffing arrangement of the first term that he felt led to staff conflict and leaks, which it did. He also wanted to make some personnel changes, but most importantly he wanted to "let Reagan be Reagan."

Regan's personal style and career suggested that he would take a different approach to running the White House than had James Baker. Regan had been an officer in the Marines and was used to being CEO of Merrill Lynch. "When I was chief executive and I said, 'Jump,' people asked, 'How high?' As secretary of the treasury, when I said, 'Jump," people said, 'What do you mean by jump? What do you mean by high'?"[67] According to one of Regan's aides, "He considers the executive branch to be like a corporation. Cabinet members are vice presidents, the president is the chairman of the board, the chief of staff is

---

[65]Smith, *The Power Game,* p. 299.

[66]See the insightful discussion of Nancy Reagan's role in the Reagan administration by Richard Neustadt, *Presidential Power and the Modern Presidents* (New York: Free Press, 1990), pp. 312–316.

[67]William R. Doener, "For Rhyme and Reason," *Time* (January 21, 1985), p. 20.

the chief operating officer."[68] Regan was used to being a principal and did not easily slide into a staff role.

Whereas Baker had brought strong subordinates to work with him, Regan would brook no rivals for influence. The staffers he brought from his days at the Treasury Department were known around the White House as "the mice" because of their meek approach to their boss. According to White House staffers, Regan's personal staff aides were "almost obsequious and scared stiff of him."[69] A former colleague of Regan said: "His weakness is that his ego was so strong he did not pick good subordinates. Or if they were, he broke them. He couldn't stand the competition."[70]

At the same time that Regan was establishing himself as chief of staff, other strong advisers to the president were leaving the White House. Baker and Meese were taking cabinet positions; Deaver was leaving the White House to make money; Darman left with Baker; David Stockman was on his way to Wall Street. Max Friedersdorf and Ed Rollins stayed for a while in the second term, but soon left.

Regan's wanting to "let Reagan be Reagan," led him to think that his own lack of strong policy preferences was a guarantee that he was serving the president's goals and no one else's. But to best serve the president, the White House staff must compensate for his weaknesses. In this case, the president's weakness was his passivity and not being willing to search out alternatives on his own. This placed the responsibility on the staff to ensure that contrasting views were brought to the president's attention. In the first term this was ensured, despite the staff's intentions to protect the president from conflict, because the rivalries among the staff and the struggle between conservatives and moderates could not be entirely suppressed.

Reinforcing the president's conviction that most policy problems were really very simple was another consequence of "letting Reagan be Reagan," but this was not a favor to the president. In criticizing Regan, David Stockman called this "the echo principle" and argued that it shielded Reagan from hard economic realities.[71] According to Richard Darman, one of the advantages of the first-term conflictual triumvirate was that the president was forced to face up to some complex realities. "Seeing the interplay between us, a lot of things happened. First of all, Ronald Reagan learned much more about reality."[72]

But Don Regan was doing his best to stifle this built-in safety valve. He asserted tight control over the White House, controlling access to the president,

---

[68]Ed Magnuson, "Shake-Up at the White House," *Time* (January 21, 1985), p. 10.

[69]Bernard Weinraub, "How Don Regan Runs the White House," *The New York Times* (January 5, 1986), p. 33.

[70]Quoted in Cannon, *Role of a Lifetime,* p. 563.

[71]Stockman, *The Triumph of Politics,* pp. 18–19, Photograph No. 42.

[72]Quoted by Bob Schieffer and Gary Gates, *The Acting President* (New York: Dutton, 1989), p. 200.

scheduling, paper flow, public appearances, appointments, and phone calls. Also, unlike other strong chiefs of staff, he attempted to assert control over national security policy. But Regan's heavy-handed attempt to control everything went too far. Long-time Reagan intimate Stuart Spencer observed that Regan "became a prime minister, he became a guy that was in every photo op, he wasn't watching the shop. And he surrounded himself with yes people. Those were all signs of weakness to me."[73]

Contrary to the Brownlowian admonition to have a passion for anonymity, Regan sought the limelight, and was constantly trying to get into photographs with the president that would appear in the newspapers. The most egregious example of this was the official photograph of Presidents Reagan and Gorbachev at the Geneva Summit. The White House photo showed the two leaders sitting on a couch with Don Regan behind them, leaning forward as if he were the orchestrator of their agreement. Regan, who as chief of staff made the final decision, insisted that this be the only photo of the summit agreement released by the White House.[74]

In "letting Reagan be Reagan" Regan acted as if the president were his only constituent. He did not seem to realize that in order to serve the President effectively, a chief of staff needs to cultivate other constituencies, especially Congress and the press. Regan soon alienated members of Congress with his disdain for Congress as an institution and his distaste for politics. He antagonized the press because of his heavy-handed attempts to control leaks and his hostility over unfavorable coverage of the administration. Unlike Baker, he did not realize that the press "serves as a bulletin board" upon which Washington insiders post notices, and use it to his (and his president's) advantage.[75]

Regan had other drawbacks as chief of staff, one of which was not getting along with the First Lady. According to Nancy Reagan, Regan liked the sound of "chief" but not the sound of "staff."[76] Nor did Regan care much for Nancy. "Mrs. Reagan regarded herself as the president's alter ego . . . as if the office that had been bestowed upon her husband by the people somehow fell into the category of worldly goods covered by the marriage vows."[77] He also resented the influence of Nancy's astrologer on the management of the presidency. "Virtually every major move and decision the Reagans made during my time as White House chief of staff was cleared in advance with a woman in San Francisco who drew up horoscopes to make certain that the planets were in a favorable alignment for the enterprise."[78] "At times the president's schedule

---

[73]Quoted by Cannon, *The Role of a Lifetime,* p. 721.

[74]Maureen Dowd, "Saving Face Means Having It in the Picture," *The New York Times* (June 16, 1991), p. 1, 18.

[75]Smith, *The Power Game,* p. 81.

[76]Cannon, *Role of a Lifetime,* p. 566.

[77]Regan, *For the Record,* p. 288.

[78]Regan, *For the Record,* p. 3.

would have to be changed at the last minute, or set for precise timing, at the behest of Joan Quigley, the Reagans' astrologer."[79]

While chiefs of staff traditionally take the blame for the president, Regan wasn't always willing to take the heat for administration failures. After the disclosure of the administration's dealings with Iran, and the failed Reykjavik summit, Regan tried to distance himself from the embarrassment. "Some of us are like a shovel brigade that follow [sic] a parade down Main Street cleaning up. We took Reykjavik and turned what was really a sour situation into something that turned out pretty well."[80] What is unsettling about this statement is that Regan is shifting blame for administration embarrassments away from himself and toward the person who was in charge of U.S. performance at the Reykjavik summit: President Reagan. The strong implication here is that Regan saw himself as cleaning up after the president made a mess of things. This public shifting of blame to the president is unacceptable for a White House staffer.

The final straw in Regan's term as chief of staff was the Report of the Tower Commission. Despite the fact that Regan denied that he had any control over foreign policy, the Tower Commission held him responsible for the Iran–Contra disaster. According to Brent Scowcroft, Regan claimed to have jurisdiction over foreign policy advice to the president. "He kept saying he did. One of the reasons McFarlane quit was because Regan wanted McFarlane to report through him."[81]

The Tower Commission that investigated the Iran–Contra scandal did not accept Regan's denials. Although it did not conclude that Regan participated in the scandal or the cover-up, it did hold him responsible for allowing it to happen on his watch. In citing the "failure of responsibility" the board pointed out that ultimate responsibility for the White House staff system belongs to the president, but that Regan was partially responsible for the disaster. "More than almost any chief of staff of recent memory, he asserted personal control over the White House staff and sought to extend this control to the national security advisor. He was personally active in national security affairs and attended almost all of the relevant meetings regarding the Iran initiative. . . . He must bear primary responsibility for the chaos that descended upon the White House when such disclosure did occur."[82]

After resisting as long as he could and after much prodding from his wife

---

[79]See Cannon, *The Role of A Lifetime,* pp. 583–588.

[80]Quoted by David Hoffman, "Regan: Chief of Risk" *Washington Post* (February 28, 1987), pp. 1, 16. The rest of Regan's comments were: "Who was it that took this disinformation thing and managed to turn it? Who was it [sic] took on this loss in the Senate and pointed out a few facts and managed to pull that? I don't say we'll be able to do it four times in a row. But here we go again, and we're trying."

[81]Quoted in Cannon, *The Role of a Lifetime,* p. 720.

[82]*Report of the President's Special Review Board* (Washington, DC, February 26, 1987), pp. IV-10–IV-11.

and other intimates, the president asked for Regan's resignation, but agreed to wait until several days after the release of the Tower Report as a facesaving gesture. But the coup de grace was administered by Nancy immediately after release of the report when it was leaked to the press from her office that Howard Baker would be Reagan's new chief of staff. As soon as he heard of the press announcement, Regan immediately resigned.[83]

After the resignation on February 27, 1987, Regan's problems were summed up by a former Reagan White House staffer:

> Don never realized that while Wall Street runs one way; Pennsylvania Avenue is a two-way street. He never realized there is a difference between being an elected and an appointed official. He never realized the distinction between being a staff person and the chief executive officer. He never realized that the White House demands talent throughout, rather than talent derived. He never realized his job was to compensate for the perceived strengths and weaknesses of others, rather than to dominate those weaknesses.[84]

BUSH'S PIT BULL

George Bush recruited a competent White House staff marked by professionalism and a low-visibility approach to White House service. The best in White House staff service was exemplified by Brent Scowcroft, assistant to the president for national security affairs, who had filled the same role in the Ford administration. Scowcroft was tireless in his service to Bush, and often provided a personal sounding board to Bush's thoughts about foreign affairs. Another model White House staffer was Roger Porter, who had served in the Ford and Reagan administrations and was made assistant to the president for domestic and economic policy in the Bush White House. He provided experience, expertise, and sound policy analysis without engaging in public disputes over policy or status or trying to strong-arm members of the cabinet.

Bush's White House staff did not tend to interpose themselves between the president and cabinet secretaries or have major fights with the cabinet departments because Bush knew his cabinet well, and unlike Reagan, made it a habit to keep in touch with them. So Bush's White House did not have major ego problems or conflicts with the cabinet, with one major exception: his chief of staff, John Sununu.

---

[83]See the account by Cannon, *The Role of a Lifetime,* pp. 722–732.

[84]David Hoffman, "Regan: Chief of Risk," *Washington Post* (February 28, 1987), pp. 1, 16. Reagan biographer Lou Cannon argued that Regan had four deficiencies as chief of staff: (1) his ego was too large; (2) he held politics in disdain; (3) he did not appreciate Nancy's role in the administration; and (4) he brought the "mice" with him to the White House instead of recruiting a strong staff, as Baker had. See Cannon, *The Role of a Lifetime,* p. 567.

President Bush, who had a chief of staff (Craig Fuller) when he was vice president, clearly wanted a chief to organize the White House and coordinate policy development. And Sununu performed well many of the traditional chief of staff roles. He made the trains run on time. He was the enforcer with respect to White House staffers, the cabinet, and Congress. He fired people, and he took the heat for unpopular decisions.

Sununu presided over the senior staff meeting every day at 7:30 AM in the Roosevelt Room in the White House. Typically, he spent from 8 AM to 9:30 AM in the Oval Office with the president for the national security briefing and setting priorities for the day, and ended the day with the president from 4:30 PM to 5 PM. During the day he would see the president about ten times and would spend a total of 35 to 45 percent of the day with the president.[85]

One common mistake of chiefs of staff that Sununu did not make was to reinforce a presidential weakness, as had Haldeman and Regan before him. He provided a sharp contrast in personal style to the president. He was the president's "pit bull" dog who would act mean and allow the president to take the "kinder and gentler" stance. Sununu, unlike the three previous strong chiefs of staff, had firm ideological convictions and advocated his own policy preferences. But what would ordinarily be a major drawback in a chief of staff worked to the president's advantage in this case. Sununu was more conservative politically than the president and was willing to play a highly visible role as keeper of the conservative flame and representative of the conservative wing of the Republican party in the White House. When Sununu would stake out a very conservative position, for instance on environmental policy, it would allow the president to take a more moderate stance, thus reassuring conservatives that their interests were being represented in the White House, while letting the president still claim to be "the environmental president."

The danger of a chief of staff who is also a policy advocate is that advice to the president might be skewed to favor the chief of staff's favored outcome. The other common danger of a strong chief of staff is that access to the president will be constricted. President Bush's style of governing minimized these dangers. He knew enough about the policy issues himself to be able to discount the bias of his staff. And his personal style of frequent communication with members of his cabinet mitigated the danger that he would become isolated, even though Sununu did control access to the Oval Office. The president was often on the phone, touching base with anyone who was involved with current policy issues.

But the president's penchant for keeping in touch, while avoiding the danger of isolation, did not entirely eliminate Sununu's attempts to control communication to the president. Sununu's personal policy agenda made it at times difficult for those in the cabinet or staff who wanted to speak with the president about a different approach to get through Sununu's gauntlet. This problem became pub-

---

[85]See Burt Solomon, "No-Nonsense Sununu," *National Journal* (September 16, 1989), p. 2251.

lic when both *Time* and *Newsweek* ran stories that senior Bush aides were so upset at being cut off by Sununu that the president was forced to open a post office box at his summer home in Kennebunkport, Maine, as a back channel so that his top advisers could contact him directly without Sununu's censorship.[86]

The existence of this avenue of communication was publicly confirmed by Health and Human Services Secretary Louis Sullivan, who admitted on television that he used the channel to communicate advice to the president.[87] After the admission, Sullivan quickly covered himself by saying that he had no trouble meeting with the president when he needed to on public policy issues, but that he had used the post office box for "political advice." The point is not what Sullivan had to say to the president; the point is the very fact that President Bush felt compelled to set up a private post office box, physically and organizationally outside the White House, was an admission of organizational failure.

Another indicator of that failure was the Council of Economic Advisers Chair Michael Boskin's attempt to see the president in the fall of 1991. After several unsuccessful attempts to get in to see Bush, on November 20, 1991, Boskin threatened to resign if Sununu did not allow him to talk to the president about economic policy.[88] In these instances John Sununu was not acting as a "neutral broker" of ideas for the president. White House staffers and cabinet secretaries did not have the confidence that their ideas would reach the president intact if they submitted them to the White House staff. Instead, Sununu was seen as a biased filter, screening out ideas he personally did not like.

Despite his rapport with the president and his ability to perform very valuable chief of staff functions, Sununu made four strategic errors as chief of staff:

1. He let his ego cloud his judgment and affect his behavior.
2. He succumbed to the "John Tower syndrome," thinking that he did not have to be nice to people.
3. He fell victim to the "Gary Hart syndrome," feeling that he was so important that he did not have to pay attention to the conventions of public morality.
4. He developed the "Don Regan syndrome": stay in the limelight, and if things go wrong, blame the president.

Professional colleagues in and out of the White House criticized Sununu for his large ego. When he came to the Republican convention in Houston it was reported that Sununu had vice presidential aspirations.[89] When he was chief of staff he had his staff do research to find out if the fact that he was born

---

[86]See *Time* (September 30, 1991), p. 19; and *Newsweek* (December 30, 1991), p. 4.

[87]"This Week with David Brinkley," ABC News, Transcript of program of February 2, 1992, p. 13.

[88]Bob Woodward, "The President's Key Men," *Washington Post* (October 7, 1992), p. A18.

[89]See Eleanor Randolph, "The Washington Chain-Saw Massacre," *The Washington Post Magazine* (December 2, 1990), p. 37.

in Cuba disqualified him from being president.[90] One of his soft spots was his stratospheric IQ, which reportedly was 180. But it struck many with whom he worked that he seemed to have to put others down in order to demonstrate how smart he was. White House staffers and assistant secretaries did not appreciate being denigrated in front of their peers when their staff work did not seem to measure up to Sununu's standards. He told one reporter who asked about his interpersonal skills that it "depends how badly the other guy's screwing up."[91]

Sununu really seemed to believe his oft-stated maxim that he had a constituency of only one, the president. This led to Sununu's strategic error number two: the John Tower syndrome. Senator Tower was President Bush's first nomination to be secretary of defense. After many years as a member of the Senate Armed Services Committee, and several years as a Reagan-appointed negotiator, there was no doubt that Tower was qualified. But after he had been nominated, people came forward with allegations about his private life, including excessive drinking, sexual misconduct, and possible conflicts of interest. Normally a senator will be given an easy time by former colleagues in confirmation hearings, but Tower had been so rude and arrogant as a senator that few of his former colleagues were willing to come to his defense when the charges of misconduct were raised. Thus, Tower was the first initial nomination by a president to a cabinet position in history to be defeated. A similar fate would befall John Sununu when he got into hot water.

Far from being responsible to a constituency of only one, strong chiefs of staff have demonstrated the lesson that serving the president means being able to cultivate other constituencies for his use. Sununu did not recognize this, and thus felt free to alienate Congress, the cabinet, the press, and interest groups, as well as his White House subordinates. It is as if his attitude were: 'I am so powerful that I do not have to be nice, or even minimally civil, to other people.' In this he was ignoring the old Lebanese proverb that holds, "One kisses the hand that one cannot yet bite."[92] When Sununu got into trouble, those who previously had to kiss his hand turned to bite it.

Sununu systematically alienated and insulted many members of Congress. He once called Republican Senator Trent Lott "insignificant," a serious insult in Washington, especially to a member of the Senate.[93] His behavior at the 1990 Budget summit, in formal meetings with the leadership of Congress, was so obnoxious that he prompted Senator Robert Byrd to chastise him: "I have had thirty years in the U.S. Senate, and I have participated in many such summits, and I have never in my life observed such outrageous conduct as that displayed

[90]Sidney Blumenthal, "So Long, Sununu," *Vanity Fair* (February 1992), p. 168.

[91]Quoted in "John Sununu: What Color Is Your Parachute?" *Spy* (March 1992), p. 31.

[92]Proverb quoted in *Time* (May 21, 1990), p. 25.

[93]Blumenthal, "So Long, Sununu," p. 168.

by the representatives of the president of the United States. Your conduct is arrogant. It is rude. It is intolerable."[94]

Sununu was also willing to alienate cabinet secretaries as well as their subordinates. He often undercut their policy proposals to the president, which may very well have been part of his job as chief of staff policing the policy development function. When he fought HHS Secretary Louis Sullivan on civil rights policy, or EPA Administrator William Reilly on environmental issues, it was arguably part of his job and carrying out the president's wishes. But the tone of his communications often left cabinet members feeling that more than policy differences were being conveyed. The gratuitous insulting of others is not a necessary part of the policy coordination function. Treasury Secretary Nicholas Brady, a close friend of the president's, told a friend that he was sick of being denigrated by Sununu.[95] Commerce Secretary Robert Mosbacher complained about being forced by Sununu to accept unwanted political appointees. Sununu also made a tactical error when he refused to let Defense Secretary Richard Cheney use the presidential helicopter to fly to Camp David on official business.[96]

Even though the U.S. Chamber of Commerce is an important Republican constituency, Sununu did not hesitate to verbally brutalize its president, Dick Lesher, when he supported a cut in Social Security payroll taxes. That Lesher was supporting a tax cut that the Bush administration might very well have backed in different circumstances (i.e., it was not a matter of principle), highlights Sununu's extreme response to a relatively minor policy difference.

In defense of his behavior, Sununu echoed other chiefs of staff in claiming he was merely doing the president's bidding. "I'm no freelancer. I meet with the president dozens of times during the day. . . . The president knows I'm following his agenda. . . . I know enough about the president to do exactly what he wants done. Exactly what he wants done."[97] In this statement, Sununu was both claiming presidential authority for all of his own actions and subtly shifting the blame for any of them to the president.

Sununu's explanation for his lack of civility is that each breach of good taste and manners was carefully calculated: "I guarantee you that contrary to the legend, any strong statements on my part are both controlled, deliberate, and designed to achieve an effect. There is no random outburst. It all is designed for purpose. And I think the efficiency of the result is underscored by what we've been able to achieve."[98] This rationalization is consistent with one

[94]Blumenthal, "So Long, Sununu," p. 168.

[95]Blumenthal, "So Long, Sununu," p. 113.

[96]Blumenthal, "So Long, Sununu," p. 168.

[97]Juan Williams, "George Bush's Flying Circus," *Washington Post* (November 24, 1991), pp. C1, C4.

[98]Quoted in Ann Devroy, "Citing Year of Triumph, Sununu Defends Actions," *Washington Post* (December 12, 1990), p. A25.

important role of the chief of staff, playing the heavy for the president, being the enforcer of tough decisions and bringer of bad tidings to others. "I don't care if people hate me, as long as they hate me for the right reasons," said Sununu.[99] But that was the problem. Washington professionals understand that the policy preferences of the president are the responsibility of the chief of staff, and they expect him to be tough for the president. Professionals are willing to accept being beaten in the policy arena, but Sununu's gratuitous ad hominem insults and rude behavior generated resentments much greater than mere policy defeats would have. Sununu acted as if he did not understand the import of his own words.

Sununu's third strategic error was the Gary Hart syndrome. Senator Gary Hart was married and running for the Democratic nomination for president in 1984. When he was confronted by the press with allegations of adultery, he denied them and challenged the press to follow him around to prove his innocence. Not surprisingly, they did, and reported the next time he spent the night with model Donna Rice. This doomed Hart's bid for the nomination. The point here is not about sexual behavior; it is rather about respect for conventional morality and appearances. Any person running for president must accept constraints on his or her personal behavior in deference to public opinion. If a person is not willing to conform his or her behavior to general standards of public morality, he or she does not have enough self-restraint to be president. The parallel with John Sununu is that he felt that he did not have to restrain himself in the use of the privileges and perks of his office.

In spring of 1991, the *Washington Post* reported that the chief of staff had taken more than seventy trips around the country aboard military aircraft. Almost all of the trips were designated (by the chief of staff) as official business, even though the purpose of some of them seemed to be to provide skiing trips for Sununu and his family. None of the twenty-seven trips to his home state of New Hampshire were designated as personal.

When the disclosures caused a public scandal in May 1991, the president (whose early priority was to have an administration above ethical reproach) ordered Sununu to clear all future flights with the White House counsel's office. But in June, Sununu had a White House limousine take him to New York for a stamp auction he wanted to attend and solicited corporations to provide air travel back to Washington and other trips. The president again was forced to restrict Sununu's travel practices.[100]

There is no argument here that Sununu's trips on government planes constituted outrageous or illegal behavior, or that White House staffers should always fly coach. Few would begrudge a few trips on official planes with occa-

[99]Quoted in Maureen Dowd, "Sununu: A Case Study in Flouting the Rules," *The New York Times* (May 5, 1991), p. 34.

[100]*The New York Times* (December 4, 1991), p. B12.

sional combinations of business with pleasure. High-level officials in Congress and the executive branch have done this for decades, and it is standard practice in corporate America. The point is that Sununu abused his privileges and pushed them to excess. His bending of the rules was routine, pervasive, and systematic. He was unable to restrain himself from taking advantage of his position and was unwilling to rein himself in, even after the president was forced publicly to admonish him. By pushing his privileges too far Sununu became an embarrassment to the president, who was forced to defend him in public. A chief of staff should never put the president in this position.

Sununu's final strategic error was the Don Regan syndrome: take credit when things go well, and when they turn sour shift blame to the president. At a November 1991 campaign fund-raising speech in New York, President Bush remarked that people in the financial community felt that interest rates charged on credit cards were higher than necessary and that it might spur the economy if they came down a bit. The next day Senator Alphonse D'Amato (R–N.Y.) introduced legislation to impose a legal limit on the interest rates credit-card companies could charge their customers. The economic wisdom of the proposal was challenged in the financial community, and the Dow Jones Industrial Average fell 120 points. The administration had to back away quickly from the proposed legislation and publicly argue against it.

When asked by reporters about this embarrassing episode, Sununu said that the remark about interest rates was not in the president's prepared text but that the president had "ad-libbed" the remarks on credit-card interest rates. This attempt to blame the embarrassing remarks on the president was rebutted by Marlin Fitzwater, the president's spokesman. He told reporters that the lines were in the printed text of the speech and were not ad-libbed. Some administration officials even said that Sununu, himself, was the author of the offending lines.[101]

The issue in this case is not whether the lines were in the speech text or not. The issue is who publicly takes the blame for an embarrassing incident. In this case, Sununu publicly tried to shift blame to the president. If Sununu were lying about the speech text, his behavior was outrageous. But even if he were telling the truth, it is not the role of the chief of staff to publicly blame the president for an administration blunder. The appropriate behavior for the chief of staff is to take the heat in order to protect the president.

Sununu's general attitude toward the press was reflected in his public reaction to a *Washington Post* reporter who covered the story of the credit card flap. After a bill-signing ceremony on the White House lawn, he told Ann Devroy, loudly and in front of others: "You're a liar. Your stories are all lies. Everything you write is a lie."[102]

---

[101] *The New York Times* (November 23, 1991), pp. 1, 10.

[102] Quoted in *The New York Times* (November 23, 1991), pp. 1, 10.

The final downfall and firing of Sununu took place soon after the credit-card incident, which was merely the final straw. The striking thing about Sununu's term as chief of staff is how long he was allowed to stay. It speaks strongly of President Bush's gratitude for Sununu's support in the New Hampshire primary and of the president's personal loyalty to his subordinate, but it also demonstrates that he was performing highly valued functions for the president.

The firing came at a low point in the Bush administration; the economy was doing poorly, the president was sliding in public opinion polls from his huge popularity after the Persian Gulf war, and the administration seemed to be in disarray. Sununu personally could only be blamed for the last of the three, but the scapegoat factor is a real one in Washington. Nevertheless, without Sununu's strategic miscalculations, he could probably have weathered the storm of problems for which he was not solely responsible.

Shortly after Sununu resigned he was replaced with Secretary of Transportation Samuel Skinner.[103] But in the summer of 1992 when President Bush was faring poorly in the polls and falling behind Bill Clinton, he persuaded James Baker to leave the State Department and return to the White House as chief of staff.

CLINTON'S CIRCUS

In the early months of the Clinton administration, the White House was like a circus in the sense that it had three rings of power, most importantly the president himself, but also First Lady Hillary Rodham Clinton and Vice President Al Gore. The First Lady played a more active role in administration across the board—politics, personnel, policy—than had any other first lady in history. Certainly other first ladies had been powerful and had played crucial roles in the administrations of their husbands, but not in the comprehensive way that Mrs. Clinton did from the beginning of the administration. Al Gore had been chosen vice president not for the usual reasons of balancing the ticket in terms of ideology, age, or geography, but because there was a definite sympatico between the two men; their relationship was personal as well as professional. The level of trust between the only two nationally elected officials was unusually high. Thus, Clinton delegated to Gore significant areas of policy for special influence (e.g., foreign policy, science, environmental policy, administrative reform). He also gave Gore a say in personnel, and he consulted him regularly.

The presence of these three circles of power made managing the Clinton White House a special challenge. But the Clinton White House in the beginning was also a circus in the sense that there was a lack of coordination among White House staffers and the policy agenda. At times there seemed to be no

---

[103]For an insightful profile of Samuel Skinner, see Marjorie Williams, "The President's Straight Man," *Washington Post Magazine* (June 7, 1992), p. 11.

ringmaster other than the president, and the president wanted to think about policy and politics rather than to manage the circus.

Bill Clinton was the first Democratic president to come to office admitting that he needed a chief of staff. Thus, in December 1992 he designated his childhood friend Thomas (Mack) McLarty to be his chief of staff. McLarty had the advantages of unquestioned trust from the president, political experience in Arkansas, and experience as a business executive. In contrast with the domineering chiefs of staff, he was unfailingly courteous and gracious, and he tried mightily to manage the White House for a year and a half. He was not successful for several reasons. He spent only about two-thirds of his time dealing with internal White House management in a position that requires 110 percent of a person's time; the rest of the time he was acting as presidential ambassador to the business community or conservatives on the Hill. He also had to deal with the three rings of power in the White House, a gargantuan coordination challenge. But most importantly President Clinton did not want to be managed or to delegate the necessary authority to anyone else to manage the White House.

Clinton was an inveterate "policy wonk" who was fascinated by the details of public policy and tended to work over problems endlessly with anyone available; he resisted coming to closure or making final decisions. It seemed that meetings were countless and endless, with nothing ever getting finally decided. As a result, staffers continued to fight for their own preferred policy outcomes and did not hesitate to lobby the president for them. The policy-development process was chaotic, and the White House suffered from a number of minor snafus that might have been avoided with a more disciplined organization.

One of the problems that McLarty had was the active White House involvement of Clinton's 1992 campaign team. Several campaign leaders, including James Carville, Paul Begalla, Mandy Grunwald, and Stanley Greenberg, decided not to take positions in the government, but continued to advise Clinton about policy in White House meetings at which they demanded that no White House staffers be present. They argued that in his approach to reduction of the budget deficit Clinton was selling out the constituency that elected him. They wanted more liberal policies and thought that the White House staff, particularly Clinton's economic team, was hijacking the policy agenda.[104]

This caused problems for McLarty and the White House staff. The problem was not that Clinton was getting advice from outside the White House. Presidents often seek the input of those not in the government; and in any case, presidents ought to be able to listen to whomever they choose. The problem was that the campaigners' advice was not being monitored or coordinated with anyone else. The only place where the campaigners' ideas and professional policy analysis came together was in Clinton's head. The outside ideas were not vetted by White House staffers, departmental policy analysts, or OMB bud-

[104]For further analysis, see James P. Pfiffner, *The Strategic Presidency: Hitting the Ground Running* (Lawrence: University Press of Kansas, 1996), chap. 8.

get staffers. Nor was outside advice balanced with the input of White House staffers on the political, policy, congressional, or budget implications. McLarty's lack of control over the campaigners' access was a problem for the administration and White House organization. The content of the advice was not a problem, the lack of coordination was.

By the summer of 1994 President Clinton realized that McLarty could not do the job that needed doing in the White House and replaced him with his Director of the Office of Management and Budget, Leon Panetta. McLarty was retained in the White House as a senior counselor, the only chief of staff to be retained in the White House after having been, in effect, fired. The fact that Panetta put some more rigor into the White House organization was due not so much to his personality, which was more authoritative that McLarty's, but to Clinton's realization that he had to delegate more authority to his chief of staff to run the White House.

When he took over in July 1994 Panetta asserted more actively some of the traditional prerogatives of the chief of staff. He tightened access to the president so that only one or two staffers, rather than ten, had "walk-in" privileges to the Oval Office. He insisted that the campaigners have access to the president only through him and only as part of the coordinated advice to the president. He insisted that all staff work and decision memoranda go to the president through him and ensured that all staff work was fully prepared before being presented to the president. He took control of White House hiring and payroll decisions. He set tighter agendas with more focus for meetings with fewer people invited and insisted on "closure," that is, coming to a decision about the issue at hand.

With these changes, the Clinton White House became more organized and the policymaking process more coherent. There were fewer minor embarrassments that leaked to the press. In 1995 and 1996 Panetta also was one of the major negotiators with the Republican-controlled Congress. But Panetta's control of the White House was compromised by the role that Dick Morris played in 1995 and 1996. After the devastating defeat in the 1994 congressional elections in which the Republicans gained control of Congress for the first time in 40 years, the President sought advice from Dick Morris who had advised him when he was Governor of Arkansas and who helped engineer his reelection in 1982 after he had been defeated for reelection in 1980. Morris, who had been working as a political consultant for Republican members of Congress, began to advise Clinton to moderate the administration's policies, and he drafted speeches for him. Morris's advice was clearly valuable to Clinton, but the problem was that in the early months of 1995 Morris was advising Clinton secretly (under the code name of "Charlie"), unbeknownst to Leon Panetta or the rest of the White House staff.

As with the campaigners in 1993, the problem was not that Clinton was receiving outside advice, but that the advice was not being vetted or balanced with those who would be in charge of implementing the policies. For the president's sake as well as the rest of the executive branch, new policy proposals should be analyzed for their budget and implementation implications as well as for their political appeal. The president needs competing policy advice in order to make the most informed decisions, and he needs administrative advice in order to weigh the policy implications and implementation dimensions of proposals. The regular and frequent access of Morris to the president without the knowledge of White House staffers reduced the effectiveness of the White House staff for the president. Finally in March and April 1995 Panetta became aware of Morris's role, and Morris along with several people he designated were brought into White House political and policy deliberations. This increased the level of conflict in the White House between more liberal and more moderate advisors, but at least the conflict was in the open and Panetta was fully informed in coordinating advice for the president.

In 1996 Panetta announced that he would retire at the end of the first term to return to California, and shortly after winning reelection President Clinton designated Erskine Bowles to be chief of staff in his second term. Bowles was an investment banker from South Carolina who had been head of the Small Business Administration in 1993 and 1994 and was then brought into the White House as a deputy to Leon Panetta. As deputy chief of staff Bowles conducted a management study of the White House and concluded that the president's time was too fragmented into 15-minute time chunks and that he should have several hours of unstructured time in the afternoon to work on his own priorities rather than being dominated by an overcrowded schedule.[105]

Bowles recruited two deputies, each of whom had experience in the first-term Clinton White House. He also designated his own chief of staff and had an executive assistant, a national security assistant, and a press secretary. Even though in some sense all White House staffers report to the president through the chief of staff, this was a more elaborate superstructure for the chief of staff office than had existed in any earlier White House. The general consensus was that Bowles imposed more order on the White House. As one White House staffer put it, "We now have *controlled* chaos."[106]

The bottom line in the White House is always what the president wants. The new order came to the White House management not because Bowles wanted to impose it, but because Clinton, after his experience in the first term wanted him to.

CONCLUSION

The experience with White House organization in the modern presidency has highlighted several important lessons. White House staff and organization will faithfully reflect the president, but should strive to counter presidential weaknesses. If the president is reclusive (as Nixon was), the staff should try to bring

---

[105]See Karen Breslau, "Clinton Goes Corporate" *Newsweek* (February 17, 1997), p. 38.

[106]Ibid., emphasis added.

ideas and people to him (as Persons did for Eisenhower). If the president is too open, the staff should impose some order on access to the president (as Cheney did for Ford). If the president is too focused on details (as was Carter), the staff should encourage him to look at the big picture. If the president is too detached, the staff should bring issues, even unpleasant ones, to the president's attention (as the Baker system did for Reagan, but Regan did not).

Beyond this we have learned that, regardless of personal style or preference, the contemporary White House needs a chief of staff to impose order on policy development, guard access to the president, and settle administration disputes that are not of presidential importance. As the Ford and Carter presidencies demonstrated, someone short of the president must be in charge, or the president will be overwhelmed. No president has successfully run the White House without a chief of staff since 1969, and since 1979 no president has tried.

But if that necessary chief of staff takes a strong and controlling approach to the job, it is a likely prescription for disaster. *Each* of the strong chiefs of staff (Adams for Ike, Haldeman for Nixon, Regan for Reagan, and Sununu for Bush):

- alienated members of Congress
- alienated members of their own administration
- had reputations for the lack of common civility
- had hostile relations with the press

And *each* of them resigned in disgrace, having done harm to their own presidents and the presidency.[107]

A number of lessons about the role of chief of staff can be gleaned from the experience over the past four decades of the presidency. These lessons, which were too often ignored by the domineering chiefs of staff, include:

1. Carrying out the president's wishes will often make some people angry, but gratuitous harshness will not help the president or the chief of staff.
2. It is appropriate to guard access as tightly as the president wishes, but a heavy-handed assertion of personal power will unnecessarily anger members of the cabinet.
3. The chief of staff has a constituency of more than one. It includes:

   a. Congress: The president (or chief of staff) will sooner or later need support in Congress, so fences should be mended carefully after congressional feelings have been hurt.

   b. The press: The president needs favorable press coverage. Having a cordial, professional working relationship with the press may not ensure favorable coverage, but it can help to mitigate bad coverage.

[107]See James P. Pfiffner, "The President's Chief of Staff: Lessons Learned," *Presidential Studies Quarterly* (Winter 1993), pp. 77–102.

4. The president should not be put in the position of having to defend publicly a White House staffer.
5. A chief of staff cannot do the job in complete anonymity, but people will notice if the chief of staff squeezes into every photo opportunity.
6. As Jack Watson says, the chief of staff is the president's "javelin catcher." The chief of staff should take the heat for the president, and in no circumstance publicly shift blame to the president.

This list may seem a bit preachy and obvious. But the lessons bear repeating because they have so often been ignored by the four domineering chiefs of staff in the modern presidency.

The ideal approach to the job is exemplified by James Baker, Jack Watson, Richard Cheney, Donald Rumsfeld, Leon Panetta, and Erskine Bowles (as well as Howard Baker, and Kenneth Duberstein for shorter periods). Each served his president well by performing as an honest broker and coordinator of administration policy. These people were in no way soft or ineffectual. They controlled access to their presidents with firm hands and enforced a discipline on the policy-development process. They performed the other chief of staff functions, such as giving credit for success to the president and taking blame for failures, without letting their own egos get in the way. Each demonstrated that the chief of staff job could be done without absolute control by one person.

But in the end, there is no salvation from staff. As presidential scholar Bert Rockman puts it: "No system or organization ultimately can save a president from himself when he is inclined to self-destruct. And no system that a president is uncomfortable with will last."[108] A president cannot manage the White House alone, but he must make sure that someone is managing it to his specifications. Presidents must be ruthless in their judgments of aides who are not serving the presidency. If they do not follow these precepts, their presidencies will be vulnerable to being run for others' purposes rather than their own.

---

[108]Bert Rockman, "The Style and Organization of the Reagan Presidency," in Charles O. Jones, ed., *The Reagan Legacy* (Chatham, NJ: Chatham House, 1988), p. 27.

Four

THE INSTITUTIONAL PRESIDENCY

The decision of how to organize the White House, the functions of the immediate staff, the relations of the staff to the president, and the relation of staff to each other are matters of individual presidential choice and personal dynamics. The choice may be conscious, as when Eisenhower chose to create the chief of staff position and Kennedy chose not to have a chief of staff, or the decisions may be made by default and depend on day-to-day presidential actions in the White House. Personality dynamics of staff members also have an impact on the relationships, for example, the contrasting styles that James Baker and Donald Regan exhibited as chiefs of staff for the same president.

But as the presidency has grown in size and the reach of the White House has extended deeper into the executive branch, functions have developed that are not at the complete discretion of each new president. For instance, the size and complexity of the White House staff had increased to such an extent that by the 1970s the function of chief of staff was necessary. Presidents Ford and Carter each tried to govern without one, and each admitted defeat.

There are many other functions of the White House that are part of what scholar Hugh Heclo calls its "deep structure," that is, the dimension of the office that "is largely a given that a president can change slowly if at all. This structure is a web of other people's expectations and needs."[1] The accumulated functions performed by the presidential staff cannot easily be sloughed off by a new president. For instance, the president needs to coordinate national security policy from his own perspective. This cannot be done at the departmental level. Thus, the National Security Council function must be performed under whatever name. The president can no longer choose not to have a legislative agenda of some sort, and the president's lobbying cannot be delegated to departments and agencies. The president's appointees must be

[1]Hugh Heclo, "The Changing Presidential Office," in James P. Pfiffner, ed., *The Managerial Presidency* (Pacific Palisades, CA: Brooks/Cole, 1991), p. 35.

screened for him by his own staffers: no longer do the political parties have the capacity to perform this function. The president's legal needs are too specialized to have them met by the attorney general's office, as they were in the past.

This chapter will begin by considering the size and structure of the White House Office and the Executive Office of the President (EOP). While the size of the White House Office has increased over the years, it is difficult to measure the growth precisely. The EOP has housed a number of presidential units since its creation in 1939, and each president has usually added or deleted a unit or two by executive order.

The theme of this chapter is that the size of the White House staff has been growing, and its functions have been increasingly institutionalized in the last half of the twentieth century. The subunits in the White House and EOP have been institutionalized by the establishment of continuing functions that survive from president to president. Yet most of the personnel in most of the units turn over with each new president. To illustrate the process of institutionalization, this chapter will briefly trace the development of several units in the presidency: the Office of Legislative Liaison, the Office of Presidential Personnel, and the Office of Communications in the White House Office; and in the EOP, the Bureau of the Budget, the National Security Council staff, and Domestic Policy staff.

WHITE HOUSE STAFF AND THE EXECUTIVE OFFICE OF THE PRESIDENT

Two major aspects of White House development are size and complexity. The size of the White House staff has never been easy to determine precisely for two reasons. For different purposes it may be relevant to count only staffers close to the president, or only professional-level staffers, or only those in the White House Office. Or it may be relevant to include military support, the Secret Service (which is technically in the Treasury Department), or White House groundskeepers. The other reason that it is difficult to count the number of White House staff is that presidents do not want to seem too imperial and would just as soon be thought of as having small, efficient staffs. This is why all modern White Houses have used workers who have been "detailed" to work at the White House from their own agencies where they are on the payroll. Detailees are usually not counted on the official White House rolls (Table 4–1).

Thus, there are many different accounts of the number of White House staff, but one of the most used categories is the number of staffers in the White House Office. By examining these numbers, we can see a trend of increasing size that we might expect from the increased duties and centralization of control of the executive branch in the White House. Looking at the changing size of the White House Office we can see an increase in the number of staffers

TABLE 4-1
Top Level Assistants to the President, 1960-1992

1960	1992
1 Assistant to the President (chief of staff)	1 Chief of Staff
1 Principle Deputy Assistant	1 Deputy Chief of Staff
6 Deputy Assistants	16 Assistants to the President
20 Special Assistants	29 Deputy Assistants
1 Deputy Special Assistant	34 Special Assistants

Source: Adapted from Paul Light, *Thickening Government: Federal Hierarchy and the Diffusion of Hierarchy,* p. 154. Copyright © 1995 by Paul Light. Reprinted by permission of Brookings Publications.

from about 60 under FDR, to 300–400 under Eisenhower, to 400–500 under Kennedy-Johnson, up to 500–600 under Nixon-Ford, slightly down to 400–500 under Carter, Reagan, Bush, and Clinton (though if the Office of Administration and Executive Residence are included, as they were in Nixon's time, the numbers are higher than the Nixon administration).[2] There are also about 1,300 full-time people in the Military Office (with 2,500 who support the White House part-time) and about 800 Secret Service personnel who support the White House, none of whom are counted on most accounts of White House staff.[3] The White House Office contains the staffers and units closest to the president and is included as a separate unit in the EOP. See Figure 4–1.

The Executive Office of the President, created in 1939, is an umbrella organization holding those offices that serve the institution of the presidency. The EOP is not really a single office, but rather a collection; and it is not really executive, since it contains units that are primarily advisory rather than executing.[4] In addition, the original intention of Roosevelt, to separate his personal staff (the six staffers the Brownlow Committee called for) from the institutional staff in the Bureau of the Budget and other units, has broken down. The EOP was to contain units that advised the president and coordinated executive branch policymaking. Over the course of the modern presidency the various units of the EOP have become progressively more responsive to individual presidents, rather than to the continuous office of the presidency, and are now the primary policymakers of the executive branch.

The membership of the units in the EOP change with each new president; the only unit to have a sizable career civil service staff with an institutional

---

[2]These general estimates are drawn from: John Hart, *The Presidential Branch* (New York: Pergamon Press, 1987), p. 101; Gary King and Lyn Ragsdale, *The Elusive Executive* (Washington, DC: CQ Press, 1988), pp. 205–206, Table 4.2; and Samuel Kernell and Samuel Popkin, eds., *Chief of Staff* (Berkeley: University of California Press, 1986), p. 201.

[3]See Bradley Patterson, *The Ring of Power* (New York: Basic Books, 1988), p. 339.

[4]Hugh Heclo, "The Executive Office of the President," in Marc Landy, ed., *Modern Presidents and the Presidency* (Lexington, MA: Lexington Books, 1985).

FIGURE 4-1
Organization Chart for the White House Office

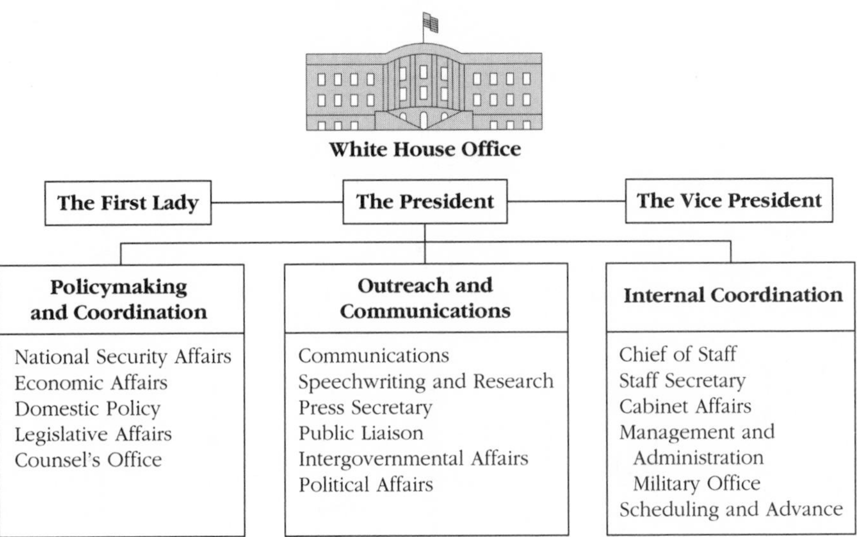

Source: Executive Clerk to the President, 1996. The units in the White House Office were specified in personal communication with the author. The functional categories are the author's.

memory is the Office of Management and Budget (OMB). Since its creation in 1939, the EOP has included more than sixty different units. Most of these had brief stays in the EOP to symbolize presidential concern (e.g., drug abuse, inflation, consumer protection, space exploration, etc.), or to incubate them before transfer to larger, more established departments in the executive branch (e.g., the Office of Economic Opportunity).

The core and continuing units of the EOP perform different functions for the president. Four of them perform coordination and enforcement as well as advisory functions: the Office of Management and Budget, the National Security Council staff, the Office of Policy Development, and the Office of U.S. Trade Representative. Each coordinates administration policy for the president and ensures that the narrower departmental perspectives and turf do not prevail over the president's priorities. Other units of the EOP primarily provide advice to the president and do not have the independent power or staff to prevail over departments and agencies. These include: the Office of Science and Technology Policy, the Council of Economic Advisors, and the Council on Environmental Quality. Finally, some offices perform administrative functions: the Office of Administration and the Executive Residence at the White House. (See Figure 4–2.)

FIGURE 4-2
Executive Office of the President, 1939 and 1997

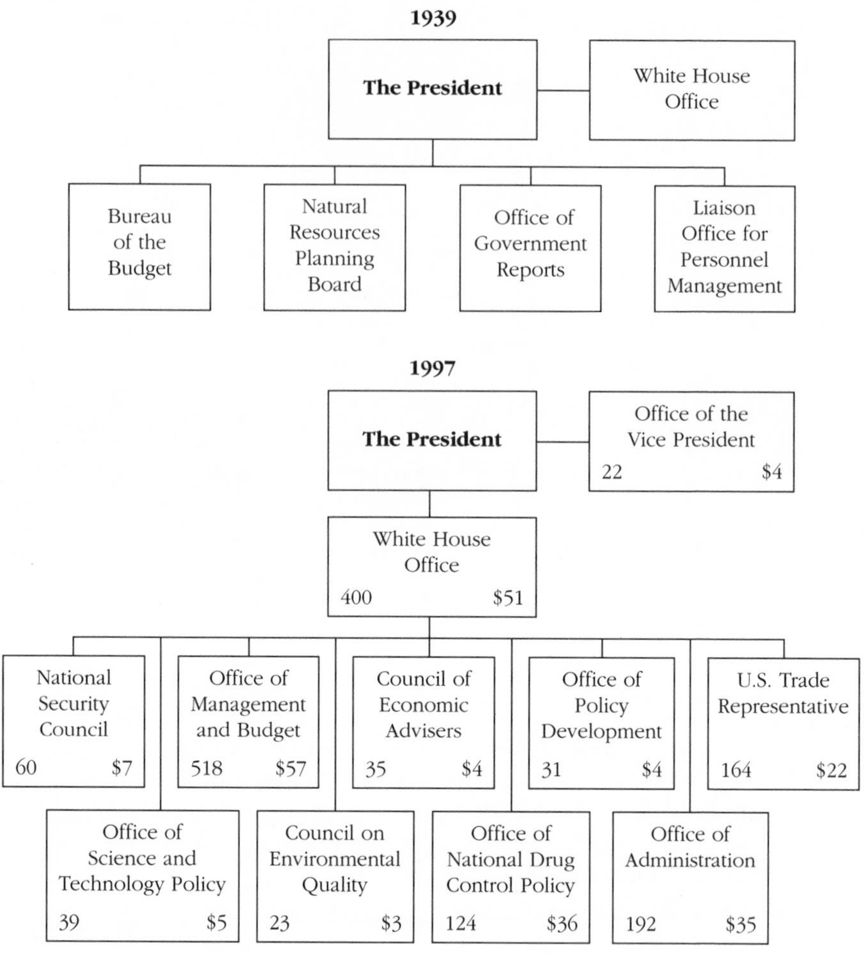

Source: Budget of the United States, Fiscal Year 1998. Numbers on left indicate authorized full-time personnel. Dollar amounts in millions indicate proposed budget authority for the 1998 fiscal year.

More than numbers of staffers and separate units are involved in the institutionalizing of the presidency. The dynamics of centralization and control have increased the capacity of the White House staff to substitute for departments and agencies in policy development and expert advice to the president. This can only be accomplished by specialized division of labor to reflect the complexity of the executive branch (which, in turn, mirrors the complexity in the domestic and international environments). The specialization is accompanied by other bureaucratic characteristics, including established decision-making and operating processes, differentiated units, and hierarchical structures.[5] The main difference with more conventional bureaucracies is that there is much less continuity of personnel in the presidency. Virtually all of the White House Office and EOP (with the exception of OMB, military support, and housekeeping units) turn over with each new president; even secretarial and clerical workers are often cleared out. Institutional memory is sacrificed, but the same functions must be replicated by the next president.

To illustrate the process of institutionalization over the years, the development of several presidential units will be traced. In the past, these functions were performed by presidents themselves and their generalist staff aides or outside the presidency entirely, i.e., by departments and agencies or political parties. As the presidency expanded and more central control was sought, more functions were drawn into the White House. The process usually began when a president would put one staffer in charge of a function and create a title for him or her. Soon the person acquired their own staff, and then a separate office would be created. For the most important functions this has been a one-way street; once the unit is created, it continues to exist across administrations, regardless of president or political party. The process of institutionalization will be illustrated with three units from the White House Office: the Office of Congressional Relations, the Office of Presidential Personnel, and the Office of Communications. We will then examine three units from the Executive Office of the President: the Office of Management and Budget, the National Security Council staff, and the Office of Policy Development.

OFFICE OF LEGISLATIVE LIAISON/OFFICE OF CONGRESSIONAL RELATIONS

Franklin Roosevelt conducted his historic legislative campaign in the first 100 days of the New Deal by himself with the help of a few White House aides. Despite his legislative activism, no one short of the president coordinated relations with Congress. The first presidential aide to be given informal charge of congressional relations was President Truman's appointments secretary, Matt Connelly, who had two assistants to help him.[6] Truman sent his legislative agenda to Congress each year, and though he was not always successful, the president's legislative priorities were always clear.

When President Eisenhower was elected he did not intend to be as active in legislation as were his Democratic predecessors. But when he decided not

[5]See the analysis by Margaret J. Wyszomirski in "The Discontinuous Institutional Presidency," in Colin Campbell and Margaret J. Wyszomirski, eds., *Executive Leadership in Anglo-American Systems* (Pittsburgh: University of Pittsburgh Press, 1991), pp. 85–108.

[6]Patterson, *The Ring of Power*, p. 152.

to send a legislative program to the Hill after taking office in 1953, he was criticized from both sides of the aisle. One administration member was told by a member of the House: "Don't expect us to start from scratch on what you people want. That's not the way we do things here. You draft the bills and we work them over."[7] This began the practice of annual legislative programs developed by the White House and sent to the Hill. But this practice also implied an active and professional staff to press the administration's agenda on the Hill.

Thus, Eisenhower was the first to establish a formal legislative liaison unit in the White House. He assigned the task to General Wilton B. Persons, who had experience in congressional liaison in the Defense Department, and several professionals. Persons hosted weekly meetings of legislative leaders with the president, and kept in touch with agency legislative liaison operations. Members of Congress being directly contacted by members of the White House staff was very unusual before Eisenhower, but with the development of the Office of Congressional Relations (OCR) it was to become much more commonplace.

Bryce Harlow, who was head of the operation at the end of the Eisenhower administration, was visited by Larry O'Brien after Kennedy was elected. O'Brien was going to handle legislative liaison for the new administration, and he was paying a visit to ask Harlow's advice. O'Brien thought he might handle relations with the Hill as a one-person operation, but Harlow quickly disabused him of that fantasy:

> You're about to ruin your president. . . . Let me explain to you why. . . . I average a hundred and twenty-five incoming telephone calls a day. Average. Bob Hampton handles the congressional appointments and presidential appointments. That office handles four hundred incoming calls a day, even now. Now then, when you first come to work in this building, and it's January 20 and it is 12:01, you won't be able to hang up this phone. For your first two years you won't be able to hang it up without it ringing, no matter how many lines you put on it. Now, if you think you can handle all that stuff by yourself and this little girl Phyllis, I'm just telling you, you're going to destroy yourself and destroy your president . . . that's absolutely mad, stark raving mad.[8]

O'Brien took Harlow's advice and expanded the legislative liaison operation into one of the most effective operations in the modern presidency.

His operatives spent much of their time on the Hill cultivating members of Congress and keeping in touch with their concerns. He reined the rest of the executive branch legislative liaison offices directly to the service of the administration's goals. He held weekly meetings of agency liaison officials and ex-

---

[7]Richard Neustadt, "The Presidency and Legislation: Planning the President's Legislative Program," *American Political Science Review* (December 1955), p. 1015.

[8]LBJ Library Oral History Interview of Bryce Harlow by Michael L. Gillette, pp. 51–52 of the transcript.

pected regular written reports on their contacts with Congress. One of O'Brien's advantages was that he reported directly to the president rather than through another staffer. According to O'Brien, "For the first time, someone from the White House could sit in the Speaker's office with the congressional leadership and be recognized as a spokesman for the president. You weren't an errand boy or a head-counter, you had the authority to speak for the president."[9]

Richard Nixon had a large congressional liaison operation, but with his conservative legislative goals and his confrontational approach to Congress, it was not able to get him what he wanted from the Democratic Congress. With the congressional reforms in the 1970s, in response to the Nixon administration, Congress became more decentralized. White House relations with Congress became more complex, and presidents had to retail rather than wholesale their priorities on Capitol Hill.

The importance of professionalism in congressional liaison was underscored when Jimmy Carter brought in his director of legislative relations, Frank Moore, to conduct relations with Congress. Moore had done a good job with the Georgia legislature, but his lack of Washington experience hurt Carter's dealings with Congress his first year. According to Jack Watson, Moore's first year in the White House was the "most awful case of on-the-job training I have ever seen in my life."[10] President Reagan hired an experienced Washington hand, Max Friedersdorf, to run his congressional liaison, and gave the legislative agenda top priority in his first year. In addition to high-profile lobbying, the Office of Congressional Liaison conducts many routine chores. In the Reagan administration, more than 600 letters a month would come in from Congress.[11]

While Congress has always been important to presidents, congressional relations has been at the center of much of the modern presidency. From the momentous to the routine, presidents cannot do without the multifaceted services of a professional legislative liaison operation. The number of professionals increased from six in the Kennedy years to thirteen under President Reagan, and that number is not likely to decrease in the future.[12]

OFFICE OF PRESIDENTIAL PERSONNEL

For most of the nineteenth and first part of the twentieth century the recruitment of political appointments for the president was mediated by the political parties. Patronage was a sustaining force for the party system, and presidents

---

[9]See Patrick Anderson, *The Presidents' Men* (New York: Doubleday, 1969), p. 307.

[10]Jack Watson's remarks at a conference on the "Origins, Development and Future of the American Presidency," at Gannon University, Erie, PA (April 25, 1987).

[11]Patterson, *The Ring of Power,* p. 154.

[12]King and Ragsdale, *The Elusive Executive,* p. 63.

were tightly tied to the parties. But with the coming of the modern presidency the political recruitment function began slowly to be taken over by the White House.

Several factors led to this centralization. The political parties began to decline with the proliferation of primary elections and the increasing independence of presidential candidates from the parties. With an activist federal government, there was a greater need by presidents for control of policy rather than merely partisan control of the government.[13] The need for policy control necessarily implied a greater degree of professionalism in presidential appointments. These factors led to the formalization of a political recruiting capacity in the White House.

Harry Truman was the first president to assign the recruitment function to one person, and Eisenhower created the position of special assistant for personnel management. White House recruitment began to be more systematic when Kennedy divided his "talent hunt" operation from the political patronage function. John Macy wore two hats in serving Lyndon Johnson as political personnel recruiter as well as chairman of the Civil Service Commission. The Nixon administration saw the development of professionalism in recruiting when White House Personnel Operation (WHPO) director, Frederic Malek, brought in professional "headhunters" from the private sector to do recruiting for the president. Malek also increased the size of the White House operation from about twelve to thirty, and ended up with a full complement of sixty in his office.

President Ford changed the name from WHPO to the Presidential Personnel Office, and Jimmy Carter was the first presidential candidate to begin organizing a personnel search operation (the Talent Inventory Program) before he was elected. But the largest and most sophisticated personnel recruitment effort of the modern presidency was organized by Pendleton James for the Reagan administration. James had been a recruiter in the Nixon administration and was a professional private-sector recruiter when Reagan convinced him to take the job. James was given the title of assistant to the president, a signal of the importance that Reagan attached to the personnel recruitment task. In the first years of the Reagan administration James had 100 people working for him, though the number dropped by about half after the administration was fully staffed.

The large number of people on his staff stemmed from the broad approach to personnel recruiting and the importance attached to it by the Reagan administration. The administration screened candidates for jobs very closely, determined to hire only those who were firmly committed to the policy goals of the administration. The number of political appointees had increased over the 1960s and 1970s, demanding greater resources. But the OPP also took on the job of screening candidates for lower-level political appointments (not requir-

[13]See G. Calvin Mackenzie, "Partisan Presidential Leadership: The President's Appointees," in L. Sandy Maisel, ed., *The Parties Respond* (Boulder, CO: Westview Press, 1990).

ing presidential nominations) in order to control more tightly the implementation of presidential priorities. This centralization of power was unprecedented and required a more elaborate operation than had existed in the White House before. The new Clinton administration sought to emulate the Reagan personnel operation, and had 130 people working in the OPP in the early months of 1993.

The modern presidency has seen the personnel recruitment function develop from a one-person job to a very sophisticated and systematic operation supported by the latest computer capabilities and scores of professionals. While the size of the operation will depend on presidential preferences and the initial recruitment task of the president, a professional personnel office is now a permanent fixture in the White House.

OFFICE OF COMMUNICATIONS

All presidents have realized that the press has an important impact on the success of presidential campaigns, and later for public support of the president in office, and the most effective presidents have placed importance on their relations with the press. By the end of the nineteenth century a professional press corps was developing in Washington with a focus on covering the presidency and the federal government. While all presidents and their top aides have had regular relationships with the press, it was not until Franklin Roosevelt that a president designated one staffer, Stephen Early, to be his formal press secretary.[14] When Truman came to office he continued to have press conferences, but he also began to permit radio broadcasts of excerpts of his news conferences. Eisenhower held fewer news conferences than Truman, but did allow the recording of press conferences to be broadcast on television.

John Kennedy was an innovator in the development of a public relations capacity in the White House. He introduced the first live televising of presidential press conferences, beginning in his first month in office.[15] Kennedy was to make several other innovations that would be of lasting significance. He held private interviews with members of the media and special informal gatherings with invited members of the press. The White House also began to cultivate the local press throughout the country, not merely the Washington press corps. These innovations marked the recognition that in order to portray the president most favorably, the White House would have to be active in doing its best to manage the image of the administration, not merely passively let the press decide what to cover.

Thus, the duties of the press secretary had broadened under Kennedy and

---

[14]See the analysis of Samuel Kernell, *Going Public* (Washington, DC: CQ Press, 1986), pp. 63–76.

[15]Kernell, *Going Public,* p. 70.

Johnson, but it was the Nixon administration that began the systematic organization of these innovations. Realizing that the duties of the press secretary were much broader than merely handling the Washington press corps, Nixon created the White House Office of Communications, headed by Herbert Klein. The Washington press corps was to be handled by the press secretary, while the Communications Office would develop the potential of television, further exploit radio opportunities, arrange more briefing sessions for the press, and develop outreach to local media around the country. Kennedy's new techniques were to be lasting, and Nixon's creation of new White House organizations to exploit those techniques were to become a permanent fixture of the presidency.

Just as Gerald Ford tried to run his White House without a chief of staff, he decided to downgrade the Communications Office and placed it under the press secretary. But just as he later decided a chief of staff would be necessary, he also decided to restore the Office of Communications with speech writing, television, and a research office in it. Carter also put the communications function under the press secretary and called it media relations. In 1978, its purview was broadened under Gerald Rafshoon.[16]

Ronald Reagan was known as "the Great Communicator," and the public presentation of the president was a major tool in the advocacy of the administration's policies. The White House communications capacity was organized under Assistant to the President for Communications David Gergen, and included a television office, a speaker's bureau, and research and writing sections. The White House also developed the capacity for the electronic distribution to local radio stations of presidential speeches and White House news releases.[17] The Reagan White House is acknowledged to have been masterful in its use of the media to project to the nation the story that it wanted to convey.

The presence in the White House of a large office for communication reflects the combination of two factors. One is the importance of communications to the modern president's policy agenda. Public statements reflect the commitment of the president to certain policies, and the way they are communicated to the public affects how they will be received. But these policymaking decisions are communicated by a very complex technology that takes a high level of professionalism to conduct. The other factor is the development of different media outlets (national TV networks, local TV stations, local and national radio, daily newspapers, weekly news magazines, etc.), which has led to the differentiation of the organization that must service these different outlets. These multiple audiences are why the White House Office of Communications has grown in size and complexity. The cause of growth is not merely bureaucratic empire-builders seeking more power and money, but rather a presidential response to a more complex environment driven by new tech-

[16]Samuel Kernell, "The Evolution of the White House Staff," in John E. Chubb and Paul E. Peterson, *Can the Government Govern?* (Washington, DC: Brookings Institution, 1989), pp. 211–217.

[17]Patterson, *The Ring of Power,* p. 185.

nologies. The office run by Herbert Klein in 1969 with four aides had developed by 1988 to a large staff that supervised five separate subunits.[18]

The continued existence of the White House Office of Communications is ensured. The president is now *not* free to decide not to have an Office of Communications, whether it is combined with the press secretary or separate. As Jody Powell put it:

> That's got to be done. Whether the press secretary should be the person to do it is a good question. . . . You had literally hundreds of people involved . . . not only with "Meet the Press" and those shows but "Good Morning Idaho" and "Hello Atlanta" . . . that takes a lot of coordination. You've got to free the people up. You've got to tell them where to go. You've got to make sure that they say what they're supposed to say when they get there. . . . There's no doubt in my mind . . . that those [Panama Canal] treaties would never have been approved . . . but for that sort of operations. . . .[19]

The need to deal with the media will continue to be important to presidents, and it will be done by professionals on the president's immediate staff.

BUREAU OF THE BUDGET/OFFICE OF MANAGEMENT AND BUDGET

The Bureau of the Budget (BOB) was created by the Budget and Accounting Act of 1921. It gave the president the capacity to formulate an executive budget that would be considered in Congress as a whole, rather than as separate appropriations requests from the many agencies of the executive branch.[20] BOB was placed in the Treasury Department, and its small staff of twenty or thirty was used to achieve economies and efficiencies over the next two decades. The bureau was to be transformed, however, when it was transferred to the newly created Executive Office of the President in 1939. Its role was to help give the president some managerial control over the agencies of the executive branch, many newly created during the New Deal. During World War II, it also played an important role in coordinating the war effort. BOB emerged from World War II, with a staff of 600 and a managerial as well as a budgetary role, as the right arm of the president in dealing with the executive establishment.

BOB's major role has been to formulate the president's budget by refining

---

[18]Kernell, "The Evolution of the White House Staff," p. 217.

[19]Quoted in Patterson, *The Ring of Power*, p. 189.

[20]For a full analysis of the development of BOB/OMB since 1939, see James P. Pfiffner, "OMB: Professionalism, Politicization, and the Presidency," in Colin Campbell and Margaret J. Wyszomirski, eds., *Executive Leadership in Anglo-American Systems* (Pittsburgh: University of Pittsburgh Press, 1991), pp. 195–218.

agency budget requests before they go to Congress for consideration. This function is accomplished by its budget examiners, who become experts in the agencies they oversee and know where cuts can be achieved with the least harm to essential programs. BOB also conducts "central legislative clearance" by examining all legislative requests from agencies to ensure they are in accord with the president's program before they go to the Hill. By the 1950s, BOB had developed a professionalism and institutional memory that was a great help to the presidency.

But in the 1960s, Presidents Kennedy and Johnson felt that the bureau was not as useful as it might be for innovation and the new ideas and programs of the New Frontier and the Great Society. They began to pull domestic policymaking into the White House and create the capacity for new initiatives there under White House staffers Theodore Sorensen, Bill Moyers, and Joseph Califano.

President Nixon came to office with the purpose of reducing the domestic functions of the government and cutting programs. He felt that BOB, with its history of coordinating agencies and building new programs, would not be responsive to his new priorities. He thus decided to reorganize BOB and change its name to the Office of Management and Budget (OMB) to signify its new functions. To ensure political control, a new layer of political appointees, the program assistant directors, was inserted between the career budget staff and the director's level. These four new positions covered the functional areas of the budget and were intended to make the bureau more directly responsive to presidential political priorities. Nixon also gave his first director of OMB, George Shultz, an office in the west wing of the White House to signify his status as personal presidential adviser as well as director of the institution of OMB. In 1973 Shultz's successor, Roy Ash, was given the title of assistant to the president as well as director of OMB.[21] The role of OMB was changed during the Nixon administration to support his controversial impoundment policies, to exert greater control over the executive branch, and to take a higher visibility role in publicly asserting the president's budgetary proposals. During the Carter administration another layer of political appointees, executive associate directors, was added to the leadership of OMB.

In the Reagan administration, OMB Director David Stockman played the major role in the administration's fiscal agenda of cutting taxes and programs on the domestic side of the government. The huge deficits generated by the administration's fiscal policy necessitated a top-down control of the budget and the ability to respond immediately to changes in budget assumptions. Thus, Stockman changed the role of OMB staffers by creating the capacity to analyze immediately, by computer, changes he was negotiating with Congress, and he put new emphasis on liaison with Congress to defend the administration's budget policies.

In the Bush administration, OMB Director Richard Darman played a major

---

[21]See Margaret J. Wyszomirski, "The De-Institutionalization of Presidential Staff Agencies," *Public Administration Review* (September/October 1982), pp. 448–458.

role in formulating administration domestic policy as well as presiding over OMB. He continued the trend toward using budget documents to justify the administration's policies and counterproposals from Congress, rather than as objective statements of the finances of the federal government. In the Clinton adminstration, Leon Panetta as OMB Director was a major force in the administration's domestic and economic policy before he took over as the Chief of Staff. His deputy, Alice Rivlin, was appointed director when he left, and when she was appointed to the Federal Reserve Board, Franklin Raines took over for Clinton's second term.

Since its inclusion in the Executive Office of the Presidency, the Budget Bureau has played an active and crucial role as the right arm of the president in policy and management. In contrast to most of the other agencies discussed in this chapter, it has not become more institutionalized, since it was established as a large bureaucracy by the end of World War II. It has, however, become more responsive to presidents over the years by becoming more involved with the personal political priorities of individual presidents at the cost of its role as custodian of the institutional presidency. But this responsiveness has developed because presidents have wanted it to play that role. To survive, it had to make a choice between responsiveness and decay. It chose to survive and has thus remained at the heart of White House centralization of control over the executive branch, a trend that has been going on since 1960. One key difference remains, however: even though it has more political appointees than ever before, the bulk of its staff are still career civil service workers. A high level of professionalism is necessary because of the expertise and institutional memory that is necessary for OMB to perform its function effectively.

NATIONAL SECURITY COUNCIL STAFF

The National Security Council (NSC) was created in 1947 and was intended to ensure that the president would take into account professional military advice in planning national security policy. Harry Truman was suspicious of the congressional creation and did not use it much until the Korean War in 1950. The council itself has four statutory members: the president, vice president, secretary of state, and secretary of defense. The council merely advises the president, and thus has little independent power; the influence of the NSC usually refers to the clout of the NSC staff and its director. In Truman's time there was an executive secretary who ran the staff. When Eisenhower came to office, he decided to raise the importance of the NSC staff and gave its director the title of special assistant to the president. The influence of the staff was ensured when Eisenhower built an advisory system of interagency subcommittees organized around the NSC staff. With his military background, Eisenhower was not dependent on his staff director for expertise, and the NSC staff was no threat to the domination of foreign policy by Secretary of State John Foster Dulles.

John Kennedy dismantled much of the NSC machinery, but after the Bay of Pigs invasion failed he leaned more heavily on his national security assistant, McGeorge Bundy. He brought Bundy's office into the west wing of the White House and encouraged him to form a "Little State Department" to give independent advice to the president. Bundy's small staff of fifteen to twenty professionals acted as a neutral conduit of information and advice for the president, but it clearly marked the centralization of policy advice in the White House, a development that continued under Lyndon Johnson.

During the Nixon administration, the White House capacity for advice to the president independent of the Departments of State and Defense was firmly established. The NSC staff under Assistant to the President for National Security Affairs Henry Kissinger was to become much more than a neutral conduit of information and advice, it was to become the central formulator of the foreign policy of the Nixon administration. Kissinger reorganized the NSC policy development process at the very beginning of the administration to ensure his domination of the committees and subcommittees set up to deal with policy planning and implementation. But in addition, Kissinger and his staff became the chief formulators of the major initiatives of the Nixon administration. Kissinger himself played the major negotiating role in the opening to China, the SALT negotiations with the Soviet Union, and the Vietnam peace talks. To support these unprecedented roles for the national security adviser, the NSC staff grew to more than fifty professionals, but if detailees are included, the real staff strength approached 200.[22]

Under Jimmy Carter NSC staff strength was cut a bit, but the assertiveness and strongly held views of Zbigniew Brzezinski ensured that the NSC adviser would play a powerful role in the administration. Despite Carter's assurances to Secretary of State Cyrus Vance, Brzezinski and his staff prevailed in many important aspects of foreign policy and process. The friction between the two men and their staffs finally led to Vance's resignation.

Ronald Reagan came to office determined to cut the influence of the national security adviser and the NSC staff, and the White House was organized to have Richard Allen report to the president through Edwin Meese. The original intent was to restore the secretary of state to preeminence as the foreign policy spokesman for the president, but the White House staff did not trust Alexander Haig. When Reagan intimate William Clark came from the State Department to the White House to be assistant to the president for national security affairs, the locus of national security policymaking returned to the White House, where it would stay throughout Reagan's term. The Iran–Contra affair demonstrated the dangers of too much secrecy and centralized control in a

[22]See Joel M. Woldman, "U.S. Presidential National Security Advisers: Changing Roles and Relationship" (Washington, DC: Congressional Research Service Report No. 87–334F, April 15, 1987), p. 34. See also Patterson, *The Ring of Power,* p. 99; and John Prados, *Keepers of the Keys* (New York: Morrow, 1991), p. 493.

White House staff that was not sufficiently supervised by the top levels of the White House. Although the Reagan administration NSC staff had a budgeted full-time staff of about sixty professionals, its full strength was at the levels of the Kissinger staff, about 180.[23]

President Bush had one of the most tightly knit national security teams in the recent past. James Baker as Secretary of State, Richard Cheney as Secretary of Defense, and Brent Scowcroft as National Security Adviser had all worked together before the Bush administration and trusted each other. This experience was invaluable during the successful conduct of the Gulf War in 1990–1991. Bill Clinton chose the low-key Anthony Lake as National Security Adviser, who did not try to dominate the foreign policy process, but worked without much visible conflict with Secretary of State Warren Christopher and Secretaries of Defense Les Aspin and William Perry. The size of the National Security Council staff was reduced in the Clinton administration to lower levels than it was in the Reagan administration, and the relationship between the National Security departments and the White House staff returned to a more even balance than it had been in the Nixon, Carter, or Reagan administrations.

Military and foreign policy advice have always been central to the presidency, but since World War II the coordination of the huge national security bureaucracies has become a major challenge. That challenge was met with the creation of the National Security Council and the growth in ensuing decades of its staff. The failure of the attempt by President Reagan, in 1981, to downgrade the NSC staff demonstrates that a strong, central, integrating capacity for national security policy in the White House is unavoidable.

OFFICE OF POLICY DEVELOPMENT (DOMESTIC POLICY STAFF)

Until the 1960s, domestic policy was not considered a separate category of the presidency. The New Deal proposals of Roosevelt were virtually all domestic policy, and FDR and his top advisers developed the legislative initiatives in the White House and sent them to Congress. Truman had a legislative staffer, but put no one in charge of domestic policy per se. Eisenhower's aides worked different aspects of domestic policy, but with no separate designation. Ted Sorensen took care of much of the domestic agenda for John Kennedy, though he was involved with foreign policy, speech writing, and other functions as well. The immediate forerunner to a formal domestic policy staff was Joseph Califano, whose primary job was coordinating Great Society legislation and implementation for Lyndon Johnson.

---

[23]See Woldman, "U.S. Presidential National Security Advisers," p. 37; Patterson, *The Ring of Power*, p. 339.

After experimenting with domestic advice from conservative Arthur Burns and liberal Patrick Moynihan, Richard Nixon decided that he wanted a formal White House capacity to formulate and coordinate domestic policy, similar to the role that the NSC played in national security policy. When the Budget Bureau was reorganized into the Office of Management and Budget, President Nixon created the Domestic Council, which was to be chaired by the president and included cabinet secretaries and EOP officials. John Ehrlichman was to be its director, and he recruited a staff of sixty to seventy by 1972, including a deputy and six assistant directors.[24] The council itself seldom met, but the staff met often and acted in effect as the president's agent with respect to domestic policy. That is, Ehrlichman acted for the president and convinced cabinet members to go along.[25]

Watergate led to the decline of the power of the Domestic Council, and it did not recover much in the Ford administration when the president delegated his domestic agenda to Vice President Rockefeller. Since President Ford was a fiscal conservative, there was not much on the domestic agenda, and much of the policymaking action on the domestic side was dominated by the newly created Economic Policy Board. But when Jimmy Carter came to office there were a number of domestic policy initiatives he wanted to pursue, and he reconstituted the function under the name of the Domestic Policy Staff. The staff was headed by Assistant to the President Stuart Eizenstat, who acted as an honest broker with the cabinet and advised the president. Eizenstat and his staff of forty to fifty were influential advisers to Carter, but did not have the independence or authority that Ehrlichman had in the Nixon administration.[26]

In the Reagan administration the name of the domestic staff was changed to the Office of Policy Development (OPD), with a staff of about forty under Martin Anderson, who reported to Edwin Meese. The main priorities of the new administration were economic and budget and were developed through the Legislative Strategy Group and David Stockman's OMB. The OPD developed second-level domestic policy initiatives but also played an important role in staffing the cabinet council system of the first term and in staffing the Domestic Policy Council during the second term. Under President Bush the Domestic Policy Council continued to exist, and the domestic policy staff was headed by Roger Porter, whose title included both domestic and economic policy. Domestic policy, however, was also heavily influenced by OMB Director Richard Darman and Chief of Staff John Sununu. President Clinton created a large Do-

---

[24]See Margaret Wyszomirski, "The De-Institutionalization of Presidential Staff Agencies," pp. 448–458.

[25]See Margaret J. Wyszomirski, "The Roles of a Presidential Office for Domestic Policy: Three Models and Four Cases," in George C. Edwards, Steven A. Shull, and Norman C. Thomas, eds., *The Presidency and Public Policy Making* (Pittsburgh: University of Pittsburgh Press, 1985), pp. 130–150.

[26]Wyszomirski, "The Roles of a Presidential Office for Domestic Policy," pp. 139–140.

mestic Policy Council, but did not meet with it often, if ever. A domestic policy staff existed in the White House, but did not function as a major force in policymaking. Clinton's National Economic Council staff, however, did play an important role in domestic policymaking.

Thus, the existence of a domestic policy capacity with a specialized staff is firmly established in the White House. Some presidents may use it more (Nixon) and others may use it less (Reagan), but the option to do away completely with a domestic policy capacity in the White House is not likely to be taken by any president. The function of domestic policy coordination and the capacity to develop new initiatives are too important to a president. The existence and legitimacy of the domestic policy staff is firmly established in the White House Office.

CONCLUSION

Since the beginning of the modern presidency the White House staff has grown as the federal government has taken on more functions in our society. In the 1930s the national government did not have a space program, run a large scale military establishment and project its force around the world, provide Social Security or Medicare benefits for most Americans, have an interstate highway system, regulate air traffic, or play an active role in education. As the tasks of government increased, the size of government grew in both personnel and budget.

The White House has had to respond to the greater complexity in its environment. The executive branch is much more fragmented now that it has to deal with the many functions of modern government, and the White House has reflected that fragmentation in its internal specialized units. Congress, though it is made up of roughly the same number of legislators, has expanded its functions as the federal government has grown, and has also increased its own staff resources to deal with the executive branch. The White House has had to respond to these changes, as well as to the increased fragmentation in Congress, since the reforms of the 1970s.

Thus, the proliferation of offices in the presidency, while striking when viewed in isolation, becomes much more understandable when seen as a series of responses to a changing political and governmental environment.

Five

THE CABINET AND THE EXECUTIVE BRANCH

The Constitution declares that the executive power shall reside in the president, but it does not go into detail about the structure or organization of the president's branch. This chapter will analyze the major components of the executive branch—the cabinet, political appointments, departments and agencies—with the emphasis on how the president uses these tools of governance. Presidents have often tried to use their cabinets as collegial sounding boards, but the experience of recent presidents has not often lived up to that ideal. Relations between cabinet secretaries and the White House staff have often been strained, and this chapter will explain the dominance of the White House staff in the contemporary presidency.

Political appointees provide managerial and policy leadership in the executive branch. Some of the appointments are presidential, but some have traditionally been controlled by cabinet secretaries and agency heads. Recent presidents have centralized the control of these appointments in unprecedented ways. Most presidents come to office harboring suspicions of the career bureaucracies of the government. We will examine the role of the two million civil servants (and three million in uniform) who serve the country at the direction of the president.

The theme of this chapter is that presidents have asserted much more centralized control over the cabinet and executive branch in recent decades and that, contrary to some assertions, executive branch bureaucracies are quite responsive to presidents. Nevertheless, presidents will still be frustrated because they must share the governmental agenda with Congress, and they are subject to the constraints of public law and the broader forces in the political system. The modern presidency exerts more centralized control over the executive branch at the end of the twentieth century, but presidential control is necessarily incomplete because of the constitutional framework.

ORIGINS OF THE CABINET

The "president's cabinet" as an institution is based on practice and precedent, for it has no basis in the Constitution or law (though some laws refer to cabinet officers). The Framers decided not to saddle the president with any council of advisers, and the Constitution merely allows the president to "require the Opinion, in writing, of the principal Officer in each of the executive Departments, upon any Subject relating to the duties of their respective Offices" (Article II, Section 2). The cabinet departments were begun when Congress, at President Washington's request, created three departments of government in the summer of 1789: the departments of state, war, and treasury.[1] While Washington continued to seek advice from his former associates, the use of his cabinet secretaries as a more formal advisory system was precipitated by the refusal of the Senate to perform the advisory role that Washington had expected. Washington went to the Senate in 1790 to seek its advice on a treaty with the Indians, but the Senate rejected his overture. Consequently, Washington turned to his department heads for advice, and since then no president has relied on the Senate for advice with respect to treaties or appointments.

Washington consulted with his departmental secretaries about matters of state, and in 1791 began meeting with them as a group. He even suggested that, when he was traveling, Alexander Hamilton, Thomas Jefferson, and Henry Knox meet in his absence if any issues arose that might require his attention.[2] Although the term "cabinet" in the U.S. government was not used until 1794, Washington began in 1793 to seek regular advice from his department heads: the secretaries of state, treasury, and war, and Attorney General John Jay (though the Justice Department was not created until 1870).

After the Federalist period presidents began to choose cabinet members with whom they were not close associates, and began to seek advice from others as well. Andrew Jackson, for instance, did not even meet with his official cabinet for his first two years in office, preferring to seek advice from old friends who became known as his "Kitchen Cabinet." James Polk, on the other hand, met with his department heads 350 times during his one term in office. Throughout the nineteenth century, presidents more or less used their cabinets as a primary advisory mechanism.

The cabinet in the United States must be distinguished from the cabinet in a parliamentary system, where cabinet members are also members of parliament. Political parties choose ministers from among the leadership of the con-

[1]For a history of the U.S. Cabinet, see R. Gordon Hoxie, "The Cabinet in the American Presidency, 1789–1984," *Presidential Studies Quarterly* (Spring 1984), pp. 209–230; for a developmental perspective on the cabinet see Ronald C. Moe, "The President's Cabinet," in James P. Pfiffner and Roger H. Davidson, *Understanding the Presidency* (New York: Longman, 1997), pp. 136–155.

[2]Hoxie, "The Cabinet in the American Presidency," p. 212.

trolling party in parliament. They retain their full voting membership in the legislature at the same time that they are the cabinet ministers in charge of the executive departments (ministries). They are thus dependent on their party in the legislature where party loyalty is expected, and the prime minister is the first among equals. In the United States, however, cabinet secretaries are wholly dependent on the president for their appointment, and the Constitution forbids membership in both branches at the same time. Cabinet secretaries serve at the pleasure of the president, who can dismiss them at any time. The U.S. cabinet as such has no formal power. Its relationship to the president was reflected by Abraham Lincoln, who announced a vote in his cabinet: "Seven nays and one aye, the ayes have it."

THE CABINET AS A DELIBERATIVE BODY

Modern presidential candidates often refer to "cabinet government" as an ideal to which their administrations will adhere. In the U.S. context, the term refers to the delegation of a certain amount of authority to cabinet secretaries and to presidential consultation with the cabinet as a deliberative body. The idea has much appeal. The U.S. government is so complex that no one person can understand it all, and the regular advice of the experts who head the major departments and agencies cannot help but be salutary to a president. In addition, the synergy of a team of highly competent people deliberating on the complex issues of governance and proffering their best collective advice to the president can be compelling.

Harry Truman expressed this ideal when he decided to replace Roosevelt's cabinet appointments with his own. "The cabinet is not merely a collection of executives administering different governmental functions. It is a body whose combined judgment the president uses to formulate the fundamental policies of the administration."[3]

Of all modern presidents, Dwight Eisenhower came closest to achieving the U.S. ideal of cabinet government. He consciously chose his cabinet appointees to be part of a team, and selected a group of men of similar backgrounds. His cabinet was a homogeneous collection, as one magazine put it: "eight millionaires and one plumber."[4] Eisenhower believed in the efficacy of the deliberation of the full cabinet on matters of importance. He told his cabinet: "My hope will be to make this a policy body, to bring before you and for you to bring up subjects that are worthy of this body as a whole."[5] Eisenhower expected that

---

[3]Quoted in Michael Nelson, ed., *Congressional Quarterly Guide to the Presidency* (Washington, DC: CQ Press, 1989), p. 978.

[4]*New Republic* (December 15, 1952), p. 3; quoted in Stephen Hess, *Organizing the Presidency* (Washington, DC: Brookings Institution, 1988), p. 57. The one "plumber" was Martin P. Durkin, who had been president of the AFL United Association of Plumbers and Steamfitters.

[5]Quoted in Fred I. Greenstein, *The Hidden-Hand Presidency* (New York: Basic Books, 1982), p. 106.

members of his cabinet would not confine their advice to their own policy areas but would speak out on the broad issues facing his administration.[6]

Eisenhower also believed in delegating matters not clearly of presidential importance to his line officers in the cabinet rather than having his White House staff make the decisions. Eisenhower's White House aide, General Goodpaster, recalled: "In the Eisenhower White House, the president would deal only with the great issues. . . . I remember that when important issues came up in staff meetings, Eisenhower would interrupt and say 'Excuse me, but that is not a staff matter. I will take that up with the secretary of defense, or interior. . . .'"[7]

The seriousness with which Eisenhower took cabinet deliberations was demonstrated by his establishment of a cabinet secretariat to prepare agendas for cabinet meetings and make sure that all background papers were in the hands of secretaries well before cabinet meetings. Members of the secretariat also made a record of each meeting and followed up on presidential decisions to ensure cabinet compliance.[8]

But even Eisenhower's cabinet did not always live up to his ideals of cabinet government. According to one participant, Elliot L. Richardson, seldom were matters of importance put before the collective body for deliberation and decision by the president. Vice President Richard Nixon, whom Eisenhower included in cabinet deliberations, recalled that most cabinet meetings were "unnecessary and boring."[9] If the pressures of the U.S. political system prevented even Eisenhower's cabinet from fully living up to his cabinet government ideal, most post–World War II presidents did not even come close. The incentives in the system all run against collaboration. Cabinet secretaries would rather do their special pleading one-on-one with the president, rather than putting their own priorities on the table for general discussion by the full cabinet.

Possibly because of his background as a member of Congress with a small staff, in contrast to Eisenhower's experience with military staff systems, John Kennedy preferred working with small groups. From the beginning of his presidency, Kennedy felt that the cabinet should meet for little more than symbolic reasons. "Cabinet meetings are simply useless," he declared. "Why should the Postmaster General sit there and listen to a discussion of the problems of Laos?"[10] Even his close adviser and brother, Attorney General Robert F. Kennedy, felt that full cabinet meetings were of such little use that he attended only about half of them.[11]

---

[6]Dwight D. Eisenhower, *Mandate for Change* (New York: Doubleday, 1963), p. 99.

[7]"Jimmy Carter on the Presidency" (Washington, DC: The Wilson Center, 1984), transcript of remarks, p. 16.

[8]For an analysis of the operation of the cabinet secretariat by one of its participants, see Bradley Patterson, *The President's Cabinet* (Washington, DC: American Society for Public Administration, May 1976), pp. 107–114.

[9]See Elliot L. Richardson and James P. Pfiffner, "Creating a Real Cabinet," *USA Today Magazine* (September 1990), pp. 10–12.

[10]Arthur Schlesinger, Jr., *A Thousand Days* (Boston: Houghton Mifflin, 1965), p. 688.

[11]Edwin O. Guthman and Jeffrey Shulman, eds., *Robert Kennedy in His Own Words* (New York: Bantam Books, 1988), p. 53.

Kennedy preferred to bring together smaller groups of people who were directly involved with an issue, whether members of his cabinet or White House staff. But more importantly, he wanted people whose judgment he could trust at these meetings. After the Bay of Pigs invasion, he felt he could not rely on people based on their experience or the positions they held; he wanted people at the table whom he personally knew.[12]

Lyndon Johnson kept Kennedy's cabinet for the first thirteen months of his administration before he began to replace them with his own appointees. In the earlier years of his administration Johnson met with his cabinet regularly, though at times they were not as productive as he hoped. George Reedy recalled LBJ's cabinet meetings: "Cabinet meetings were held with considerable regularity, with fully predetermined agendas and fully prewritten statements. In general, they consisted of briefings by cabinet members followed by a later release of the statements to the press. It was regarded by all participants except the president as a painful experience."[13]

In the latter years of his administration, marked by controversy about the continuing war in Vietnam, President Johnson came to distrust even his own cabinet members. As he told President-elect Richard Nixon in December 1968, "Let me tell you, Dick, I would have been a damn fool to have discussed major decisions with the full cabinet present, because I knew that if I said something in the morning, you could sure as hell bet it would appear in the afternoon papers."[14]

Richard Nixon began his presidency with the intention of rejecting the Democrats' more casual approach to the cabinet and return to a model closer to Eisenhower's. His initial intention was to delegate personnel selection and most of domestic policy to his cabinet and concentrate most of his own energy on foreign affairs. "I've always thought this country could run itself domestically without a president. All you need is a competent cabinet to run the country at home. You need a president for foreign policy."[15] Nixon wanted a strong cabinet to run the government for him. He intended that his cabinet secretaries would be experienced leaders who would use their independent judgment in advising him and running their departments.

But Nixon soon became disillusioned with his cabinet appointees and felt that they were too attached to their own policy and organizational interests and not committed enough to his reelection. After his landslide reelection in 1972 Nixon demanded the resignation of his entire cabinet and their political subordinates, a devastating blow to the loyal political appointees who had faithfully served in the administration and had worked for his reelection. In his second term, Nixon replaced his first-term cabinet with people who had less

[12]Guthman and Shulman, *Robert Kennedy in His Own Words,* p. 54.

[13]Quoted in Nelson, *Congressional Quarterly Guide to the Presidency,* pp. 978–979.

[14]Richard Nixon, *RN: The Memoirs of Richard Nixon* (New York: Grosset & Dunlap, 1978), p. 357.

[15]Rowland Evans, Jr., and Robert D. Novak, *Nixon in the White House* (New York: Random House, 1971), p. 11.

independent political stature of their own and were more personally loyal to him.[16] Nixon's first-term experience changed his mind about the possibilities of cabinet deliberation and delegation: "Cabinet government is a myth and won't work, . . . a president should never rely on his cabinet . . . no [president] in his right mind submits anything to his cabinet. . . ."[17]

Nixon's disdain for his cabinet appointees was reflected in their frustration with him. Many of them felt that, as cabinet secretaries, they had a certain claim on the president's time to discuss issues that fell within their jurisdictions. Secretary of the Interior Walter J. Hickel, in a letter to Nixon shortly before he was fired, said, "Permit me to suggest that you consider meeting, on an individual and conversational basis, with members of your cabinet. Perhaps through such conversations we can gain greater insight into the problems confronting us all, into solutions of these problems."[18] Nixon's attitude toward his cabinet led to his sweeping reorganization proposal and White House restructuring, which would have placed several layers of counselors between the president and most cabinet secretaries.

While Gerald Ford, in reacting to the Nixon administration, wanted to restore the status of the cabinet, he made himself much more accessible to his cabinet and refurbished its stature. But just as his "spokes of the wheel" White House organization gave way to a chief of staff system, after a year his cabinet declined in importance. The Ford administration did, however, make use of a cabinet subcommittee, the Economic Policy Board (EPB), to deliberate about economic policy. The EPB was a frequently used forum in the Ford presidency and included both White House staffers and members of the cabinet.[19]

In reaction to Nixon's centralized control and neglect of his cabinet secretaries, Jimmy Carter intended to "restore the cabinet to its proper role as the president's first circle of advisers."[20] Carter promised that his White House staffers would clearly be subordinate to members of his cabinet and not dominate them as the Nixon staff had. Carter's White House aide and later chief of staff, Jack Watson, articulated four principles of cabinet government: (1) cabinet officers should be free to select their own subordinates; (2) they should be able to set their own priorities; (3) they should be able to administer their own agencies free of White House interference; and (4) the president should delegate significant policy-making authority to cabinet secretaries.[21]

---

[16]See Nelson Polsby, "Presidential Cabinet Making: Lessons for the Political System," *Political Science Quarterly* (Spring 1978), pp. 15–16.

[17]Joan Hoff-Wilson, "Richard M. Nixon: The Corporate Presidency," in Fred I. Greenstein, ed., *Leadership in the Modern Presidency* (Cambridge, MA: Harvard University Press, 1988), p. 170.

[18]Quoted in Nelson, *Congressional Quarterly Guide to the Presidency,* p. 979.

[19]See Roger Porter, *Presidential Decision Making* (New York: Cambridge University Press, 1980).

[20]Quoted in Joseph Califano, *Governing America* (New York: Simon & Schuster, 1981), pp. 26–27.

[21]Joel Havemann, "The Cabinet Band—Trying to Follow Carter's Baton," *National Journal* (July 16, 1977), p. 1105.

Carter's early intentions did not escape the reality of executive branch politics. According to his domestic policy adviser, Stuart Eizenstat, the cabinet was important for expertise, information, and implementation, but it was not effective as a collective decision-making body. In the beginning of his administration Carter held cabinet meetings weekly, but the cabinet's effectiveness as an advisory body soon declined, and meetings decreased in frequency. By the middle of the Carter administration, the White House staff began to feel that some members of the cabinet were not fully on board with the president's program but were pursuing their own policy priorities on the Hill. This feeling led Carter to demand the resignations of all of his cabinet appointees and accept those of five in the summer of 1979.

During President Reagan's transition into office, Caspar Weinberger wrote an article describing how Reagan's cabinet system was intended to work. The president would:

> meet with his cabinet appointees on a regular basis with a planned agenda . . . to discuss with them all of the major problems facing the government that week, as well as some of the longer range problems, and to take counsel with his appointees not just on subjects relating to each member's department, but on an overall basis aided by a collegial discussion, arguments and differing points of view, presented by all members of this small group.[22]

Weinberger's description fit squarely into the traditional post–World War II cabinet ideal. But this idealized version of cabinet government did not work for Reagan any better than it had for his immediate predecessors. The Reagan administration was one of the most staff-directed and centralized presidencies in the modern era. Administration policy, budget priorities, and political personnel selection were tightly controlled by the White House staff. The people who planned the Reagan presidency self-consciously learned lessons from the experiences of Nixon and Carter with their cabinets. They were determined that Reagan would not make the same mistakes (as they saw it) of delegating personnel discretion to cabinet secretaries or of allowing budget priorities to be driven by departmental needs.

To ensure central control of policy development, but also to include cabinet secretaries, they organized a cabinet council system. Seven cabinet councils were formed around specific policy areas (economic affairs, commerce and trade, resources and environment, human resources, management and administration, food and agriculture, and legal policy), and the cabinet secretaries responsible for these areas would meet with White House staffers to develop policy. The important part of this system was to get the White House staff and

---

[22]Caspar W. Weinberger, "Yes, Washington, We *Can* Have Cabinet Government," *Washington Post* (November 25, 1980).

cabinet members sitting down together to discuss policy. Though some of the councils were much more active than others and not all major policy initiatives went through the system, it was a useful contribution to White House–cabinet relations and helped to avoid some of the usual fighting between the two groups. By the beginning of the second term, however, it was evident that the seven council system was too cumbersome and time-consuming. So the seven councils were reduced to two: economic policy and domestic policy. Along with the National Security Council, these were intended to be the primary policy development mechanisms for the administration, though as in the first term, the issues of highest priority were handled directly by top White House aides.

President Bush was one of the few modern presidents who did not promise cabinet government in campaigning for the presidency; yet he made more effective use of his cabinet than had most of his recent predecessors. Cabinet secretaries did not complain about being left out of policy deliberations in the first half of his term. Bush's first chief of staff, John Sununu, tried to dominate domestic policy, and the White House dominated policy-making in the areas of civil rights, budget priorities, and the environment. The president himself made and conducted the most important foreign policy initiatives, but entrusted much operating leeway to Secretary of State Baker and Secretary of Defense Cheney, who were very close to him. Bush cabinet meetings fit into the typical trend of declining importance as his term wore on.

During his transition, president-elect Clinton spent a considerable amount of time choosing his cabinet. He brought candidates to Little Rock and met with them individually for hours to ensure that he felt comfortable with them personally and in policy terms. He felt that his cabinet appointments were important because they would send a symbolic message of inclusion to the country about his priorities. He said he wanted to appoint "a cabinet that looks like America." He had to scramble to meet his self-imposed deadline of December 24 for completing his cabinet designations, but he did appoint a more diverse cabinet than any of his predecessors, with four African Americans, two Latinos, and three women, including the nation's first woman Attorney General, Janet Reno. His careful selection paid off in that only four positions turned over during his first term (including the accidental air crash death of Commerce Secretary Ron Brown).

For his second term Clinton replaced seven of his cabinet secretaries, about average for turnover for a second term. In his second-term appointments, Clinton continued to value diversity, with two Latinos, three African Americans, and four women, including Madeline Albright, who was the first woman appointed Secretary of State. He also appointed a Republican to be Secretary of Defense: former Senator William Cohen of Maine. In appointing his second-term cabinet team Clinton said, "I believe that one of my jobs at this moment in history is to demonstrate by the team I put together that no group of people should be excluded from service to our country and that all people are capable of serving. So I have striven to achieve both excellence and diversity. . . . But I would not have appointed a single one of them because of their gender or their racial or ethnic background had I not thought that they could succeed."[23]

In addition to the Secretaries of the fourteen cabinet departments, President Clinton accorded "Cabinet-level rank" to the following officials[24]:

Chief of Staff to the President
Director, Central Intelligence Agency
Director, Office of Management and Budget
Chair, Council of Economic Advisors
Director, Environmental Protection Agency
United States Trade Representative
Director, Office of National Drug Control Policy
Director, Federal Emergency Management Agency
Director, Small Business Administration
U.S. Representative to the United Nations
Counselor to the President

Other presidents had granted cabinet rank to officials other than the secretaries of departments, but not to the extent that Clinton did.

President Clinton's use of his cabinet as a symbol of the representative nature of his administration and his unprecedented granting of cabinet status to many other administration officials was consistent with his disinclination to use the cabinet as a working group or deliberative body. Twenty-five people is too many for a working meeting. The same point held for Clinton's National Economic Council with eighteen members and his Domestic Policy Council with twenty-three members. Clinton also added nine officials as participants in National Security Council meetings (see Chapter 7). The large memberships of these policy groups emphasize the symbolic nature of their membership. Actual policy deliberations were most often conducted in informal subsets of the groups' members along with the staffs of the groups who actually do most of the policy development work.[25]

Clearly, the main policy initiatives of the Clinton administration were run out of the White House, not in the departments or in the cabinet policy groups set up by the president. For instance, the economic program of the first term was formulated by Robert Rubin, director of the National Economic Council. After he was appointed Treasury Secretary, Rubin continued to play the dom-

[23] *Washington Post* (December 21, 1996), P. A 16.

[24] *United States Government Manual 1996/1997* (Washington, DC: Government Printing Office, 1997), p. 89.

[25] See James P. Pfiffner, *The Strategic Presidency: Hitting the Ground Running,* 2nd ed. (Lawrence: University Press of Kansas, 1996), pp. 155–159.

inant role in economic policy. The national health care planning task force symbolized Clinton's approach, with a task force of 500 people set up in the White House led by the First Lady and directed by White House adviser, Ira Magiziner. President Clinton's approach to his cabinet was indicated by the fact that, in the four years of his first term Clinton had formal cabinet meetings only eighteen times, an average of fewer than five per year.[26] He of course met with members of the cabinet many times, but not as a deliberative body.

Presidents have been disappointed in their attempts to use their cabinets as a deliberative body. The synergy that should result when presidents convene these highly intelligent men and women, all with the highest ideals of serving the president and the nation, is somehow missing. Why is the ideal of the cabinet as the president's primary advisory body so difficult to achieve? Part of the problem is size. The cabinet now has fourteen members in addition to the president and vice president and others whom presidents often invite to attend cabinet meetings.[27]

But the more important impediment to true collegial deliberation is that each cabinet secretary feels a strong need to defend departmental political and policy interests, and is thus unwilling to expose his or her special interests to the crossfire of fellow cabinet officers who may be battling for the same turf and resources.[28] As FDR's secretary of commerce, Jesse H. Jones, declared: "My principal reason for not having a great deal to say at cabinet meetings was that there was no one at the table who could be of help to me except the president, and when I needed to consult him, I did not choose a cabinet meeting to do so."[29]

DEPARTMENTAL SECRETARIES VERSUS THE WHITE HOUSE STAFF

The inability of presidents to take advantage of their cabinets as collective, deliberative bodies is rooted in cabinet members' individual roles as departmental secretaries and the consequent rise of the White House staff as the president's primary advisers. Departmental secretaries are the highest ranking appointed positions in the executive branch and are the line officers of the government. As line officers they possess statutory authority to carry out their du-

---

[26]Number of meetings provided by the Office of Cabinet Affairs, March 4, 1997.

[27]For an analysis of why cabinet government does not work see Shirley Warshaw, *Power Sharing: White House-Cabinet Relations in the Modern Presidency* (Albany, NY: State University of New York Press, 1996).

[28]See Elliot L. Richardson and James P. Pfiffner, "Creating a Real Cabinet," *USA Today Magazine* (September 1990), p. 12. See also Richardson and Pfiffner, "Our Cabinet System is a Charade," *The New York Times* (May 28, 1989).

[29]Quoted in Nelson, *Congressional Quarterly Guide to the Presidency*, p. 980.

ties, and they make major decisions about the allocation of resources and the deployment of personnel. In contrast, the power of White House staffers is derived from their personal relationship to the president; they do not have independent legal authority. Given this official status of cabinet secretaries and the resources at their command, why have they been overshadowed by the White House staff in the modern presidency? The answer lies in the roles they play in the political system and the need of presidents to control the government. (See Table 5–1.)

The role of departmental secretaries is Janus-like in that they must face both the president as the person who appointed them and at whose pleasure they serve, but each must also face downward to his or her department. This places them in a bind: they must prove themselves loyal to the president, yet at the same time they must be effective leaders of their own departments. In order to be effective in implementing programs and advocating presidential priorities, department secretaries must provide effective leadership for their departments. But this requires loyalty to departmental staff and career civil servants as well as to the president. The irony is that at times cabinet secretaries can be of most long-term use to the president by paying close attention to the needs of their own departments and their constituencies.

White House staffers often complain that cabinet secretaries tend to be special pleaders, and they are mostly correct in that evaluation. According to Miles's Law: where you stand (concerning policy) depends on where you sit (organizationally).[30] Thus, cabinet secretaries are virtually always advocates for their own departments. Just as this is predictable, it is also mostly legitimate. If departmental secretaries do not defend their programs, who will do it with credibility? Department heads cannot be expected to judge impartially the merit or priority of their own programs. The secretary of health and human services is obliged to make the best case for the value of medical research and public-health programs. The secretary of transportation is equally obliged to assert the priorities of air-travel safety.

But departmental advocacy stems from resource as well as policy grounds. In order to do an effective job, department heads need resources, money, and people, and they will fight for those resources. This is why Charles G. Dawes, the first director of BOB and Calvin Coolidge's vice president, said: "Cabinet secretaries are vice presidents in charge of spending, and as such are the natural enemies of the president."[31]

The differences in perspective of cabinet secretaries and White House staffers becomes more understandable if you consider the reasons why each group is selected. While White House staffers are recruited based on personal loyalty to the president, there are a number of criteria that are considered in

---

[30]Rufus Miles was Assistant Secretary for Administration of the Department of Health, Education, and Welfare for many years, as well as a Public Administration scholar.

[31]Quoted in Richardson and Pfiffner, "Creating a Real Cabinet," p. 12.

TABLE 5-1
Cabinet Departments

Department	Year	President	Personnel (1996)
State	1789	Washington	24,692
War/Defense	1789	Washington	810,424 (civilian)
Treasury	1789	Washington	151,379
Interior	1849	Polk	73,750
Agriculture	1862	Lincoln	112,503
Justice	1870	Grant	109,384
Commerce (formerly part of Commerce and Labor, 1903)	1913	Wilson	35,779
Labor (formerly part of Commerce and Labor, 1903)	1913	Wilson	15,399
Housing and Urban Development	1965	Johnson	11,511
Transportation	1966	Johnson	63,141
Energy	1977	Carter	18,636
Health and Human Services (formerly part of Health, Education and Welfare, 1953)	1980	Carter	59,490
Education (formerly part of HEW, 1953)	1980	Carter	4,753
Veterans Affairs	1988	Reagan	253,317

Source: Office of Personnel Management, *Federal Civilian Workforce Statistics* (July 1996), p. 16.

putting together a cabinet. The appointments of cabinet secretaries are often the first signals of how a president will act in office. Thus, these early decisions are fraught with symbolic importance. A newly elected president may want to unite the political party by naming a member of the opposite ideological wing to the cabinet. A president may even appoint a member of the other party, as did President Kennedy in naming Douglas Dillon to be treasury secretary, or Eisenhower his first secretary of labor, Martin Durkin. Richard Nixon's first choice to be secretary of defense was Democratic hawk, Senator Henry Jackson (though Jackson refused the offer). Carter's first secretary of energy, James Schlesinger, had been secretary of defense in the Nixon and Ford administrations.

Traditionally, presidents have paid attention to geographic and religious distribution in selecting their cabinets. Some departments are usually filled with representatives of certain constituencies: the Department of Agriculture is usually headed by a former farmer, Interior by someone from the West, Treasury by someone from the financial community, etc. Presidents have also demonstrated their commitment to racial diversity by naming African Americans or Latinos to cabinet posts. Recent presidents have usually named at least one woman to their cabinets, and President Clinton appointed five. With these different criteria affecting the choice of cabinet secretaries, it is predictable that the collective members of the cabinet will not be as personally close to the president as will the senior White House staff. President Clinton made much of his promise to make his cabinet "look more like the American people" and ended up with more women, African Americans, and Latinos in his cabinet than previous presidents.[32]

The roles that departmental secretaries play for the president are diverse. Each must be an effective political representative for the president with the public and an effective lobbyer with Congress, which controls departmental budgets and programs. Each must effectively manage the department's bureaus and agencies, and be an effective leader of the career and political officials of the agency, as well as a visible symbol of the president's commitment to that particular policy area. The internal management function is challenging because most departments are more of a holding company of different bureaus and agencies than a single-purpose agency. This calls for adept use of budgetary, organizational, and personnel skills by the secretary. At times these levers of control are sufficient, but in other cases bureaus have ties to sympathetic members of Congress who may try to influence departmental policy independent of the secretary.

Because of these multiple obligations, departmental secretaries often seem to be "captured" by the interests of their departments and swayed by their career personnel, who have a stake in the well-being of their programs. According to Nixon aide John Ehrlichman, departmental secretaries go off and "marry the natives." Of course, the perspective of the departmental secretary is that he or she is faithfully serving the president's best interests, and that White House staffers have their own agendas that they claim presidential authority to pursue. The frustrations of presidential appointees in the agencies is expressed by Donald Devine, former Reagan administration director of the Office of Personnel Management: "The president's staff at times pursues its own interests, not necessarily the president's. . . . If the agency head is loyal to the president, he should never be dictated to by the White House staff. Otherwise, every clerk in the White House will feel at liberty to call him and tell him the president wants this or that."[33]

In explaining departmental advocacy, the background of departmental secretaries is also a factor. They have often spent most of their careers becoming experts in the policy area they are now administering. But lack of absolute loyalty to the president by department secretaries is inherent in the American political system, both because of the reasons for their recruitment and because they are legally bound to carry out the law and may be called before Congress to account for their actions and justify their budgets.

From the White House perspective, however, these forces are not sufficient reason when cabinet secretaries do not seem to be toeing the administration

---

[32]The public disputes over the initial appointments to President Clinton's White House may signal that symbolic criteria are also becoming more important in the staffing of the White House.

[33]Donald Devine, "So You Want To Run An Agency," *Policy Review* (Winter 1989), p. 9.

line. As one Kennedy White House staffer put it, "Everybody believes in democracy until he gets to the White House and then you begin to believe in dictatorship, because it's so hard to get things done. Every time you turn around, people resist you and even resist their own job."[34] From the White House perspective, only advisors close to the president have the breadth of perspective to make the cross-cutting policy decisions that are necessary at the top of the federal government. In the words of Stuart Eizenstat, Jimmy Carter's domestic policy advisor: "No matter how good a cabinet secretary is there is a certain predictability to the outlook and response of his agency. The White House staff, as opposed to the cabinet, is perhaps the only arm of the president that offers some integrative capacity."[35]

The perspective of cabinet secretaries, however, is different. They often feel that they are forced into the role of advocacy because they so seldom get to see the president. According to one executive branch official:

> domestic cabinet members are so rarely with the president that when they do have a chance to see him, they have to advocate and plug their departmental program. . . . But precisely at such times, the senior White House aide present can adopt or strike a pose as the more objective, rational statesman taking a non-advocate and more "presidential" position. . . . The White House aide knows, on the other hand, that he can see the president later that day or the next, and so can afford to play a more reasonable and restrained role in such meetings."[36]

The natural friction between cabinet secretaries and White House staffers is exacerbated by differences in age and stature, with young White House aides often having the clout to be able to tell senior administration officials what to do. Jeb Stuart McGruder, a young Nixon staffer, put it this way:

> From our perspective in the White House, the cabinet officials were useful spokesmen when we wanted to push a particular line—on Cambodia, on Carswell, or whatever. From their perspective, however, it was often a rude awakening to have Jeb Magruder or Chuck Colson calling up and announcing, "Mr. Secretary, we're sending over this speech that we'd like you to deliver." But that was how it was. Virtually all the cabinet members had to accept that they lacked access to the president and that their dealings would be with Haldeman and his various minions."[37]

These differing perspectives represent the inherent tensions in the modern presidency. Cabinet secretaries are the line officers of the executive branch,

---

[34]Quoted by Thomas Cronin, *The State of the Presidency* (Boston: Little, Brown, 1980), p. 223.

[35]"Jimmy Carter on the Presidency," p. 17.

[36]Quoted in Thomas Cronin, *The State of the Presidency* (Boston: Little, Brown, 1980), p. 284.

[37]Jeb Stuart Magruder, *An American Life: One Man's Road to Watergate* (New York: Atheneum, 1974), p. 102.

and they are pulled by strong centrifugal forces. White House staffers enforce presidential needs to have greater control of the large and complex executive branch.

Since the 1970s, the centralization of control of the executive branch in the White House has been a continuing reality in domestic as well as foreign policy. In 1971, Senator Ernest F. Hollings stated the perceived reality:

> It used to be that if I had a problem with food stamps, I went to see the secretary of agriculture, whose department had jurisdiction over that program. Not any more. No, if I want to learn the policy, I must go to the White House and consult John Price. If I want the latest on textiles, I won't get it from the secretary of commerce, who has the authority and responsibility. No, I am forced to go to the White House and see Mr. Peter Flanigan. I shouldn't feel too badly. Secretary [of Commerce] Stans has to do the same thing.[38]

The fragmenting forces in American politics have intensified with the growth of the scope and size of government. The modern presidency has dealt with this fragmentation by increasing the size and power of the White House staff. Regardless of campaign promises, the reality of the modern presidency is that the White House staff will continue to compete with and often overshadow departmental secretaries.

PRESIDENTIAL APPOINTMENTS

Cabinet secretaries are the president's most important line officers, but they comprise only a very small percentage of the total number of political appointments that presidents make. Most government officials in most nations in the world are not temporary political appointees but rather are appointed for indefinite periods, often for their careers. So are most government employees in the United States. What sets the United States apart from other modern industrialized democracies is the number of political appointees available for each newly elected president. The European parliamentary democracies of Britain, France, and Germany change only a maximum of several hundred officials with a change in party control of the government. A U.S. president, however, can make a total of about 3,000 appointments to the executive branch, and can control about 2,000 more political appointments. (See Table 5–2.)

Even if the total of about 5,000 is reduced by the 2,000 appointees who are only part-time, and the almost 2,500 who are technically not presidential, but rather agency-head political appointments (Noncareer Senior Executive Service and Schedule C), that still leaves about 650 appointments to run the executive branch, more than any other modern democracy.

---

[38]Harold Relyea, "Growth and Development of the President's Office," in David Kozak and Kenneth Ciboski, *The American Presidency* (Chicago: Nelson Hall, 1985), p. 135.

TABLE 5-2
Political Appointments Available to Presidents

PAS*	
Part-time	505
Ambassadors	165
U.S. Attorneys and Marshals	187
Executives and Commissioners	663
PA†	
Executive branch	24
White House	438
Part-time	1,405
Agency appointments‡	
SES§	711
Schedule C‖	1,725
Total	5,823¶

*Presidential appointment with the consent of the Senate.

†Presidential appointment not requiring Senate confirmation.

‡Legally made by agency head, but the president can instruct appointees whom to appoint.

§Senior Executive Service: 10 percent of authorized total SES positions can be political appointees, about 700 of 7,000.

‖Created in 1953, political appointments at GS 15 and below. Must have a confidential or policymaking role in the administration.

¶Presidents can also appoint about 1,000 federal judges, who serve for life. But any individual president will only have the opportunity to make a portion of these appointments.

Source: PAS and PA data derived from information provided by the executive clerk to the president (February 19, 1992). Agency appointments data from General Accounting Office reported in the *Washington Post* (November 20, 1992), p. A23.

The purpose of these presidential appointees is to help lead the two million civilian employees and three million military personnel who comprise the executive branch. The premise is that the American people elect the president, but that the president cannot manage the government alone, and thus he or she can appoint executives and managers to help lead, direct, and control the executive branch of government. When the people elect a president, they also, by implication, help select the people the president will appoint to lead the government.

The Framers of the Constitution were greatly concerned with the quality of those chosen to run the government, feeling that their character would determine the overall quality of the U.S. government. Those Framers favoring a strong executive wanted to give the president exclusive authority to make appointments. But those distrustful of executive power preferred to give the appointment power to the Senate. At the end of the Constitutional Convention the issue was finally settled by the compromise calling for presidential nomination and Senate confirmation of the major appointments to the executive branch.[39]

---

[39]An excellent analysis of the Framers and the appointment power can be found in Charles Ross, "The Accidental Elite: Senate Confirmed Federal Executives," Doctoral Dissertation, George Mason University, 1993, chap. 2.

Senate confirmation hearings on particular nominees can be grueling for the nominee and tense for the administration. Occasionally there will be an acrimonious fight and the Senate will reject a nominee, such as George Bush's nomination of John Tower to be secretary of defense in 1989. But such rejections are very unusual. From 1789 to 1990 only fifteen cabinet nominations (and twenty-seven Supreme Court nominees) have been formally rejected by the Senate, and only four of these in the twentieth century.[40] No president since Herbert Hoover has been forced to withdraw more than one percent of his nominations, and no president since FDR has had more than six nominations rejected by the Senate.[41]

There is a tension in the modern nation-state between political responsiveness and technical competence. The American government of the twentieth century is a huge, fragmented, and highly complex congeries of organizations. Government organizations put satellites into space, search for cures for cancer and AIDS, make judgments about patents for biotechnology, control nuclear missiles and regulate nuclear energy, and make sure that computers generate accurately the millions of Social Security checks that go out each month. Running these programs is no job for amateurs.

So each new president is faced with the duty to appoint competent professionals to leadership positions in the government, but presidents also face pressures to reward political supporters with government jobs. Before the modern presidency, the job of recruiting presidential appointees was dominated by the political parties. From the early nineteenth century presidents had used patronage—that is, government jobs—to build support for their political parties. When the party's candidate won, the party faithful expected that they would be rewarded with jobs.

The modern appointments system, though greatly changed, still has some resemblance to the traditional patronage system. The major changes stem from two factors: the decline of political parties and the need for expertise in the government. The types of people now needed to run the government must be highly qualified, and their qualifications must be more than merely party loyalty. The people needed to fill technical positions in defense systems, nuclear energy, biotechnology, patents for intellectual property, space exploration, or strategic defense are "unlikely to be found hanging out at party headquarters on election night."[42]

The other major developments that have affected presidential appointments are the decline of political parties and the simultaneous rise of the White House staff. As the White House staff grew in size, importance, and influence

---

[40]See Rogelio Garcia, "Cabinet and Other High Level Nominations that Failed to be Confirmed, 1789–1989," Library of Congress, Congressional Research Service Report No. 89–253 GOV (April 14, 1989).

[41]Morris Fiorina, *Divided Government* (New York: Macmillan, 1992), p. 97.

[42]G. Calvin Mackenzie, "Partisan Presidential Leadership: The President's Appointees," in L. Sandy Maisel, ed., *The Parties Respond* (Boulder, CO: Westview Press, 1990), p. 283.

in the modern presidency, political parties enjoyed less control of traditional patronage. As the number of primary elections increased, political parties lost control of the nominating process, and thus when presidents were elected they owed less in the way of patronage to the parties. In making appointments presidents were unwilling to accept whoever happened to be a loyal party worker, but wanted to recruit people who would be loyal to them and who were competent enough to the do the jobs for which they were recruited.

Presidents began to designate White House staffers to specialize in political recruitment. Harry Truman put one person in charge of presidential appointments. John Kennedy had his three-person "talent hunt." Richard Nixon had Frederic Malek put together a thirty- to forty-person White House personnel office. Jimmy Carter's transition operation had its "Talent Inventory Program." Ronald Reagan's Office of Presidential Personnel had 100 people at work during the first months in office. And President Clinton had 130 people recruiting presidential appointees in the early months of 1993. As the White House personnel operation grew in size it also increased in professionalism, with people directing it who had had professional executive recruiting experience in the private sector.

In the contemporary presidency the professionalism and competence of the Office of Presidential Personnel is crucial, especially at the very beginning of a presidency. In order for a new president to take control and give direction to the government, appointees must be in place to provide leadership to the many bureaucracies. At the beginning, efforts must focus on the top 300 or so positions in the executive branch: the cabinet and immediate subcabinet (under, deputy, and assistant secretaries). But the need for speed in making these appointments is countered by the volume of work that must be done.

Each new administration is besieged by people who want government jobs. Those who have worked in the campaign expect special consideration, and members of Congress are not at all reticent in recommending constituents or staffers for appointments in the new administration. In recent administrations, thousands of applications and recommendations flowed into transition headquarters. President Bush's director of the Office of Presidential Personnel, Chase Untermeyer, reported that the Bush administration received more that 45,000 applications and recommendations in its first five months in office.[43] The Clinton transition team received up to 2,000 applications per day, and expected to receive a total of 100,000.[44]

The Office of Presidential Personnel must separate out the wheat from the chaff in the applications. But even the chaff cannot be ignored with impunity. If the recommendation comes from the Hill, the president's personnel office must write cordial letters explaining why Senator X's favorite nephew is not qualified to be assistant secretary for research in the Energy Department. So a

---

[43]Interview with Chase Untermeyer, The White House, June 6, 1990.

[44]*U.S. News & World Report* (February 1, 1993), p. 9.

contemporary president cannot afford to begin an administration without a large and professional personnel operation.

With the volume of applications for presidential appointments, what criteria are used to narrow down the list of final nominations? The sine qua non of presidential appointments is loyalty. But the definition of loyalty has shifted over the years. Loyalty used to be defined by party service. If one was a good Republican or Democrat that was deemed to be sufficient to attest to one's loyalty. But party affiliation began to decline in importance as the need for professional competence rose. President Eisenhower, a professional public servant for all of his career, felt very uneasy with the claims of partisanship. John Kennedy and Richard Nixon both said early in their terms that competence was more important than partisanship; they wanted the person best qualified for the job.

But recent presidents have felt an increasing need for loyalty in presidential appointees in order to control the government. In their initial commitment to cabinet government both Presidents Nixon and Carter delegated to their cabinet appointees the authority to select their immediate subordinates (the subcabinet), even though these were presidential appointments. But several years into their administrations both came to feel that they had delegated away too much presidential leverage. When conflicts between cabinet departments and the White House staff arose, the White House felt that the presidential appointees out in the agencies were loyal to the cabinet secretary who appointed them rather than to the president. Each administration tried to pull the appointment authority back into the White House, but once appointment authority has been delegated, trying to bring it back to the White House is like trying to put toothpaste back into the tube after it has been squeezed out. (See Table 5–3.)

Top Reagan advisers decided before they took office that they would control political appointments in the White House. Pendleton James, Reagan's first personnel recruiter, was given an office in the west wing and the title of assistant to the president; both were unprecedented and intended to symbolize the importance that the administration gave to personnel. They argued that policy control was not possible without personnel control.

In order to ensure White House primacy, the Reagan administration insisted that all presidential appointments be tightly controlled by the White House. Cabinet secretaries could suggest candidates for their management teams, but final decisions would be made in the White House. In another unprecedented action they insisted that all political, not just presidential, appointees be cleared through the White House. These included noncareer SES and Schedule C appointments, which are technically at the discretion of the agency head.

The other component of the Reagan administration plan to control the government was their definition of loyalty. A loyal Republican heritage was insufficient. People who had worked for the Nixon and Ford administrations were called "retreads." The right wing of the Republican party wanted people in the administration who were committed "Reaganites" and who were committed to the conservative policy agenda. Those who were not "movement conservatives"

TABLE 5-3
Political Appointees by Cabinet Department (1992)

Department	PAS	Noncareer SES	Schedule C
State	64*	33	97
Defense	51	48	103
Treasury	32	22	75
Interior	19	38	54
Agriculture	17	49	131
Justice	48†	58	64
Commerce	32	52	152
Labor	19	14	91
Housing and Urban Development	14	26	83
Transportation	19	37	57
Energy	25	38	107
Health and Human Services	20	67	89
Education	19	21	116
Veterans Affairs	15	4	13

*Plus 165 Ambassadors.

†Plus 93 U.S. Marshals and 94 U.S. Attorneys.

Source: PAS from executive clerk to the president (February 19, 1992). Noncareer SES and Schedule C from General Accounting Office reported in the *Washington Post* (November 20, 1992), p. A23. Copyright © 1992 The Washington Post. Reprinted with permission. Veterans Affairs noncareer SES and Schedule C from VA Office of Public Affairs (February 18, 1993).

felt that the criteria were an unfair "litmus test" that excluded loyal Republicans who were competent and qualified for positions because of their service in previous Republican administrations. The tension between professionalism and ideological commitment characterized the appointment process for the first year of the administration.[45]

In the Bush administration the definition of loyalty shifted from ideological to personal loyalty to, and past service with, George Bush. An administration "scrub team" went over potential nominations to ensure that those with past service to Bush were not passed over. The Bush administration paid more attention to professional competence and delegated more discretion to its cabinet secretaries in choosing their immediate subordinates than Reagan had, but still insisted that agency heads find jobs for campaign workers at the Schedule C level.

The main criterion for personnel selection in the Clinton administration (aside from competence) was diversity, often known as the "EGG" standard, standing for ethnicity, gender, and geography. The Clinton White House played a very active role in selecting political appointees throughout the government. While the White House accepted suggestions from departmental secretaries,

[45]For an analysis of the presidential appointments process, see James P. Pfiffner, "Nine Enemies and One Ingrate: Presidential Appointments During Transition," in G. Calvin Mackenzie, ed., *The In and Outers: Presidential Appointees and the Problems of Transient Government in Washington* (Baltimore: Johns Hopkins University Press, 1987).

the lists submitted were often rejected for lack of diversity. One of the results of this commitment to diversity was a greater percentage of women and African Americans than served in any previous administration. Another result was a slower appointment process than any other administration.[46]

As the White House has taken a larger and more controlling role in the political appointment process, the time it takes to get the top levels of the executive branch staffed has increased. It took President Kennedy an average of 2.1 months from inauguration day to fill a position, but since then the period has steadily increased to 8.5 months for President Clinton in 1993. Despite Bush's service as vice president, his personnel transition was one of the slowest in history.[47] The reasons for the increasing time necessary to staff an administration include the new ethics laws, closer scrutiny by presidential recruiters, more thorough FBI checks, and more drawn out Senate confirmation procedures.

Several other trends have marked the development of the political appointments process in the modern presidency. As the government has grown in size and complexity, the number of political appointees has grown, at the PAS as well as at lower levels. From the 1930s to the 1970s, the White House gradually took control of appointments from the political parties by developing a professional recruitment capacity in the White House. After the 1970s appointments have been more tightly controlled by the Office of Presidential Personnel, with much less leeway for department and agency heads to choose their immediate subordinates. All of these factors point to the importance of a professional White House recruitment office that is ready to go immediately after a presidential election.

THE EXECUTIVE BRANCH BUREAUCRACY

The modern career bureaucracy that comprises the executive branch is the successor to the spoils system of the nineteenth century. President Andrew Jackson provided the justification for the spoils system by arguing that all government jobs were essentially simple and that incumbents of government positions tend to abuse their power. In the middle decades of the nineteenth century, presidents newly coming to office brought with them party loyalists to fill the government jobs. The spoils system helped to build political parties in the U.S., but reformers argued that spoils led to incompetence, inefficiency, corruption, and the need to train a new cadre of campaigners to do government jobs every four years. Presidents complained that they spent too much time making patronage decisions and acting as petty job-brokers. (See Table 5–4.)

---

[46]For a detailed analysis see Pfiffner, *The Strategic Presidency,* chap. 8 and Conclusion.

[47]See Paul Light, *Thickening Government* (Washington, DC: Brookings Institution, 1995), p. 68.

TABLE 5–4
More Officials at the Top Layers of the Executive Branch

	1960	1992
Secretary	10	14
Deputy Secretary	6	21
Under Secretary	15	32
Assistant Secretary	87	212
Deputy Assistant Secretary	78	506

Source: Adapted from Paul Light, *Thickening Government: Federal Hierarchy and the Diffusion of Hierarchy,* pp. 191–193. Copyright © 1995 by Paul Light. Reprinted by permission of Brookings Publications.

The arguments of the reformers came to fruition when Charles Giteau, a disappointed office-seeker, assassinated President Garfield in 1881. This act galvanized the Congress to pass the Pendleton Act of 1883, which created the merit system under which civil servants would be chosen on the basis of ability rather than party affiliation. The act also forbade executive branch officials from making personnel decisions—hiring, firing, promotions, demotions—on the basis of party. It also created the Civil Service Commission, which was to run personnel recruitment for the government and act as a watchdog for the protection of merit principles throughout the government.

Initially the Pendleton Act covered only 10 percent of the civil service, with presidents having the option of including by executive order other categories of workers ("blanketing in"), thus protecting their own political appointees from being dismissed by the next president. By the 1930s over 70 percent of government workers were in the Civil Service, and by the 1980s well over 80 percent were covered.

The trade-off for the protections of the merit system for civil servants was the commitment to "neutral competence." That is, professional civil servants would be selected on the basis of competence, but they would be neutral with respect to political party. They would be responsive to any president, regardless of party. But as the system of protections against political abuse grew—for instance, limits on demoting or firing personnel—the system was seen to be more insulated from political control. And complaints about the insulation and lack of responsiveness of "the bureaucracy" were increasingly heard. (See Figure 5–1.)

Modern presidents have tended to be skeptical of the career bureaucracy. When Eisenhower was elected, Republicans felt that the career people promoted during the past twenty years of Democratic control would be biased against the new administration. His administration thus created a new category of political appointments, Schedule C positions, which would be at lower levels (GS 15 and below) in the agencies. Those committed and loyal in a partisan way to the president would no longer be limited only to the highest positions in the executive branch.

John Kennedy was doubtful whether the leadership of the career services,

FIGURE 5–1
The Government of the United States

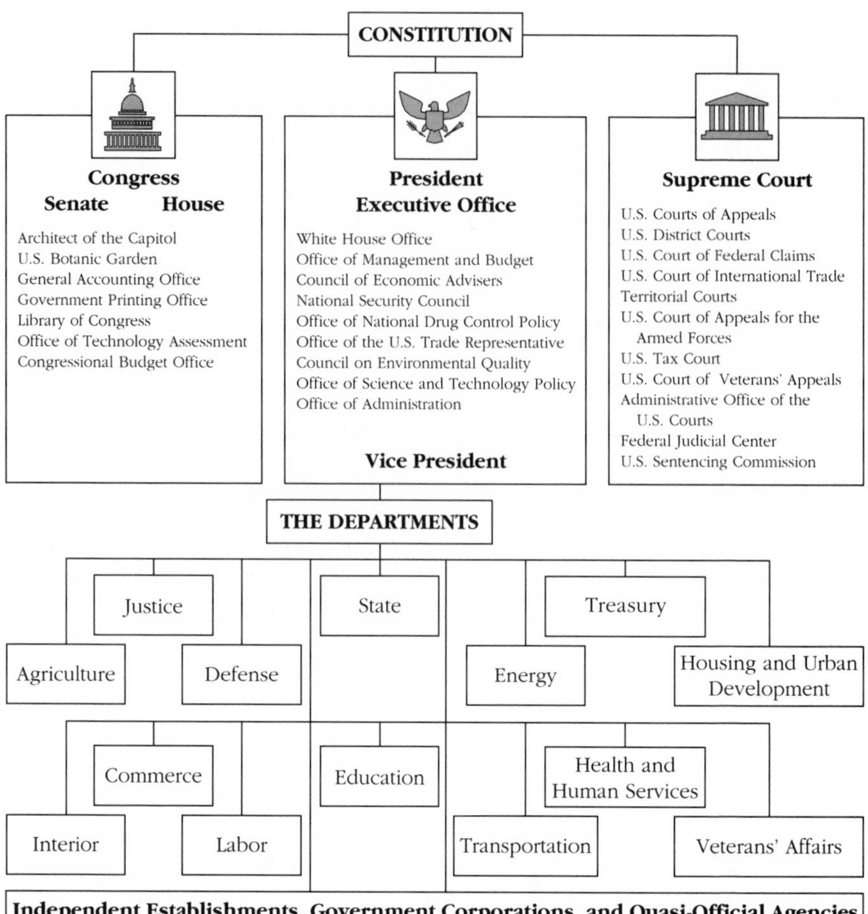

Independent Establishments, Government Corporations, and Quasi-Official Agencies

Administrative Conference of the U.S.
African Development Foundation
Central Intelligence Agency
Commodity Futures Trading Commission
Consumer Product Safety Commission
Corporation for National and Community Service
Defense Nuclear Facilities Safety Board
Environmental Protection Agency
Equal Employment Opportunity Commission
Export-Import Bank of the U.S.
Farm Credit Administration
Federal Communications Commission
Federal Deposit Insurance Corporation
Federal Election Commission
Federal Emergency Management Agency
Federal Housing Finance Board
Federal Labor Relations Authority
Federal Maritime Commission
Federal Mediation and Conciliation Service
Federal Mine Safety and Health Review Commission
Federal Reserve System
Federal Retirement Thrift Investment Board
Federal Trade Commission
General Services Administration
Inter-American Foundation
Interstate Commerce Commission
Merit Systems Protection Board
National Aeronautics and Space Administration
National Archives and Records Administration
National Capital Planning Commission
National Credit Union Administration
National Foundation on the Arts and the Humanities
National Labor Relations Board
National Mediation Board
National Railroad Passenger Corporation (Amtrak)
National Science Foundation
National Transportation Safety Board
Nuclear Regulatory Commission
Occupational Safety and Health Review Commission
Office of Government Ethics
Office of Personnel Management
Office of Special Counsel
Panama Canal Commission
Peace Corps
Pennsylvania Avenue Development Corporation
Pension Benefit Guaranty Corporation
Postal Rate Commission
Railroad Retirement Board
Resolution Trust Corporation
Securities and Exchange Commission
Selective Service System
Small Business Administration
Social Security Administration
Tennessee Valley Authority
Thrift Depositor Protection Oversight Board
Trade and Development Agency
U.S. Arms Control and Disarmament Agency
U.S. Civil Rights Commission
U.S. Information Agency
U.S. International Development Cooperation Agency
U.S. International Trade Commission
U.S. Postal Service

Source: United States Government Manual, 1995/96 (Washington, DC: Government Printing Office, 1995), 22.

who had developed their careers during the Eisenhower years, would be flexible or bold enough to develop proposals for the "New Frontier" and to "get the country moving again." After the Bay of Pigs disaster, Kennedy became even more suspicious of the judgment of career executives and began to centralize control in the White House. Lyndon Johnson prodded the Budget Bureau to think boldly in designing his Great Society legislation, but was never fully satisfied by their efforts.

Richard Nixon had a legendary distrust for the career bureaucracy. He regarded them as "built-in establishmentarians fighting for the status quo," and told his White House aides: "We have no discipline in this bureaucracy. We never fire anybody. We never reprimand anybody. We never demote anybody. We always promote the sons-of-bitches that kick us in the ass. . . ."[48] The Nixon White House waged "guerilla warfare" with the bureaucracy, according to his aide, John Ehrlichman.

Jimmy Carter ran for president as an outsider complaining about the "horrible bureaucratic mess in Washington." Part of his motivation and support for the 1978 Civil Service Reform Act came from the desire to make it easier to fire civil servants. Ronald Reagan also ran a "bureaucracy bashing" campaign, promising to "get the government off our backs." He recruited a number of political appointees who were openly hostile to the agencies to which they were appointed and did his best to cut spending and personnel for the domestic agencies of the government. President Bush provided a sharp contrast to his immediate predecessors with his respect for career professionals and his ideals of public service.

Notwithstanding the attitudes of some newly elected presidents, their distrust of career civil servants is mostly misplaced. The vast majority of career professionals believe in the Constitution and respect the outcome of elections. Political executives have the necessary managerial tools to motivate career civil servants. Presidential appointees control promotions and can heavily influence the career prospects of people in their agencies. They can, although with some difficulty, fire people who are incompetent or who resist legitimate directives. Each agency head can also move most top career executives to different assignments because of the personnel authority granted in the 1978 Civil Service Reform Act. There will always be scattered instances of resistance to any policy, regardless of the incumbent party, but these are unusual.

Most presidential appointees gradually come to have a high respect for their career subordinates. This reality is reflected in the responses of presidential appointees who served between 1964 and 1984 to questions about the competence and responsiveness of career executives they worked with. From 77 to 92 percent of them rated career executives as "responsive" or "very responsive" (four or five on a five-point scale). Most administrations are marked by a

---

[48]The latter quote is from the Presidential Transcripts made from the Watergate recordings, quoted in Thomas Cronin, *The State of the Presidency* (Boston: Little, Brown, 1980), p. 223.

"cycle of accommodation" in which new political appointees gradually gain respect for the career subordinates with whom they work.[49]

But this responsiveness does not guarantee that presidents will always get everything they want from the executive branch. Congress, especially when it is of the opposite political party, can be depended on to compete with the president for control of administration. Congress holds the key levers of power over much of the bureaucracy and is often willing to use that power. The very existence of programs depends on the enabling legislation that creates programs and agencies, and most programs face periodic reauthorization. Each agency's budget must be defended each year, and the purse strings can be very specific.

Presidential appointees can be compelled to testify before congressional hearings that can be used to put pressure on agencies. Political power is also wielded by organized interest groups who can weigh in on issues affecting them directly. Even presidential appointees will be pulled by these centrifugal forces.

Thus, presidents will often be frustrated by outside political forces when they are seeking to achieve their policy goals. But the source of these frustrations is most often not "those damn bureaucrats" but the power of Congress and opposing political factions in the broader society. Bureaucrats may respond to these diverse political forces, but they seldom initiate them, and by themselves can seldom effectively resist presidential wishes. If bureaucrats, in and of themselves, could effectively counter presidential wishes, the Reagan administration would not have been able to achieve the budget and personnel cuts in domestic agencies that it accomplished in 1981 and 1982.

The career bureaucracy is the implementer of almost all programs and policies of presidents and the national government. But the separation-of-powers system ensures that presidents will not have exclusive control of the executive branch. It is thus not the independent power of bureaucrats that frustrates presidents; it is the division of powers guaranteed by the Constitution.

CONCLUSION

The reality of the modern presidency is the domination of policy and administration in the executive branch by the White House. Presidents Nixon, Ford, Carter, and Reagan all came to office with expectations that their cabinets would play a greater role in their administrations than they ultimately did. This chapter has explained some of the reasons that these presidents' expectations were not met.

The causes of the centralization of policy control in the White House relate to broad historical forces in American politics. Ever since the Progressives

[49]See James P. Pfiffner, "Political Appointees and Career Executives: The Democracy-Bureaucracy Nexus in the Third Century," *Public Administration Review* (January/February 1987), pp. 57–65.

saw the presidency as the engine of national progress, public expectations of the president have continued to grow. The New Deal and World War II expanded the size of the national government and the role of the government in the economy. The resulting fragmentation of power led presidents to want to pull together the threads of control in the White House. The proliferation of primaries and the rise of the personal, rather than party-dependent, candidate for president led to the need for personal loyalty and responsiveness in modern presidents.

The causes of White House staff domination of the executive branch stem from the administrative incentives of presidents and the advantages of personal staff over institutional bureaucracies. White House staffers are physically closer and immediately responsive to presidential wishes; they can drop everything and concentrate on the needs of the moment. In contrast to cabinet officials, they have no managerial duties to distract them, no budgets to balance, people to hire, or programs to run. No congressional mandates constrain them, nor will they be called to testify on the Hill. No wonder presidents tend to rely on their White House staffs rather than cabinet officers.

But these advantages bring with them drawbacks for the ongoing government on which presidents and their successors must depend. Cabinet departments possess the institutional memory, expertise, planning capabilities, and orderly policy processes to run the ongoing programs that are necessary to all modern governments. Insofar as presidents ignore these essentials, their decisions will be less well informed and government programs will be less well administered.

When too much policymaking is pulled into the White House, presidential capacity can be stretched too thin. Matters that can best be handled at lower levels can create problems that bog down presidents and create expectations that the president should solve every problem that arises. When political appointees penetrate the career bureaucracies too deeply, the capacity of the career services to do their jobs is undercut. Loyalist political appointees may not have the expertise to run technical programs.

The short-term perspectives of appointees may distort longer-term planning and rob the government of the ability to serve the next president equally well. The more leadership positions at lower levels that are taken by political appointments, the fewer talented career civil servants will stay in the government throughout their careers. Insofar as presidential appointees manage agencies with a close coterie of intimates to the exclusion of career executives, the capacity of agencies to serve the next president will be undercut. David Stockman, as director of OMB, and James Baker, as secretary of state, were justly praised for their competence. But their failure to include career executives in much of their policy deliberations left their agencies weaker than if they had fully utilized their career subordinates and tried to strengthen the institutional capacities of their agencies.

The centralization of power and control in the White House is understandable, and to a certain extent inevitable. The calls of some reformers to cut drastically the size of the White House staff or to delegate most policymaking to departmental secretaries are based on assumptions that no longer hold. We cannot go back to the time when the president personally knows all of the White House staffers or when cabinet secretaries could expect to discuss their agencies' matters regularly with the president. But it would not hurt to tilt back slightly in that direction. The analysis of this chapter leads to three paradoxes of the modern presidency:

1. With respect to the cabinet: The best way for a president to "control" the executive branch is to delegate most issues that are not clearly presidential to department and agency heads. Presidential involvement should be very selective.
2. With respect to political personnel: The president should play a positive role in setting the tone for recruiting political appointees, but should delegate the selection of most subcabinet appointments to department and agency heads. Personal or ideological loyalty to the president does not guarantee the effective implementation of presidential priorities.
3. With respect to the permanent bureaucracy: The career bureaucracy is often seen by new presidents as an obstacle to the achievement of presidential priorities. But cooperation with the career services is essential to accomplishing presidential goals, and enlisting the bureaucracy's enthusiastic support can enhance the probability of presidential success.[50]

[50]James P. Pfiffner, "Can the President Manage the Government? Should He?" in Pfiffner, ed., *The Managerial Presidency* (Pacific Grove, CA: Brooks/Cole, 1991), p. 4.

Six

THE PRESIDENT AND CONGRESS

In dividing constitutional powers among the branches, the Framers intended the legislative power to reside in Congress and gave the president only minimal tools to affect the legislative process. In the last half of the twentieth century, however, one of the president's main roles is that of "chief legislator." This transformation is the result of broad-scale economic and societal changes in the United States. The turning point was Franklin Roosevelt's famous "100 Days." Since then, presidents have developed the institutional capacity to influence and sometimes dominate the legislative process. But more importantly, both the public and Congress now expect that presidents will have a legislative agenda and actively fight for it on Capitol Hill.

Modern presidents are much more active in the legislative process; however, this does not mean that they dominate Congress. The success rate of presidents with legislation on which they take a position usually ranges between 50 and 80 percent and typically declines over the course of a term. This chapter will examine the constitutional and political fundamentals of presidential relations with Congress. It will then turn to contrasting examples of how modern presidents have tried to influence Congress and the legislative agenda. The varying success rates of the modern presidents demonstrate that, despite increased presidential power, the balance the Framers designed in the Constitution still exists, often to the frustration of presidents.

THE CONSTITUTIONAL FUNDAMENTALS

For the president to achieve public-policy goals and deliver on campaign promises, Congress must at least go along with, and often must actively support, the president. Even in national security policy, where the president has most leeway, money must be appropriated, and Congress can thwart presidential initiatives if it is provoked to do so. In most policy areas, legislation must be passed to initiate and implement policies.

The Framers of the Constitution, however, did not make this an easy task. In their fear of allowing power to be concentrated in any one branch of government, they separated powers and provided each of the three branches with checks on the other two. This would be accomplished, according to James Madison in *Federalist* No. 51, by "giving to those who administer each department the necessary constitutional means and personal motives to resist encroachments of the others."

In dividing governmental powers, the Framers gave the legislative power to the Congress. Article I, Section 1, provides that: "All legislative Powers herein granted shall be vested in a Congress of the United States, which shall consist of a Senate and House of Representatives." Section 8 of Article I enumerates the substantive powers of Congress and gives Congress the power "To make all Laws which shall be necessary and proper for carrying into Execution the fore-going powers. . . ." The president's legislative powers are minimal. Article II provides for the president to inform Congress on the state of the union, to recommend "necessary and expedient" measures to Congress, to convene both Houses on extraordinary occasions, and to adjourn them in cases of disagreement between them. The Constitution also gives the president the power to veto legislation, the most important formal power of the president in the legislative process.

In addition to the formal provisions for dividing the legislative power, the structure of government virtually guarantees conflict between the two branches. They have different constituencies. The president and vice president are elected by a national constituency, while each member of the House represents one congressional district of about five hundred thousand people and each senator represents one state. Local and regional interests will often pull Congress, or important parts of it, in different directions than the president wants to go.

Differing terms of office were designed to ensure that a popular wave of public opinion could not easily change the entire leadership of the country. Only one-third of Senate seats are up for election in any presidential election year. And even though all House seats are at risk each presidential election year, turnover in the House seldom exceeds 20 percent, and is most often much less than that. In addition, House seats are not often heavily influenced by the presidential election, especially in recent decades. In fact, the political dynamics of House elections in the twentieth century almost guarantee frustration for presidents, who predictably lose support in the House during off-year elections. Voters may be disillusioned by presidential performance, or the opposition party may be particularly active, but for whatever reason, the president's party can count on losing seats in the House and most often in the Senate. (See Table 6–1.)

Congress and the president are also likely to be in conflict because of the different characteristics of the two branches. Congress is necessarily collegial because of the principle of one vote per member. The executive branch, however, is hierarchical because the president holds most of the authority. The president can thus present a much more coherent and unified facade than can Congress, where disagreements are public and often dramatic. It is often said that public policymaking is like producing sausages. The difference between the two branches is that in the executive branch the public only sees the end product, whereas in Congress the public gets to witness the ingredients (polit-

TABLE 6–1
Midterm Losses by President's Party

Year	President's Party	House	Senate
1934	D	+9	+10
1938	D	−71	−6
1942	D	−55	−9
1946	D	−55	−12
1950	D	−29	−6
1954	R	−18	−1
1958	R	−48	−13
1962	D	−4	+3
1966	D	−47	−4
1970	R	−12	+2
1974	R	−48	−5
1978	D	−15	−3
1982	R	−26	+1
1986	R	−5	−8
1990	R	−8	−1
1994	D	−52	−8

Sources: Congressional Quarterly Weekly Reports, December 19, 1992, p. 3896; updated data added from December 21, 1996, p. 3428. Reprinted by permission.

ical fights, compromises, etc.) that go into the machine, as well as the product. This gives the president a rhetorical advantage in fights with Congress.

THE VETO POWER

The most important formal legislative power granted to the president is the right to veto a law that has been passed by both houses of Congress. To do so, the president returns the bill to the house of its origin with a message explaining the objections. The president's veto can be overridden, but only by the vote of a two-thirds majority of each house.

If, however, Congress sends a bill to the president and then adjourns within ten days (Sundays not included), the president can veto the bill by doing nothing. This "pocket veto" procedure is useful for presidents because it cannot be overridden. The bill must be reintroduced when Congress comes back into session and passed anew for it to be reconsidered. Although some presidents have tried to exercise a pocket veto during short congressional recesses or at the end of a session, it is generally used at the end of a Congress.[1]

Early presidents did not use the veto power very actively, and some felt that it should be used only to protect the constitutional prerogatives of the pres-

[1]Constitutional law on the use of the pocket veto is not settled. It is clear that the pocket veto is not available over a three-day recess, though some presidents have claimed that they can exercise it in a recess of five days. The question of an adjournment between sessions of one Congress is uncertain. See Jay R. Shampansky, "The Pocket Veto: A Legal Analysis," Library of Congress, Congressional Research Service, Report 90–43A (January 11, 1990).

ident. George Washington vetoed only two bills, and John Adams and Thomas Jefferson did not use the veto at all. Andrew Jackson used the veto twelve times, more than the total number of vetoes cast until that time, and established that the veto could be used to disapprove any bill the president did not think was wise. After the Civil War, the veto came into much more common use, with Cleveland using it 414 times in his first term.

The veto is a powerful tool because it is so difficult to override. The president needs merely to get the votes of one-third plus one vote in either House for a veto to be sustained. Since a president can usually find this many votes among his party cohorts in Congress, only 104 of 2,514 vetoes were overridden between 1789 and 1992.[2] From 1988 to 1992, the Democratic Congress was able to override only one of President Bush's thirty-seven vetoes. While 2,500 vetoes between 1789 and 1992 may seem like a lot, the total number of bills vetoed by presidents amount to only about 2.6 percent of the more than 92,000 bills that have been passed and sent to the president.[3] As we would expect, vetoes are more likely when the president and Congress are not controlled by the same party. For instance, in his first two years in office President Clinton cast no vetoes; but after the Republicans captured Congress in 1994, he vetoed seventeen measures during the rest of his first term, with one veto being overridden by Congress.

Yet this very effective and seemingly powerful tool, when depended on too heavily, is a sign of weakness. That is, a president who is able to convince the Congress to pass his agenda, or who is able to modify bills to his liking before passage, is in a much more powerful position than one who must wait until an unacceptable bill is presented to him and then exercise his formal veto power. President Ford used a veto strategy, vetoing sixty-eight bills and having twelve overturned. But by resorting to the veto strategy he reflected the weakness of his situation, being an unelected president following the Watergate scandals and facing the liberal Democratic Congress brought into office in the 1974 elections. (See Table 6–2.)

One legislative technique that came into frequent use in the modern period has been called the "legislative veto." It has no constitutional foundation, but has been written into legislation since 1932. The legislative veto is used when Congress is delegating power to the executive branch to make decisions in a broad program area. The legislation provides that whenever the power is used in a specific instance, such as passing a regulation or shifting funds among appropriation accounts, that Congress (or one house or a committee) be notified of the specific action and have the chance to disapprove that one application of the general delegated power. It was a technique intended to give Congress

---

[2]See Office of the Secretary of the Senate, *Presidential Vetoes, 1789–1991* (Washington, DC: Government Printing Office, 1991), update to 1992 by Gregory Harness, Head Reference Librarian, 1993.

[3]Gary L. Galemore, "Veto Overrides by Congress 1969–1988," Library of Congress, Congressional Research Service, Report No. 89–436 GOV (July 20, 1989), pp. 2–3.

TABLE 6-2
Presidential Vetoes (1789–1996)

President	Regular Vetoes	Pocket Vetoes	Total Vetoes	Vetoes Overridden
George Washington	2	—	2	—
John Adams	—	—	0	—
Thomas Jefferson	—	—	0	—
James Madison	5	2	7	—
James Monroe	1	—	1	—
John Q. Adams	—	—	0	—
Andrew Jackson	5	7	12	—
Martin Van Buren	—	1	1	—
W. H. Harrison	—	—	0	—
John Tyler	6	4	10	1
James K. Polk	2	1	3	—
Zachary Taylor	—	—	0	—
Millard Fillmore	—	—	0	—
Franklin Pierce	9	—	9	5
James Buchanan	4	3	7	—
Abraham Lincoln	2	5	7	—
Andrew Johnson	21	8	29	15
Ulysses S. Grant	45	48	93	4
Rutherford B. Hayes	12	1	13	1
James A. Garfield	—	—	0	—
Chester A. Arthur	4	8	12	1
Grover Cleveland	304	110	414	2
Benjamin Harrison	19	25	44	1
Grover Cleveland	42	128	170	5
William McKinley	6	36	42	—
Theodore Roosevelt	42	40	82	1
William H. Taft	30	9	39	1
Woodrow Wilson	33	11	44	6
Warren G. Harding	5	1	6	—
Calvin Coolidge	20	30	50	4
Herbert Hoover	21	16	37	3
Franklin D. Roosevelt	372	263	635	9
Harry S. Truman	180	70	250	12
Dwight D. Eisenhower	73	108	181	2
John F. Kennedy	12	9	21	—
Lyndon B. Johnson	16	14	30	—
Richard M. Nixon	26	17	43	7
Gerald R. Ford	48	18	66	12
Jimmy Carter	13	18	31	2
Ronald Reagan	39	39	78	9
George Bush	29	16	45	1
William Clinton (first term)	17	0	17	1
Total	1,465	1,066	2,531	105

Source: Presidential Vetoes, 1789–1991 Office of the Secretary of the Senate (Washington, DC: Government Printing Office, 1992). Update by Gregory Harness, Head Reference Librarian, 1993.

some control when a broad grant of discretion was delegated to the president, and it was used some 250 times between 1932 and 1980.[4]

Presidents, however, objected to its increasing use and argued that it was an unconstitutional restraint on the executive power. In 1983, the Supreme Court agreed with this argument in *Immigration and Naturalization Services v. Chadha*.[5] The Court ruled the legislative veto unconstitutional and argued that it violated the separation of powers principle. It said that if Congress wanted to change legislation once passed it must present it to the president as specified in the Constitution and give him a chance to veto it. While the formal decision stood, the legislative veto provided the kind of flexibility useful to both branches, and after 1983 the technique continued to be used both formally and informally.[6]

Although the Framers considered giving the president an absolute veto, one that could not be overridden, they never considered an "item veto," allowing the president to veto part of a bill while approving the rest of it. This type of partial veto, however, was included in the Confederate Constitution and has been adopted in the constitutions of forty-three of the fifty states. The item veto gives governors quite a bit of flexibility, particularly in appropriations legislation, in that they can strike out one or several projects from a broad bill that includes hundreds of itemized expenditures.

Contemporary presidents have sought such power, and Presidents Reagan and Bush proposed constitutional amendments to give it to the president, arguing that it would allow them to save the taxpayers' money by vetoing unwise "pork barrel" projects. But it was to Bill Clinton that Congress gave this legislative power. In the spring of 1996 Congress passed a law granting to the President in effect an item veto for spending measures. The procedure, technically called "enhanced rescission," allows the president to reduce appropriation bills (or cancel part of narrowly targeted tax cuts) by rescinding within five days the portion to which he objects. These portions would then be sent back to Congress, which could then pass them separately within thirty days, but these bills would be subject to a regular veto, which would have to be overridden by the usual two-thirds majority in order for them to become law.

Proponents of the item veto argued that such power would help reduce the deficit, but most federal spending is in uncontrollable expenditures such as entitlements, rather than in appropriations measures. Their expectation was also that presidents will be more fiscally responsible than Congress, an unproven assumption. But one of the effects of this innovation will be to give the president significant potential new power in bargaining with individual members of Congress. The president might very well pressure members for support

---

[4]Larry Berman, *The New American Presidency* (Boston: Little, Brown, 1987), p. 42.

[5]*INS v. Chadha* (1983); Louis Fisher, "A Political Context for Legislative Vetoes," *Political Science Quarterly* 93 (Summer 1978), pp. 241–254.

[6]Louis Fisher, "Congress as Micromanager of the Executive Branch," in James P. Pfiffner, ed., *The Managerial Presidency* (Pacific Grove, CA: Brooks/Cole, 1991).

on large spending measures by threatening relatively smaller projects in their districts with an item veto. The actual effect of this new legislative power of the president will depend on how presidents choose to use it and on whether it survives constitutional challenges in court.[7]

The law providing this new power to the president, the Line Item Veto Act, was challenged in Court by several members of Congress. In April 1997 a Federal District Court judge ruled that it was an unconstitutional delegation of power to the president. Judge Thomas P. Jackson ruled that, ". . . the Act effectively permits the President to repeal duly enacted provisions of federal law. . . . The power to 'make' the laws of the nation is the exclusive, non-delegable power of Congress. . . ."[8] In June of 1997, however, the Supreme Court delayed a final disposition of the issue by refusing to make a definitive ruling. It decided by a 7–2 majority that the members of Congress who challenged the statute did not have the "standing" to bring the case before the courts because none of them had actually been injured by the new law, since the president had not yet used the power. Thus the constitutionality of the law, which was set to expire in 2005 was still in doubt.

In addition to the veto power, the other major *formal* power of the president in the legislative process is the duty to inform Congress from time to time on the state of the union and to recommend measures that are "necessary and expedient." While these powers would not seem to give the president too much power, in the last half of the twentieth century the president has come to dominate the legislative process through the regular formulation of a legislative agenda and the institutional capacity to lobby for it on the Hill.

THE PRESIDENT AS LEGISLATIVE LEADER

Early presidents were not very active in the legislative process. George Washington proposed only three specific laws to Congress, and after he was frustrated in seeking advice from the Senate about an Indian treaty, he carefully avoided the appearance of participation in legislative activities. Members of his cabinet, however, did attempt to influence legislation, and cabinet secretaries of Thomas Jefferson even helped formulate legislation.[9] For most of the rest of the nineteenth century, presidents, particularly the Whigs in the 1840s, who believed in legislative supremacy, were not active in the legislative process. Lincoln was aggressive about legislation and presidential constitutional prerogatives, but after his administration Congress returned to domination for the rest of the century. Just as the federal government was not active in the national economy, so were presidents not active in the policy arena.

---

[7]See Ronald Moe, "Prospects for the Item Veto at the Federal Level: Lessons from the States," (Washington, DC: National Academy of Public Administration, February 1986).

[8]Quoted in *Congressional Quarterly Weekly Reports,* April 12, 1997, p. 836.

[9]Michael Nelson, ed., *Guide to the Presidency* (Washington, DC: CQ Press, 1989), p. 1118.

In the nineteenth century, Congress dominated the government to such an extent that the young scholar, Woodrow Wilson, entitled his doctoral dissertation *Congressional Government,* and argued that congressional domination of the national government after Lincoln led to ineffectual governance.[10] The twentieth century, and a more active federal government, brought changes in the presidency. President Theodore Roosevelt, with his activist view of the powers of the presidency, argued that "a good executive under the present conditions of American political life must take a very active interest in getting the right kind of legislation. . . ."[11] But even Roosevelt was hesitant to intrude too visibly in the legislative process. "Are you aware," he wrote to a critic, ". . . of the extreme unwisdom of my irritating Congress by fixing the details of a bill, concerning which they are very sensitive. . . ."[12]

Foreshadowing the modern presidents, William Howard Taft's first attempt to present legislation formally to Congress was greeted with resentment for his meddling in the legislative process.[13] Woodrow Wilson, with the model of the British prime minister in mind, played an aggressive role in the legislative process, working with members in drafting some legislation in the White House. He symbolized his activism by personally addressing Congress in his 1913 state of the union message, the first time a president had formally addressed Congress since Thomas Jefferson.[14]

But the real breakthrough for presidential participation in the legislative process was the unprecedented, and unequalled since, legendary "100 Days" of Franklin Roosevelt. Roosevelt was elected with the hope that he could do something about the Great Depression that was wracking the country. The stock market crash of 1929 left the nation's economy in a shambles, with almost a quarter of the work force unemployed. Roosevelt was able to provide the leadership the country needed to regain its confidence.

Immediately after he was sworn into office on March 4, 1933, Roosevelt declared a bank holiday and, on March 9, called the Seventy-third Congress into special session to pass the Emergency Banking Act. Over the next 100 days, Congress passed a flurry of laws meant to deal with the economic crisis. All of the bills save one were drafted in the White House, with occasional participation by members of Congress, and while some amendments were considered, none of the proposals emanating from the White House was fundamentally changed. The

---

[10]Woodrow Wilson, *Congressional Government: A Study in American Politics* (New York: Meridian Books, 1956).

[11]Nelson, *Guide to the Presidency,* p. 461.

[12]Quoted by James Sundquist, *The Decline and Resurgence of Congress* (Washington, DC: Brookings Institution, 1981), pp. 129–130.

[13]James Sundquist, *The Decline and Resurgence of Congress,* p. 130.

[14]Nelson, *Guide to the Presidency,* p. 461.

president, for the first time, was acting as a prime minister in controlling the legislative agenda and directing the legislative process.[15]

The legislation passed during this historic period between March 9 and June 16 included, among other laws:

Emergency Banking Act (to reform the banking system)

Civilian Conservation Corps (conservation for unemployed youth)

Abandonment of the gold standard

Federal Emergency Relief Act (national welfare program)

Agricultural Adjustment Act (national agricultural policy)

Emergency Farm Mortgage Act (refinanced farm mortgages)

Tennessee Valley Authority Act (provided a government corporation to develop the Tennessee valley)

Truth in Securities Act (required full disclosure of the financial situation of a firm selling new securities)

Home Owners Loan Act (refinanced home mortgages)

National Industrial Recovery Act (public works program and a system of industrial regulation)

Farm Credit Act (reorganized federal farm credit programs)

Emergency Railroad Transportation Act (coordinated the national railroad system)[16]

The significance of the 100 days was not just the number of laws passed but their effect in changing the role of the federal government in the economy and reversing the fundamental nature of the role of the federal government in the economic life of the nation.

Roosevelt's impressive legislative juggernaut was unequaled in American history, and has not been matched since. The only periods of comparable importance were Lyndon Johnson in 1965 and Ronald Reagan in 1981. Johnson took advantage of the nation's grief over the death of Kennedy and the huge Democratic legislative majority that was elected in 1964 to push through Congress his Great Society legislation and to launch the War on Poverty, creating scores of programs and expanding the role of the federal government in social welfare areas in unprecedented ways.

In 1965 Johnson and his legislative cohorts pushed through a prodigious amount of legislation, and Congress refused only three of the eighty-three major bills of the administration. The laws created included, among others:

---

[15]See the discussion in James Sundquist, *The Decline and Resurgence of Congress,* pp. 129–136.

[16]Adapted from Nelson, *Guide to the Presidency,* p. 462.

Medicare and Medicaid
Civil Rights Act of 1965
Elementary and Secondary Education Act
Higher Education Act
War on Poverty
Head Start
Air Pollution Control Act
Educational Opportunity Act
Safe Streets Act
Model Cities
Department of Housing and Urban Development
Department of Transportation
National Endowment for the Arts
National Endowment for the Humanities
Federal Water Pollution Control Act[17]

It is significant that future conservative Republican presidents (Nixon, Ford, Reagan, and Bush), though denouncing active government, did not move to repeal any of the major components of the New Deal or the Great Society.

President Reagan's triumph in 1981 was not due to the volume of legislation passed by Congress, but to the far-reaching nature of the changes enacted. They included the largest tax cut in history, the largest peacetime increases in defense spending, and major cuts in the funding of domestic programs. Reagan's legislative victories symbolized a major change toward a more conservative direction of public policy and a change in attitude about the role of the federal government in the economy.

These historic legislative landmarks, however, were initial victories that came early in each president's term, and were not followed by equivalent success. Each suffered legislative setbacks and frustrations at the hands of Congress. Thus, periods of cooperation between the president and Congress in passing major legislative programs are unusual in American history. The typical relationship is one of conflict and occasional victories by presidents, along with occasional thwarting of their wishes by Congress—much as the Framers seemed to intend.

The Political Fundamentals

Although Roosevelt's participation in the legislative process was active and intense, it was not institutionalized. He approached relations with Congress in an ad hoc manner, delegating to members of his cabinet and White House staff

[17]From Berman, *The New American Presidency,* p. 252.

specific assignments to lobby Congress on particular pieces of legislation. It was left to his successors to institutionalize presidential participation in the legislative process.

When Harry Truman took over from FDR, he continued an activist approach to legislation and began the practice of formulating detailed legislative packages to send to Congress on an annual basis. Even though the Republicans in the Eightieth Congress elected in 1946 were not very cooperative in passing his legislative proposals, Truman continued to submit legislation in the spirit of FDR's New Deal.

President Eisenhower initially declined to send a legislative agenda to Congress, but under pressure from public and congressional expectations he began to formulate an annual legislative program. To assist him and to serve as a buffer to demands from his own partisans on the Hill, Eisenhower established the Office of Congressional Relations (OCR) as a unit in the White House Office. In 1960, when Larry O'Brien, who was going to handle legislative liaison for John Kennedy, came to ask the advice of Eisenhower's OCR director, Bryce Harlow, he was convinced of the necessity to retain the formal structure and organized his operation much as Harlow had. O'Brien effectively led Kennedy's and Johnson's legislative liaison operation teams in pushing the liberal legislation championed by these activist presidents. Since then the OCR has become an institutionalized unit in the White House Office, and has played an important role in lobbying Congress for each succeeding administration.

The OCR cajoles members of Congress and occasionally twists arms, but presidential success in the legislative arena is most often determined by the fundamental political realities of the American political system. The basic reality is that the president is in a constitutionally weak position with respect to passing legislation, and the major factor that can bridge the constitutional gap is the party system. To get the votes to pass laws, presidents must start with the members of their party in each house. That is why the partisan balance is so important to a president's policy priorities. If presidents could determine only one factor to help their programs with Congress, it would be the number of members of their party in each house.

While presidents can count on their party members for a core of support in legislation they propose, they cannot count on consistent or unanimous support. This contrasts with parliamentary systems of government, in which party discipline is expected. In important legislative votes, the failure to vote with the party can result in exclusion from the party and being dropped from the ballot at the next election. Thus, on important issues, a prime minister can almost always count on the vote of members of his or her party in the parliament. In the United States, however, members of Congress run for office on their own and declare their membership in one political party. The political party cannot even prevent a person from running for office under the party banner. In 1990, David Duke ran a racist campaign for governor of Louisiana as a Republican, despite attempts by the national Republican party to prevent him from using their party as a vehicle for his campaign.

If party members refuse to adhere to the party platform, or to vote with the party in Congress, there are few sanctions that can be imposed to punish them. But more importantly, the norms of Congress dictate that members' first allegiance is to their own political interests, even if constituent interests conflict with their party's position. While party cohesion in Congress has been increasing for the past decade or so, it does not solve the problem of lack of party discipline for presidents. While higher levels of party polarization can help presidents with their own party, it can also hurt them with members of the other party.

What this means to presidents is that they cannot count on the full vote of their party contingent in Congress. In fact, even in key votes, presidents cannot count on support from members of their own party more than two-thirds of the time. But they can count on substantial opposition from the other party most of the time.[18] Thus, U.S. presidents are in the position of having to seek votes actively on most significant bills they support or oppose. The greater the margin of party members in each house presidents have, the better their chances are when they begin to seek a majority of votes on any particular measure.

In general, on those initiatives that presidents have introduced for them in Congress the president is successful slightly more than half the time. But if the measure is all bills on which presidents take a position, the average success rate goes up to slightly over 75 percent of the time.[19] (See Figure 6–1.) While large majorities of partisans in each house help, there is no guarantee of legislative success. Nor is the lack of partisan majorities necessarily fatal.

Popularity with the public is one factor that may help a president in dealing with Congress, and presidents follow their public-opinion polls carefully. The link between presidential popularity and success with Congress, however, is tenuous. It may be a necessary, but not sufficient, condition for congressional victories for the president. Public popularity certainly helped make possible FDR's 100 Days, Lyndon Johnson's huge victories in 1965, and Ronald Reagan's 1981 budget victories. Falling public popularity also hurt President Truman from 1949 to 1952, and President Nixon in 1973 and 1974. But relatively high sustained public approval did not guarantee legislative success to presidents Eisenhower or Reagan in their second terms or George Bush in his first two and one-half years in office.

Presidential Skills

Given the guaranteed difficulties of presidents with Congress, what can they do to increase their chances of success with their legislative agendas? Despite fundamental constitutional and political problems, presidents can affect the fate of their proposals in Congress, and there is a rich lore on how presidents ought to handle Congress. One thing that a president can do is take a

---

[18]See George C. Edwards, III, *At the Margins* (New Haven, CT: Yale University Press, 1989), p. 40.

[19]See the discussion by Michael Mezey, *Congress, the President, and Public Policy* (Boulder, CO: Westview, 1989), pp. 110–115. See also, Edwards, *At The Margins,* pp. 39–46.

FIGURE 6-1
Presidential Success

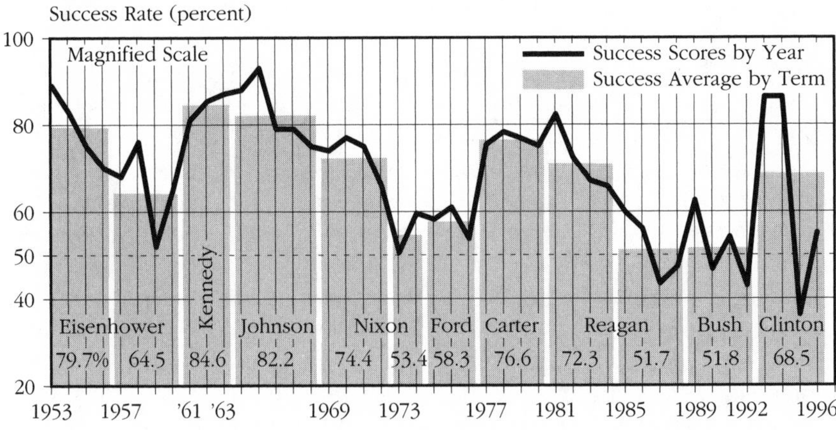

Success Rate History

Eisenhower	
1953	89.0%
1954	82.8
1955	75.0
1956	70.0
1957	68.0
1958	76.0
1959	52.0
1960	65.0

Kennedy	
1961	81.0%
1962	85.4
1963	87.1

Johnson	
1964	88.0%
1965	93.0
1966	79.0
1967	79.0
1968	75.0

Nixon	
1969	74.0%
1970	77.0
1971	75.0
1972	66.0
1973	50.6
1974	59.6

Ford	
1974	58.2%
1975	61.0
1976	53.8

Carter	
1977	75.4%
1978	78.3
1979	76.8
1980	75.1

Reagan	
1981	82.4%
1982	72.4
1983	67.1
1984	65.8
1985	59.9
1986	56.1
1987	43.5
1988	47.4

Bush	
1989	62.6%
1990	46.8
1991	54.2
1992	43.0

Clinton	
1993	86.4%
1994	86.4
1995	36.2
1996	55.1

Source: Congressional Quarterly Weekly Reports, (December 19, 1992), p. 3896, and December 21, 1996, p. 3428.

strategic approach to the administration's legislative agenda. This involves choosing which measures to put forth: should they be ambitious or narrowly cautious? It involves volume: should a president push many measures or concentrate on only a few? It involves timing: in what order and at what pace should measures be sent to Congress?

There is no one formula that will guarantee success, because presidents come to office with different political assets and at different times in the country's political history. President Johnson was successful with many legislative proposals, while President Carter was criticized for sending too many things to Congress at one time. President Reagan achieved impressive victories in his first year by concentrating on only a few priorities of sweeping character.

One generalization that seems to hold for modern presidents is that measures sent to Congress early in their first terms have a better chance of being passed than if they wait until later to send their most important initiatives. Scholar Paul Light has calculated that, from 1961 to 1978, 72 percent of those measures sent to Congress in the first three months of an administration eventually became law. During the second three months the rate of success dropped to 39 percent, and in the third three months to 25 percent.[20]

Several factors account for this predictable decline in legislative effectiveness. A new president usually enjoys a "honeymoon" with the public at the beginning of an administration, when the country wants to see the new president succeed. This feeling of goodwill is often reflected in Congress, which is willing to be more open-minded about presidential proposals than later in the term. Presidential popularity almost inevitably falls after the beginning of an administration, and as the midterm elections approach, members of Congress will begin to get nervous about their reelections and will be less likely to be sympathetic to presidents. According to Lyndon Johnson: "I keep hitting hard because I know this honeymoon won't last. Every day I lose a little more political capital. That's why we have to keep at it, never letting up. One day soon, I don't know when, the critics and the snipers will move in and we will be at stalemate. We have to get all we can, now, before the roof comes down."[21] The beginning of a term is also the best time to take advantage of the "mandate" of the voters from the election. Any mandate applies more to the person of the president than to any specific policy preferences, but managed skillfully, a claim for a mandate can be used to the president's advantage.

Presidents are also well advised to "court" Congress, that is, build up a reservoir of goodwill that can be called upon when it is needed in a close vote. Most presidents, being successful politicians, are sensitive to the need to pay their respects to members of Congress as individuals and Congress as an institution. At the beginning of administrations, they often invite members of their own party (and sometimes the opposition) to the White House for various political and social functions. Presidents Truman through Ford used to invite members of Congress to social gatherings on the presidential yacht, the *Sequoia,* for dinner, drinks, socializing, and even (in Truman's case) poker games. These were not occasions for arm-twisting or lobbying for specific votes, but rather for low-key socializing and building up the rapport that might help in later situations.

It is the job of the Office of Congressional Relations to keep in touch with

---

[20]Paul Light, *The President's Agenda* (Baltimore: Johns Hopkins University Press, 1982), p. 45.

[21]Quoted in Light, *The President's Agenda,* p. 52.

An example of the Johnson "treatment." President Lyndon B. Johnson was legendary for his ability to persuade members of Congress to support his bills. This series of photographs shows him in action with Democratic Senator Theodore E. Green of Rhode Island. (George Tames/New York Times Pictures)

members of Congress and be sensitive to their political needs. OCR also helps the president dole out favors to the administration's best advantage. Presidents consciously use a variety of carrots and sticks to reward friends and to punish political enemies. Social invitations to the White House are used to help cement support on the Hill. Those who do not vote with the president are removed from invitation lists.[22] Members of Congress can be invited to a photo session with the president and sent autographed copies of photos of them with the president.

They can be invited for flights on Air Force One or be given tickets to the presidential box at the Kennedy Center. Favors can also be arranged for key constituents, such as tours of the White House or birthday greetings from the president. Campaign help from popular presidents is in high demand during election years, and presidential campaign trips are used to good effect. President Kennedy once excluded a California congressman from a speech platform in his own district because of the member's failure to consistently support the president's foreign policy legislation.[23] Small mementos are also used consciously and effectively. Members of Congress prize cufflinks with the presidential seal, and Richard Nixon kept careful track of who received them.[24]

Presidents often present to key supporters and members of Congress the pens they use to sign bills into law, which are mounted and framed along with a reproduction of the first page of the law that was enacted. Lyndon Johnson, wanting to make the most of these opportunities, often used multiple pens to

---

[22]Cary Covington, "Guess Who's Coming to Dinner: The Distribution of White House Social Invitations and Their Effects on Congressional Support," *American Politics Quarterly,* 16 (3) (July 1988), pp. 243–265.

[23]Theodore Sorensen, *Kennedy* (New York: Bantam Books, 1965), p. 392.

[24]See testimony reprinted in Berman, *The New American Presidency,* p. 268.

sign the different letters of his name and the date of the signing. He set what must be a presidential record by using seventy-two pens to sign the Economic Opportunity Act of 1964; each pen was presented to one of those who worked with him on passage of the bill. One indicator of President Carter's rational rather than political approach to being president was his refusal to use more than two pens to sign legislation.[25]

Personal appeals for votes from the president can be very effective, because no member of the president's party wants to say no directly to the president, and no one wants to be subject to presidential wrath. President Reagan was able to win a key vote for his budget package in the spring of 1981 by placing a personal call to a member of Congress from Pennsylvania during a call-in radio talk show. A call from the president can even be effective with members of the opposition party. In March 1993, President Clinton was searching for votes on a bill and called Republican Senator James Jeffords, who was in Damascus, Syria. Senator Jeffords admitted that the call had an impact on him. "It was unbelievable," said Jeffords, "No matter how long we've been around the Hill, there's nothing more exciting than a call from the President."[26]

Presidents can even occasionally be persuasive when the vote they want seems to conflict with the political self-preservation of members of Congress. In August 1993 President Clinton was desperate for one vote in the House to break a 216–216 tie in order to pass his deficit-reducing budget package, the centerpiece of his first-year agenda. Every Republican had voted against it, and Clinton made a personal appeal to Democratic Representative Marjorie Margolies-Mezvinsky of Pennsylvania to save his agenda. Despite grave reservations about the feelings of her constituents about tax increases, she cast the tie-breaking vote for the president. Unfortunately, her loyalty to the president cost her the election in 1994, when she was defeated by her Republican opponent who exploited her loyalty to Clinton and vote for the tax increase portion of his deficit reduction package.[27]

But personal appeals must be an unusual occurrence or their effectiveness will be diluted. According to a Carter aide: "You see, you have to be careful when you use the president. A visit with the president or a call from the president has to be an event in the life of a senator or representative, or it loses its magic. Or they, say, 'Why should I give you a commitment? I want to talk to the president. John has talked to the president. And George has talked to the president. Are you taking us for granted?' You've got to be sure that you don't squander him."[28] The same point holds for patronage appointments or support on pork barrel projects. In an important battle for a key vote on an important

---

[25]Nigel Bowles, *The White House and Capitol Hill* (Oxford, England: Clarendon Press, 1987), pp. 105, 213.

[26]Richard L. Berke, "Courting Congress Nonstop, Clinton Looks for an Alliance," *New York Times* (March 8, 1993), p. B8.

[27]See Burdett A. Loomis, *The Contemporary Congress* 2nd ed. (New York: St. Martin's Press, in press).

[28]Quoted in Edwards, *At the Margins,* p. 72.

bill, the president might trade a nomination for an appointment or make an administrative decision on the location of a federal project. But if these favors are used too freely, everyone will expect the same treatment, and there are not enough appointments or projects to please everybody.

Using appointments or projects as sticks to punish uncooperative members of Congress can also be done sparingly. The principle is: once in a while to make a point is acceptable, but not too often. Presidents do not want to be seen as too heavy-handed or too quick to seek revenge. But it is useful to be seen "cracking heads" occasionally to get what you want. When the Reagan administration wanted to get the vote of a Republican representative from Pennsylvania on a vote for selling planes to Saudi Arabia, the director of public affairs for the president said: "We just beat his brains out. That's all. We just took Jepson and beat his brains out."[29] In another example, President Clinton decided to get tough after Democratic Senator Shelby of Alabama publicly opposed and consistently voted against his budget package in the spring of 1993. The administration transferred a NASA space program involving more than $300 million and ninety jobs from Alabama to Texas. To add insult to injury, Senator Shelby received only one ticket to a White House reception for Alabama's championship football team while his fellow senator from Alabama received more than twenty-five.

CASES OF PRESIDENTIAL LEADERSHIP

This section will consider several cases of presidential leadership of Congress. The cases illustrate the different relationships recent presidents have had with Congress. The Kennedy and Johnson cases show the different approaches to the Democratic Congress that each president employed. Nixon and Reagan took different approaches to achieving their agendas in the face of divided government. Jimmy Carter, despite a Democratic Congress, had mixed success with his legislative agenda. The final case shows Bill Clinton first facing a Democratic Congress, which gave him mixed support, and then a Republican Congress with which he had a much lower success rate and several confrontational showdowns.

Kennedy and the House Rules Committee: Behind-the-Scenes Leadership

The 1960 election was a squeaker. Kennedy won by a very narrow margin and could claim no mandate with which to convince the Congress that his program was the overwhelming preference of the American electorate. The congressional elections were no help for Kennedy's liberal agenda. Despite the advantage of being the first president in 100 years that had served in both houses of Congress, the Democrats lost twenty-one seats in the House.

The overall partisan margins in Congress were substantial and should have

---

[29]Quoted in Edwards, *At The Margins,* p. 87.

been reassuring to the Democrats, with a 262–174 advantage in the House and a 65–35 majority in the Senate. But the political reality was that a conservative coalition of Republicans and southern Democrats had made a common cause since the 1930s of defeating liberal, and especially civil rights, legislation. (The same coalition would combine three decades later, in 1981, to pass Ronald Reagan's conservative agenda.) The reason that the southern Democrats were so conservative was that the South had been a conservative region but it was solidly Democratic, and no budding ambitious politician could have won running as a Republican. So southern conservatives ran as Democrats and were returned year after year to Congress, since for all practical purposes the South was a one-party region. The combination of this certain longevity with the seniority system in Congress magnified the power of the southern block beyond its mere numbers. The member with the most seniority on a committee was automatically its chair, and many key committees were chaired by southern conservative Democrats. In 1964, the twenty-one House committee chairmen averaged 76.6 years of age.[30]

The House Rules Committee is the "traffic cop" for all House legislation and has to act on each bill before it goes to the floor for consideration. Since the House has so many members, allowing legislation to be introduced in a free-for-all fashion would lead to chaos. Thus, House procedures provide that each piece of legislation has to have a "rule" from the rules committee that specifies when it will be taken up and under what conditions of amendment and debate. In the early 1960s, when the committee chair held most of the reins of power, the chairman of the rules committee was the conservative Howard Smith of Virginia. In addition to Smith, the other key member was a fellow conservative, William Colmer of Mississippi. Neither Smith nor Colmer, though Democrats, had supported Kennedy in the campaign, and together with the six Republicans on the rules committee would be able and willing to block any legislation they deemed too liberal, for example, most of Kennedy's legislative agenda.

Not even Speaker of the House Sam Rayburn had the power to overcome this procedural barrier to getting legislative proposals out of committee and on to the floor of the House for a vote, where Kennedy's proposals would at least have a chance. So Rayburn and Kennedy decided soon after the convening of the Congress, and even before Kennedy was inaugurated, to attempt to enlarge the rules committee by three members, two Democrats (who would be liberals) and one Republican, which would give the liberal supporters of Kennedy a thin 8–7 majority that would vote to get Kennedy's legislative proposals to the floor for a vote by the whole House.

Kennedy was well aware of the sensitivities of members of the House who might resent a president interfering with its internal procedures, so Kennedy decided not to take a visible role in the conflict. In a public statement, he said merely: "It is no secret that I would strongly believe that the members of the

[30]Charles and Barbara Whalen, *The Longest Debate* (New York: New American Library, 1985), p. 30.

House should have an opportunity to vote . . . on the programs which we will present—not merely the members of the rules committee. . . . But the responsibility rests with the members. . . . I merely give my view as an interested citizen."[31] But when it became clear that the fight would be close and victory was not ensured, Kennedy entered the fight behind-the-scenes and put the full lobbying power of his new administration behind the vote on enlarging the rules committee. Head of legislative liaison, Larry O'Brien, took head counts and was very active in using all of the tricks of his trade to win votes, including patronage and promises of executive branch action.

Members of the cabinet were also pressed into service to change the minds of those who would have opposed the new rules. At the end, Kennedy made several personal phone calls to try to persuade wavering members. The final vote was victorious for the Kennedy forces, with a vote of 217–212 in favor of expanding the rules committee. Sixty-four Democrats had voted against the rules change and twenty-two Republicans voted for it.

The striking thing was that, with all of the stops pulled and an all-out effort by a newly elected president and House leadership, the margin of victory was only five votes. This foreshadowed the future difficulties the administration would have with much of its liberal agenda. Members of the conservative coalition, who were briefly defeated in the fight over the rules committee, would combine again to frustrate liberal Kennedy initiatives in Medicare, federal aid to education, creation of an Urban Affairs Department, and most visibly, civil rights legislation. Experience with Congress during his first two years in office led Kennedy to be pessimistic about the use of presidential power to get his way with legislation. "Party loyalty or responsibility means damn little. They've got to take care of themselves first." The Congress, Kennedy said, "looks more powerful sitting here [in the White House] than it did when I was . . . one of a hundred in the Senate."[32]

This early experience with Congress explains in part Kennedy's reluctance to introduce bold and sweeping legislative proposals. The president's brother, Robert F. Kennedy (his attorney general), argued that the House rules committee fight was indicative of Kennedy's lack of influence with Congress, particularly southern conservatives. ". . . [H]ere we had Sam Rayburn and, therefore, the Texas delegation. . . . [W]e had the maximum strength. . . . [Y]et we only won it by a couple of votes. . . . How much more difficult it was when the odds were much higher against us!"[33]

LBJ's Activist Approach: The 1964 Civil Rights Act

For the seventy years since the withdrawal of Union troops from the South in 1876 no civil rights legislation had been passed by Congress. Southern con-

[31]Sorensen, *Kennedy,* p. 381.

[32]Quoted in Sorensen, *Kennedy,* p. 387.

[33]Edwin O. Guthman and Jeffrey Shulman, eds., *Robert Kennedy in His Own Words* (New York: Bantam Books, 1988), p. 52.

servatives, all Democrats, had been able to prevent any consideration of legislation through the skillful use of parliamentary tactics. As national attitudes began to change in the midtwentieth century and the civil rights movement began to become more active, liberals began to make some progress in Congress, though not with major breakthroughs. The Civil Rights Act of 1957 was historic, not for its substance, for its provisions were substantially watered down by the time conservatives allowed its passage, but for the very fact that it was passed at all. The 1960 Civil Rights Act was passed in a similarly weak state.[34]

As president, John Kennedy was liberal with respect to civil rights, but his election in 1960 was very close, and he needed the support of southern Democrats in Congress and southern states' votes for his reelection in 1964. Though he supported civil rights as president, he was unwilling early in his term to introduce serious legislation to change the reality of segregation in the country. But his attitude changed in May 1963, when the city police chief of Birmingham, Alabama, Bull Connor, used police dogs, fire hoses, and cattle prods to break up nonviolent demonstrations. The televised film of these brutal tactics moved the nation, and John Kennedy decided to send to Congress a serious civil rights bill.

The bill written in June 1963 would enforce equal access to all public accommodations and would cut off federal funds to states that allowed segregation in their schools. The bill was being considered in the House judiciary committee when Kennedy was assassinated in Dallas in November 1963.

When Johnson became president after the assassination he was in a relatively weak position because of the way he had become president. He had succeeded to the office rather than being elected in his own right, and thus could not argue that he had a mandate for his policy agenda. He also faced the same partisan and regional situation in Congress that Kennedy had faced. Johnson did, however, have several advantages with respect to civil rights. First, he was a southerner, and his decision to support civil rights for blacks would not hurt him as much in the South as it would the northeastern Kennedy. Secondly, Johnson had been Senate majority leader and was a master legislative tactician. He would have to use all of his skills in seeking passage of Kennedy's civil rights bill, which he decided to back without any of the compromises that had been expected to water down the bill.

The first step Johnson had to take was to get the bill through the House. Since the judiciary committee, which had jurisdiction, was chaired by liberal northern Democrat Emanuel Celler, the bill was dealt with favorably. The real problem was going to be the House rules committee. Despite the expanded membership, its chairman, Howard Smith of Virginia, was going to use every trick at his disposal to prevent the bill from being considered before the full House, where it would have passed. In the past, when he wanted to block civil rights legislation, Chairman Smith would disappear from the Capitol and go out to his

---

[34]This section is based on the article by Robert D. Loevy, "The Presidency and Domestic Policy: The Civil Rights Act of 1964," in David C. Kozak and Kenneth N. Ciboski, eds., *The American Presidency* (Chicago: Nelson-Hall, 1985), pp. 411–419.

farm in rural Virginia, thus preventing the committee from meeting. When he used this tactic in opposing the 1957 Civil Rights Act, his staff said that he had to return to his farm to inspect a barn that had burned down. When Speaker Sam Rayburn heard this he said, "I knew Howard Smith would do most anything to block a civil rights bill, but I never knew he would resort to arson."[35]

Smith was using his wiles again in 1963 to fight the Kennedy/Johnson proposal. And since the bill could not be considered by the floor unless it was reported out by the rules committee, the only way to pry the bill from Smith's clutches was to have a majority of House members sign a discharge petition, which would force the bill to floor consideration. By Christmas 1963 the petition was still fifty votes short of the needed majority, but Johnson and the leadership in the House put enough pressure on unwilling members and Smith that Smith finally bowed to the inevitable and allowed the bill to go to the floor before the discharge petition forced him to do it. On the floor of the House the bill's proponents were able to defeat every amendment in the ten days of debate, and it passed the House on February 10, 1964, by a 290–130 margin.

But the Senate would bring an even tougher battle. Senator James O. Eastland of Mississippi was chair of the judiciary committee and had been able to use his powers as chair to kill more than 100 proposed civil rights bills in the 1950s and 1960s. But his powers as chair were effectively evaded when the Senate leadership, which held much of the scheduling power that the rules committee held in the House, was able to place the bill directly on the Senate calendar, thereby bypassing the judiciary committee completely.

The roadblock to Senate floor consideration and a vote on the civil rights bill, which was likely to pass if it came up for a vote, was the filibuster. Unlike the House, which due to its greater numbers must be run more tightly, the Senate, through Rule XXII, allows unlimited debate by members before a measure is brought to a vote. The only route around a filibuster is a vote for cloture, which takes a three-fifths majority to pass. A vote for cloture places a limit on debate and allows a bill to be brought to the floor for a vote. The filibuster is a parliamentary tactic that can be used by a few senators to prevent legislation from coming to a vote, and the support of only two-fifths plus one of the Senate will keep the filibuster alive and prevent a vote on a bill.

There is no requirement that debate has to be relevant to the legislation under consideration, and senators in marathon talk fests would read from the Bible or cookbooks, merely to keep the floor until, on the verge of exhaustion, they would yield the floor to a colleague who would keep up the fight. Leadership tactics to fight a filibuster included round-the-clock sessions to wear out the talkers, but they were often up to the challenge, with the record being held by Democratic Senator Strom Thurmond of South Carolina in the filibuster against the

[35]Whalen and Whalen, *The Longest Debate,* p. 92.

Civil Rights Act of 1957, who talked for more than twenty-four hours.[36] Cloture is very difficult to achieve because many senators feel that it is one of the few tactics they can use as a last resort to protect their own vital interests.

By use of the filibuster, or its mere threat, southern conservatives had been able to stop civil rights legislation from being considered by the Senate for years, and senators had never been able to get the votes to invoke cloture to end the debate on a civil rights bill. In the 1964 battle Johnson knew that the southerners would use the filibuster, and he arranged for the decks to be cleared by getting the Senate to pass all the legislation he wanted considered in the first half of 1964 so that a filibuster would not create pressure to give up the civil rights fight merely to get other legislation considered.

So Johnson let the filibuster drone on through April and the beginning of May before he made his move to get the necessary votes for cloture. In his move, Johnson called in favors from years as Senate majority leader and used all of his leverage as president. To get the necessary votes, Johnson knew he had to enable moderate Republicans to vote for the bill. To convince them and to provide them political cover Johnson courted his old colleague, minority leader Everett McKinley Dirksen of Illinois, and maneuvered so that Dirksen would get credit for his contribution to the civil rights victory. "I deliberately tried to tone down my personal involvement . . . so that a hero's niche could be carved out for Senator Dirksen, not me."[37]

Senate Democratic whip Hubert Humphrey represented Johnson in negotiations with Dirksen to work out a compromise that would satisfy both the civil rights advocates and Republican moderates. During May and early June an acceptable compromise was worked out, and on June 10 the Senate, for the first time in its history, used a cloture vote to force consideration of a civil rights bill. The historic breakthrough civil rights bill went through Congress and was signed by Johnson on July 2, 1964.

When Johnson was elected in his own right—by a landslide—in the November 1964 elections, he went on to push through his Great Society legislative agenda that was historic in its scope and volume. But his sweeping success—eighty of eighty-three of his major proposals were enacted in 1965—was due in large part to the Democratic majorities in Congress that came in with him after the 1964 elections. In the Eighty-ninth Congress, the Democrats had a 295–140 majority in the House and a 68–32 advantage in the Senate. While the legislation of the Eighty-ninth Congress was of historic proportions, the battle for the 1964 Civil Rights Act demonstrated that presidents usually have to fight for what they get from Congress and showed how skillful a fighter Lyndon Johnson was before the 1964 elections.

---

[36]William Safire, *Safire's Political Dictionary* (New York: Random House, 1968), pp. 226–227. In 1993, Republican Senators were able to hand President Clinton a significant defeat when they conducted a filibuster to prevent a vote on an economic stimulus package that was pushed by the new administration. Since the Democrats held only 57 seats in the Senate, they could not muster the 60 votes necessary to invoke cloture and cut off debate.

[37]Lyndon Johnson, *The Vantage Point* (New York: Holt, Rinehart and Winston, 1971), p. 159.

Richard Nixon: The Politics of Confrontation

In 1968 Richard Nixon was elected in a very close race, winning only 43.4 percent of the vote to Hubert Humphrey's 42.7 percent, with third-party candidate George Wallace winning most of the remainder. Despite his lack of a majority at the polls, Nixon felt that he had a mandate from the people because the electorate of the presidency is national, while the electorate of Congress is confined to individual states and congressional districts. Nixon initially intended to be an activist president, but when he tried to get the Congress to go along with his conservative proposals he became disillusioned. He found that the Democrats who controlled Congress, many of whom had voted for the Great Society legislation of Lyndon Johnson, were not about to be accomplices in its dismantling. Nixon's response to his inability to dominate the domestic agenda of the country was to "*take over* the bureaucracy and *take on* the Congress."[38] That is, Nixon used his powers as chief executive officer of the government, to their fullest extent, to achieve his policy goals. He also used, to the fullest extent, his constitutional powers as president against the Congress. In the end, he pushed some of his claimed authority beyond legal and constitutional bounds.

One of the main levers of power in government is the control of money to run programs. That is why the Framers split the power of the purse between the two branches, giving Congress the power to appropriate money, subject to presidential veto, and to the president the authority to spend the funds in carrying out the laws. Nixon decided that if he could not get Congress to make the cuts and programmatic changes in the budget that he proposed that he would do it himself by refusing to spend money that had been provided by Congress in law.

Other presidents, to save money and to cancel particular projects within broader programs, also refused to spend appropriated funds. Presidents Truman, Eisenhower, and Kennedy cancelled some military spending, and President Johnson impounded some domestic funds, though he released them when Congress made a fuss. With these precedents in mind, President Nixon decided to make impoundment the cornerstone of his domestic budget policy by refusing to spend funds on programs he disapproved of, regardless of the law or Congress.[39]

But Nixon's impoundments departed from the actions of all previous presidents in several important ways.

1. He impounded larger amounts than any previous president, from 1969 to 1972 impounding 17 to 20 percent of controllable expenditures.[40]

38Richard Nathan, *The Plot that Failed* (New York: John Wiley, 1975), p. 8.

39For a full treatment of the impoundment issue, see James P. Pfiffner, *The President, the Budget, and Congress: Impoundment and the 1974 Budget Act* (Boulder, CO: Westview Press, 1979).

40Nile Stanton, "The Presidency and the Purse: Impoundment 1803–1973," *University of Colorado Law Review* (1973) in U.S. Congress, Senate, *Congressional Record* (December 14, 1973), p. S22925, S22926.

2. He refused to spend funds despite explicit expressions of intent by Congress in law, and preambles to laws, that they be spent.
3. He tried to use impoundment to eliminate entire programs, rather than merely individual projects within larger programs.
4. He withheld funds from programs that were not included in his budget proposal to Congress, though Congress had not yet acted on his proposed budget.
5. He claimed to have the constitutional power to impound funds.

According to Nixon, "The Constitutional right of the President of the United States to impound funds, and that is not to spend money, when the spending of money would mean either increasing prices or increasing taxes for all the people—that right is absolutely clear."[41] No other president had ever made that claim.

What is important about Nixon's constitutional claim is that if it were true, Nixon would be free to ignore the will of Congress and the law of the land. Thus, President Nixon proceeded to impound funds from programs that he thought should not be funded, and his actions were challenged in federal courts throughout the country. One of the cases that finally got to the Supreme Court provides a useful illustration of Nixon's interpretation of the Constitution.

In the fall of 1972, Congress and the president were engaged in a battle over spending priorities with the president seeking to cut expenditures. When Congress refused to grant him the unilateral authority that he had requested to cut spending for fiscal year 1973, he decided to veto the Federal Water Pollution Control Act amendments that provided $11 billion in 1973 and 1974 for building water-pollution abatement plants. His grounds for the veto were that it was too much money to spend. So far things were perfectly constitutional, but when both houses of Congress voted to override his veto, he decided to impound the funds anyway. He instructed the Environmental Protection Agency to expend less than half the funds provided in the legislation.

As might be expected, this action was appealed in federal court along with scores of other impoundment cases. The Nixon administration did not fare well when its impoundment actions were examined by judges. The administration was not able to convince even one judge to declare that the president had the power to impound funds unilaterally. Some cases were dismissed on the basis of standing or justiciability, but none were won on their merits by the administration. The court of appeals found that:

> When the executive exercises its responsibility under appropriation legislation in such a manner as to frustrate the Congressional purpose, either by absolute refusal to spend or by a withholding of so substantial an amount of the appropriations as to make impossible the attainment of the

---

[41] *Weekly Compilation of Presidential Documents* 9 (5), pp. 109–110.

> legislative goals, the executive trespasses beyond the range of its legal discretion. . . .[42]

The Supreme Court also decided against President Nixon in a 9–0 decision. It decided the case on the legislative provisions of the Water Pollution Control Act, but made a broad statement about the arguments of the Nixon administration:

> As conceived and passed in both Houses, the legislation was intended to provide a firm commitment to substantial sums within a relatively limited period of time in an effort to achieve an early solution of what was deemed an urgent problem. We cannot believe that Congress at the last minute scuttled the entire effort by providing the Executive with the seemingly limitless power to withhold funds from allotment and obligation.[43]

The alarming aspect of the use of impoundment by President Nixon is that it amounted to a unilateral and absolute veto power for the president. If the president could refuse to spend money appropriated in law, even after an override of a veto, the president would possess a power that was explicitly rejected by the Framers.

In reaction to the Nixon claims to impoundment power, Congress passed the Congressional Budget and Impoundment Control Act of 1974. The act reformed the congressional budget process and severely limited the president's ability to impound funds. In the future, presidents would have to submit their proposed impoundments to Congress before they could legally take effect.

The impoundment controversy was not the only way that President Nixon decided to confront Congress. He also attempted to assert a pocket veto during a five-day Christmas recess, when Congress had made provisions to receive any regular veto message. He appointed an acting director to the Office of Economic Opportunity in order to avoid the Senate's confirmation authority. When the acting director began to dismantle the agency and impound funds while the laws for its existence and funding were still on the books, he was taken to court. President Nixon lost both of these court battles over his constitutional power.

Nixon also confronted the Congress over presidential war powers, resulting in the passage, over his veto, of the War Powers Resolution of 1973. He asserted a blanket authority for executive privilege with respect to the Watergate tapes, and was rebuffed by a 9–0 decision of the Supreme Court. These assertions of presidential power by the Nixon administration were the culmination of what some called the "Imperial Presidency."[44] Congressional reaction to them, in laws that limited actions by the executive and reformed internal pro-

---

[42]489 F.2nd. p. 492 (December 10, 1973).

[43]Quoted in Pfiffner, *The President, the Budget, and Congress,* p. 103.

[44]Arthur M. Schlesinger, Jr., *The Imperial Presidency* (Boston: Houghton Mifflin, 1973).

cedures in Congress, transformed relations between the branches, though all of the reforms did not have the results intended by their proponents.

Jimmy Carter: The Moral Equivalent of War

When Jimmy Carter was elected, Democrats in Congress held high expectations for a productive legislative relationship. The Nixon period of divided government was ended, with the presidency and both houses of Congress controlled by the Democrats: 292–143 in the House and 61–38 in the Senate. Carter intended to be an activist president and had a number of legislative proposals tackling major policy problems, such as welfare reform, health care, the tax system, and energy.

The major legislative effort in his first year was energy legislation. Since the 1973 oil embargo by OPEC, U.S. dependence on foreign nations for oil had become obvious and worrisome, but the United States had not been able to do anything to change it. Between 1973 and 1976 the price of gasoline almost doubled, but still the United States increased its dependence on imported oil from 35 percent to almost 50 percent.[45]

Carter had talked about the energy problem in his presidential campaign, but had not laid out specific proposals or made it a centerpiece of his drive for the presidency. After the election he designated James Schlesinger, an economist who had been appointed CIA director and secretary of defense by President Nixon, to take charge of the administration's energy policy and to be his secretary of energy when the department was created in 1977. Carter gave Schlesinger ninety days from the inauguration to come up with a comprehensive proposal to deal with the nation's energy problems. This was a tight time frame, given the complex nature of the policy problem as a technical issue and the formidable political obstacles that would have to be overcome if basic changes were to be proposed.

Schlesinger and his team carried out the task in virtual complete secrecy. This was useful from a technical perspective, since the issues were so complex, and politically it kept the various provisions from being leaked piecemeal and shot down before they could be formally presented. But from another political perspective the secrecy was a major hindrance. Members of Congress, who would have to vote on all of the provisions, were not brought into the process or even informed of the provisions. They felt left out, and they did not have advance warning to formulate their own reactions or explain them to their constituents. But even Carter administration officials whose jurisdictions would be affected by the policies were not informed until very late. Two weeks before the plan was unveiled Vice President Mondale, CEA Chairman Charles Schultze, and OMB Director Bert Lance had not been informed of the plans.[46]

Schlesinger's plan was ready in the required ninety days, and on April 18 Carter appeared in a nationally televised speech to announce his energy pack-

---

[45]Jimmy Carter, *Keeping Faith* (New York: Bantam Books, 1982), p. 71.

[46]Haynes Johnson, *In the Absence of Power* (New York: Viking Press, 1980), p. 189.

age. Carter preached to the American people that they had been wasteful in the past and that his plan would call for sacrifice. "Ours is the most wasteful nation on earth. We waste more energy than we import." His energy plan would "test the character of the American people" and would amount to "the moral equivalent of war."[47] By his secrecy and rhetoric, Carter was staking the administration's prestige on passage of the energy package. Two days later he presented the specifics of his proposal to a joint session of Congress.

The major elements of the proposal included a gasoline tax increase (if gas consumption exceeded the previous year's), a tax on gas-guzzling cars, a tax on crude oil, conservation tax credits, continued control of natural-gas prices (with some price increases), utility rate reforms, mandatory industrial conversion from oil to coal, and the development of alternative energy sources such as nuclear and solar power.[48] One of the problems was that all of the elements did not fit neatly into one piece of legislation. The plan had 113 interlocking provisions that fit together in a complex way and affected different parts of the economy in different ways.[49]

Another problem was that there was no natural constituency for the legislation. Even though most observers would admit that dependence on foreign oil had hurt the U.S. economy and was a potential threat to U.S. security, there was no consensus about what to do about it. The Carter plan promised diffuse benefits (i.e., everyone would benefit a little through a sounder economy) but concentrated costs. Costs would be borne by consumers in the form of higher prices for car fuel and heating oil, and the plan would hurt producers by cutting into their profits. In his appeal to the public, Carter was not able to convince people that the crisis was as bad as he judged it to be or that his package was the solution to the problem. Industries that opposed the legislation were very effective in lobbying Congress, and oil-producing states had powerful representatives on the Hill. Carter complained that "The influence of the special interest lobbies is almost unbelievable, particularly from the automobile and oil industries."[50]

The administration wanted the legislation considered in Congress as a single package rather than in separate pieces, a difficult task since the various provisions fell into the jurisdictions of seventeen House committees and subcommittees. But Speaker of the House Thomas P. "Tip" O'Neill was able to manage this tactical problem by creating a special Ad Hoc Select Committee on Energy. The administration bill passed the House relatively intact (except for the gas

---

[47]Quoted in Barbara Kellerman, *The Political Presidency: The Practice of Leadership* (New York: Oxford University Press, 1984), p. 190.

[48]See Charles O. Jones, *The Trusteeship Presidency* (Baton Rouge, LA: Louisiana State University Press, 1988), pp. 135–143; Michael J. Malbin, "Rhetoric and Leadership: A Look Backward at the Carter National Energy Plan," in Anthony King, ed., *Both Ends of the Avenue* (Washington, DC: American Enterprise Institute Press, 1983), pp. 212–245; and Barbara Kellerman, *The Political Presidency* (New York: Oxford University Press, 1984), pp. 185–219.

[49]Jones, *The Trusteeship Presidency,* p. 138.

[50]Carter, *Keeping Faith,* p. 99.

tax increase) by early August 1977. The Senate, however, was another story. The package was split into five separate bills to be considered by the Energy and Natural Resource and the Finance Committees. Carter did not have the help in the Senate that he got from Speaker O'Neill in the House, and the debate dragged on over two months, with an attempted filibuster by liberals, who did not want to see natural-gas prices deregulated. The Senate finally passed an energy bill in late October, but several key provisions of the Carter package were significantly changed. The Senate voted to deregulate natural gas, it rejected the crude-oil tax, rejected the gas-tax increase, and rejected the declining rate structures for utilities.[51]

Carter renewed his efforts in 1978, and was much more effective in his approach to Congress. A conference committee was created to consider the different House and Senate bills and compromises were worked out over the next eight months. The several provisions were put together in a fivepart package that passed in the Senate, but survived in the House by only one vote. The bill got through Congress on October 15, 1978, a year and a half after Carter had presented his proposals to Congress. The National Energy Act provided for the gradual deregulation of natural gas, a major change from Carter's original intention. It increased energy taxes a bit and required that electric power plants convert to coal. It required states only to consider restructuring of rates for utilities, and included a number of other conservation measures.[52]

Thus, President Carter got an energy package passed, but it did not contain a good portion of what he had proposed in 1977. What were the problems that prevented Carter from getting most of what he wanted in the most important legislative priority of his first year in office? The first problem was the nature of the policy itself. Energy policy is complex, and the Carter proposals did not guarantee a solution to the problem of dependence on foreign oil. Second, the plan distributed a lot of pain without promising concrete benefits that were certain to follow.

But changed relations between the presidency and Congress also affected the outcome. The reaction of Congress to the Nixon administration made the institution less willing to be cooperative with any president, even a Democrat. The internal reforms of the 1970s had fragmented power within the Congress. The leadership held less power to coerce their party troops to go along, and there were more individual members who wanted a piece of the action. Thus, presidents had to retail, rather than wholesale, their appeals for support on legislation. Carter expressed his frustration in his memoirs: "I learned the hard way that there was no party loyalty or discipline when a complicated or controversial issue was at stake—none. Each legislator had to be

[51]See Malbin, "Rhetoric and Leadership," pp. 224–227.

[52]See Kellerman, *The Political Presidency,* p. 209.

wooed and won individually. It was every member for himself, and the devil take the hindmost!"[53]

But Carter was also at fault. Part of the lack of party loyalty to Carter may have resulted from Carter's decision to run for president as an outsider rather than as a traditional Democratic party regular. Despite his effectiveness in electoral politics, Carter held a disdain for bargaining with Congress and communicated this in his dealings with its members. He felt that his policy proposals were best for the country and that members of Congress ought to support them on their merits without special efforts by him to court their votes or bargain for support. His first legislative liaison team was inexperienced, and the administration committed some early mistakes that alienated some members of Congress.

By the end of 1977, the Carter administration had learned many of the hard lessons about Congress and was much more effective in its relations with the Hill. Carter's overall legislative record compares favorably with the other modern presidents, but his early mistakes with Congress kept him from being as successful as he might have been.[54]

Ronald Reagan: The 1982 Budget Juggernaut

In 1980, Ronald Reagan won a resounding electoral victory over Jimmy Carter and promised to cure the economy of high inflation and balance the budget by 1984. He promised to cut taxes, to reduce drastically domestic spending, and to restore America's military forces. No one doubted his intentions, but many doubted his ability to make good on these campaign promises. Skeptics said the momentum of federal spending, combined with the power of both the Democrats in Congress and of the beneficiaries of federal programs, would be too powerful even for a popular president to reverse.

But contrary to most expectations, Reagan was able to accomplish much of his agenda, though not with his charisma alone. The historic budget victories of Reagan's first year were the result of careful planning, singleness of purpose, and speed of execution. At the same time, broader forces favored the administration: there were no major foreign policy crises, the electorate was in the mood for a change, the economy was in a mess, and the Democrats were in disarray.[55]

David Stockman, who had spent two terms as a member of Congress from Michigan, began planning for the budget changes before the election. Stockman's intimate knowledge of the budgetary process, his command of the bud-

---

[53]Carter, *Keeping Faith,* p. 80.

[54]For a more complete analysis of the Carter administration's early relations with Congress, see James P. Pfiffner, *The Strategic Presidency* (Pacific Palisades, CA: Brooks/Cole, 1988), chap. 7.

[55]For a more complete analysis of the Reagan budget victories in 1981, see James P. Pfiffner, "The Reagan Budget Juggernaut," in James P. Pfiffner, *The President and Economic Policy* (Philadelphia: ISHI Press, 1986), pp. 108–134.

get details, and his skills in congressional procedure were crucial to the Reagan budget victories. As soon as Stockman took over as director of OMB, he put the OMB staff to work reversing their efforts to construct the last Carter budget and planning the drastic changes that Reagan sought.

The capture of the Senate by Republicans for the first time since 1954 made the task of the administration much easier. Senate backing of early Reagan proposals could be taken virtually for granted. The House was another matter because it was controlled by the Democrats by a 243–192 majority. The new administration contemplated drastic changes, and getting the Democratic House to go along was a major challenge. The soft spot in Democratic control of the House was the block of forty-seven conservative southern Democrats in the Conservative Democratic Forum, better known as the "Boll Weevils." In its campaign to win House support for its budget priorities, the White House decided that these members were particularly vulnerable to administration pressure.

The administration used its most important asset, the president, very effectively. The public campaign was conducted by a series of formal presidential addresses, as well as hundreds of informal comments to the press. In a February 5 televised address, the president warned of an "economic calamity of tremendous proportions" if Congress refused to pass his program. On February 18, he addressed a joint session of Congress to present his "Program for Economic Recovery" along with an inch-thick document explaining his approach to fiscal and monetary policy. This was followed by another address to Congress on March 10 and the release of "Fiscal Year 1982 Budget Revisions, the detailed OMB proposals. During the same period, members of the cabinet and the Council of Economic Advisors were also pushing the administration's proposals throughout the country.

The first crucial votes on the administration program came in the House on May 7, when the first concurrent resolution came up for a vote. The purpose of the resolution was to lay out the total revenues, spending, and deficit targets for the next fiscal year. In a tactical maneuver, the Republicans had succeeded in forcing consideration of the package of budget cuts and spending priorities as a whole rather than in pieces that might have been defeated one at a time by the Democrats. After several weeks of intense lobbying by the administration sixty-three Democrats defected, and the House passed the budget package for the first concurrent resolution 253–176. These first crucial votes demonstrated the Reagan team could control the Democratic House in the budget battle.

The details of the cuts still had to be worked out in the reconciliation package in June. The Democrats put together a package that provided 85 percent of what the administration wanted, but with a smaller deficit. But the Republicans refused the compromise and proposed a substitute called "Gramm-Latta II" for the administration's vehicle. The administration again pulled out its heavy guns to lobby the House Democrats. The president himself called or telegraphed each of the sixty-three Democrats who had voted with him on the first budget resolution, and compromises were made to capture enough votes to win. Again the Republicans were able to keep the proposals in one package rather than allowing separate voting on different pieces, and the reconciliation measure passed 232–193 on June 26. After being passed by the Senate, the omnibus reconciliation package cut from the budget a total of $35.1 billion in 1982 and $130.6 billion by fiscal year 1984.

The other major part of the Reagan economic plan was a large tax cut predicated on the "supply-side" theory that a cut in taxes would stimulate the economy enough to wipe out the deficit in the near future. The Democrats also were preparing a tax-cut package, but the administration was determined to win. What resulted was a bidding war to include the most "sweeteners" and "ornaments" on the "Christmas tree bill" to attract the most votes in the House. According to David Stockman, "The basic strategy was to match or exceed the Democrats, and we did. . . . Do you realize the greed that came to the forefront? . . . [T]he hogs were really feeding. The greed level, the level of opportunism, just got out of control."[56]

After another massive lobbying effort by the administration, including a televised presidential address that helped create public pressure on Congress, forty-eight House Democrats defected to vote for the administration's tax-cut bill. In the Senate, thirty-seven of forty-seven Democrats voted for the bill. The total five-year loss to the treasury would amount to $750 billion.

President Reagan's first budget defied the predictions of scholars and old Washington hands alike. Very few predicted that he would be able to make such drastic shifts in priorities so suddenly. The changes included what House Budget Committee Chairman James Jones called "clearly the most monumental and historic turnaround in fiscal policy that has ever occurred."[57] The measures included the largest spending cuts in U.S. history, affecting hundreds of programs. It included the largest peacetime buildup of military spending. It also included the largest tax cuts in history.

The problem, of course, was that the domestic cuts neither made up for the military increases nor for the loss of revenues to the treasury. The immediate results of this fiscal policy, plus the recession of the early 1980s, were unprecedented deficits of over $200 billion that approached 6 percent of GNP. At the end of Reagan's term in office, the national debt had nearly tripled and approached $3 trillion.

But no one can dispute the historic nature of the changes made, or the skillful way the Reagan administration "hit the ground running" and accomplished its major priorities in its first nine months in office. But as with Franklin Roosevelt and Lyndon Johnson, Ronald Reagan could not maintain his string of victories

---

[56]Quoted by William Grieder, "The Education of David Stockman," *The Atlantic* (December 1981), p. 51.

[57]*Congressional Quarterly Weekly Report* (August 1, 1981), p. 1371.

throughout his term. Reagan's conservative policy victories galvanized opposing political forces, limiting his ability to continue winning further conservative initiatives. Even Republicans in Congress were not willing to back many of his budget proposals after the first few years. Reagan's legislative success steadily declined after 1981 until it fell below 50 percent in his last year in office.

Clinton and Two Congresses: A Study in Contrast

Clinton and the 103rd Congress: Winning Battles and Losing Wars

There are several perspectives from which to evaluate the way a president deals with Congress; at the personal level presidents can be relatively skilled or clumsy; at the agenda level they can put together a policy agenda designed to make the most of a particular congressional situation; and at the environmental level they can decide whether the time is ripe for constructive legislative cooperation or confrontation. President Clinton had a mixed record in his first two years in office in terms of both his overall legislative record and in the way he approached his policy agenda.

Earlier in this chapter I discussed how presidents were urged to "court" Congress. At the personal level Clinton was an impressive lobbier of Congress. He took pains to court members of both parties with invitations to the White House and personal phone calls. He combined the personal affability of Ronald Reagan with the detailed policy expertise of Jimmy Carter. In addition, he was empathetic and could communicate that he understood and sympathized with the perspective of his listener. He was willing to compromise on substance as well as pass out favors in seeking the votes he needed. His personal politicking was crucial in several very close votes on his initial budget agenda, twisting arms and making deals to win last-minute votes that he won by only one vote in both the House and the Senate. His active and public campaign for the North American Free Trade Agreement (NAFTA) was effective in winning congressional approval despite the opposition of the Democratic leadership on the Hill.

Earlier in this chapter it was also argued that presidents should focus their initial agendas tightly by using the "rifle strategy" to narrow their agendas and not to include so many issues that priorities are not clear. In this respect, the new Clinton administration did not do as well. The campaign had raised a number of issues that Clinton promised would be priorities if he were elected. Despite his promise to "focus like a laser beam" on economic policy, the new administration was not ready to go with its economic plan until February 1993. This delay allowed the press to focus on minor embarrassments like the withdrawal of his first nominee for Attorney General and his proposal to allow gay citizens to serve in the military. Clinton did sign the family medical leave act and the "motor voter" voting registration bills as well as issuing several executive orders early in his term.

His economic package included a five-year deficit-reduction package of spending cuts and tax increases amounting to about $500 billion. It was skillfully introduced to Congress and the public and well on the way to passage when the momentum was interrupted by Clinton's introduction of a "stimulus" package of less than $20 billion. The Republicans were able to label the package as "pork" and to stop it with a filibuster. This small defeat of the administration slowed momentum on the whole budget and made success more problematical. The budget fight was finally won by the administration with not a single Republican vote in the House or Senate, and it came down to a 217–216 victory in the House on the reconciliation bill and a 50–50 tie in the Senate that was broken by the vice president's vote. Thus, the administration's initial agenda did not have the level of timing, coherence, and momentum that would have helped them. Even Leon Panetta, Clinton's OMB Director and later Chief of Staff admitted: "There were so many initiatives and so many efforts that were made that we lost the message. . . ."[58]

At the systemic level (the political environment and tenor of the times) the mood of the country was not ripe for large new public programs, which doomed the Clinton health plan. Health care reform was a centerpiece of the 1996 campaign, and the administration was determined to introduce basic reform that included at least covering those who were uninsured. To signal how important health care was, the President appointed Hillary Rodham Clinton to be in charge of the huge effort that involved a White House task force of 500 people.

This major priority was finally defeated in the fall of 1994, for a number of reasons. The plan was not ready for unveiling until September 1993 when Clinton gave a well-received speech to Congress. But the draft bill was not finished until a month later. In the spring of 1994 interest groups and Republicans campaigned against the plan. But perhaps most important, the health care reform plan was exceedingly complex, calling for the creation of organizations that did not yet exist. The consequences of the reform plan were not clear and the public felt uncertain enough about it to turn against it. The complexity arose from the administration's attempt to rely on private-sector employer mandates, create universal coverage, and have no cost increase all in the same package. The resulting proposal was so complex that it was vulnerable to Republicans' charges that it was too much "big government."

Thus, Clinton's legislative record in his first two years was decidedly mixed. He won major victories in his budget package and the NAFTA votes; he won other victories in the Brady Bill (waiting period for handgun purchases), motor voter, medical leave act, and Hatch Act changes; but he was defeated in the centerpiece of health care reform. This seems to conflict with his legislative support scores of 86.4 percent in each of his first two years, according to *Congressional Quarterly*[59]—the highest since LBJ's 1965 record. But the score is misleading, as the above analysis implies, probably because the Democrats

---

[58]Quoted in Ruth Marcus, "Administration Now Sees Its Record at Risk," *Washington Post* (January 24, 1995), pp. A1, A6.

[59]*Congressional Quarterly Weekly Report* (December 21, 1996), p. 3428.

were able to structure votes so that if they were not going to win, they would not schedule a vote. Also, health care was abandoned without even a vote in the full House or Senate.[60]

But given the political environment in 1993–1994 we should not be surprised that Clinton had a mixed record in his legislative priorities. He was elected with a 43 percent plurality; he ran behind most members of Congress; he had fewer Democrats in Congress than other recent Democrats, and his party lost seats in the election. Combine these negatives with a very ambitious policy agenda and you have a prescription for high conflict and low success. Clinton won a significant number of legislative victories, but the broader war for public approval was lost when voters rejected the administration in the 1994 congressional elections and turned Congress over to the Republicans.

CLINTON AND THE 104TH CONGRESS: LOSING BATTLES AND WINNING THE WAR Clinton's mixed success with the 103rd Congress was a cakewalk when compared with his relations with the Republican-controlled 104th Congress. The irony, however, was that despite his frustration and much lower success rate with the 104th Congress, his record led to his reelection in 1996. How did this amazing turnabout occur?

The 1994 elections were widely seen as a rejection of the Clinton administration and the Democrats in Congress. Despite the relatively small margin of votes that switched, virtually all of the switches went in the Republicans' favor. They took control of the House of Representatives and of the Congress for the first time in forty years. They gained fifty-two seats in the House and eight Seats in the Senate, giving them margins of 230–204 and 53–47, respectively. (Later defections of Democrats gave the Republicans a 55–45 advantage in the Senate and a 232–202 advantage in the House.) Not one Republican incumbent lost an election. The Republican sweep of Congress was also reflected in Republican victories in state legislatures and governorships.

The Republicans in Congress, led by Newt Gingrich, newly elected as Speaker of the House, felt that they had a clear mandate from the voters. They had campaigned on an agenda of issues, known as the "Contract With America," and they were determined to push their conservative priorities through Congress. The seventy-three freshmen in the House were particularly determined and loyal to Speaker Gingrich, to whom most felt that they owed their elections. The conservative agenda in the Contract included a balanced budget amendment to the Constitution, transforming welfare entitlements into block grants to states, a tax cut, a missile defense system, cuts in capital gains taxes, and term limits for members of Congress.

During the first several months in 1995 the House worked overtime to pass the Contract items, creating an impressive record. In April, President Clinton

---

[60]For a detailed analysis of Clinton and the 103rd Congress see James P. Pfiffner, "President Clinton and the 103rd Congress: Winning Battles and Losing Wars," in James Thurber, ed. *Rivals for Power: Presidential-Congressional Relations* (Washington, DC: CQ Press, 1996).

was reduced to the point of insisting to the press that he was still "relevant" to the policy processes. As the Contract items went to the Senate, however, they were slowed down by the relative ideological moderation of the Senators and the procedural constraints of the Senate, which is subject to filibusters that can effectively bring the Senate to a halt.

By the summer of 1995 the Republicans had been insisting on balancing the federal budget within seven years, and Clinton felt that this was important enough to the public that he had to agree with balance in principle. In doing this, he was able to shift the debate from *whether* to balance the budget to *how* to balance the budget and highlight the differences between himself and the Republicans in Congress.

In the fall of 1995 the Republicans passed a budget for Fiscal Year 1996 that would have put the budget on a path toward balance; but it also contained serious cuts in the projected expenditures for programs in education, environment, Medicare, and Medicaid. Clinton said that he was also for a balanced budget, but that he would not accept the Republicans' formula. He said that he was protecting important programs from extreme cuts and vetoed the Republicans' budget. The Republicans stood firm, arguing that they were elected to implement conservative priorities and that they would not make the changes in priorities that Clinton demanded. Their problem was that they did not have the votes to override the president's veto.

With no budget passed to fund much of the government, the government would have to shut down all programs that did not yet have appropriations except those necessary to protect life or property. Ordinarily in such a situation a continuing resolution is passed, allowing the government to operate at present levels of funding until appropriations are finally passed. But the Republicans thought that Clinton would cave in and agree to their priorities rather than have the government shut down. They were wrong. Clinton refused to change his mind, and the government was shut down for six days in October and again for about two weeks at the end of the year. In January 1996, Senate Majority Leader Robert Dole convinced the Republicans to agree to continuing resolutions until regular appropriations could be passed.

The first session of the 104th Congress ended with Clinton having the lowest success rating of any president in the CQ survey of presidential success: 36.2 percent.[61] The partisanship of the session was also reflected in the highest party unity scores since 1954 when *Congressional Quarterly* began recording them. The majority of the Republicans voted against a majority of the Democrats in the Senate in 62.4 percent of the total votes and 56.4 percent of the time in the House.[62]

But this dismal legislative record set the stage for Bill Clinton's amazing comeback in 1996. The public saw the government shutdown as irresponsible and extreme on the part of the Republicans. Clinton's approval ratings began

[61] *Congressional Quarterly Weekly Report* (December 21, 1996), p. 3427.

[62] *Congressional Quarterly Weekly Report* (December 21, 1996), p. 3432.

to rise above the 50 percent level, and in the spring 1996 primaries he did not have to run against any Democratic challenger. During the spring of 1996 little legislation was passed, although appropriations measures were enacted to fund the government's programs.

By summer, members of Congress were intensely engaged in running for reelection, and members of both parties wanted positive legislative records to run on. Republicans could also see that their confrontational tactics had not worked, and they began to soften their stances in order to cooperate with Democrats to pass legislation before the fall elections. Thus in the spring and summer of 1996, a number of significant pieces of legislation passed, including an increase in the minimum wage, the phasing out of some farm benefits, deregulation in the telecommunications industry, and changes in portability of health insurance.

Even though there was no love-fest between the two parties, they saw the necessity of cooperation for their mutual benefit. Thus, the legislative record of the second session of the 104th Congress was significantly better than the first session, and the president's success score took the largest single-year leap in the history of the survey to 55.1 percent, though this was significantly lower than most post-war presidents.

The 1996 Congressional campaigns reflected the change in public attitude from the 1994 elections. In 1994, Democratic candidates were trying to distance themselves from their president for fear that association with him would hurt their chances for reelection. Republican congressional candidates were attacking Clinton as a big government liberal and promising to cut government severely if they were elected. In 1996, Democrats were clamoring to have President Clinton campaign for them, and even Republicans were taking credit for compromises with him, such as the minimum wage increase.

Clinton ran a strong campaign, staying consistently well ahead of Robert Dole, who suffered from the age factor and a lackluster campaign. Even though Clinton won the election 49 percent to Dole's 42 percent, the Republicans maintained control of both the House and the Senate.

Thus, Bill Clinton's first-term legislative record was a paradox. In the 103rd Congress, working with the Democratic majority, he had near record legislative support scores, but a mixed policy record and he lost the war for Congressional elections. Against the 104th Congress his legislative success was much lower, but he was able to prevail in the broader war over the policy agenda of the Republican Congress and win reelection easily, a feat that no one could have predicted at the beginning of the 104th Congress.

THE PROBLEM OF DIVIDED GOVERNMENT

When the Framers designed the constitutional system they consciously built into the government conflict between the president and Congress. With two branches sharing the powers of governance, each with different constituen-

FIGURE 6-2
Divided and Unified Control of the Government, 1944-1998

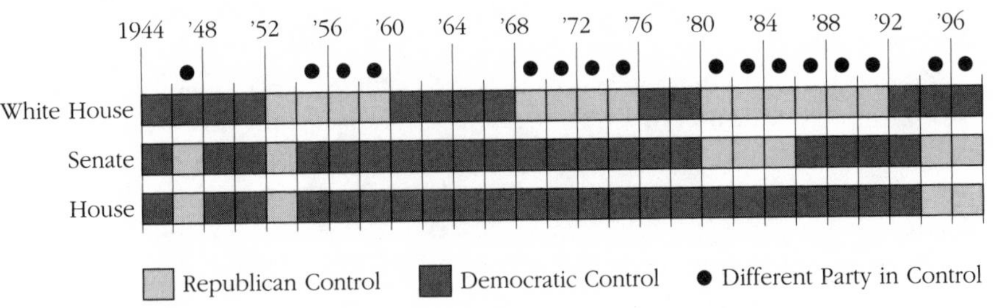

Source: The Washington Post, October 27, 1996, p. A24.

cies and terms of office, ambition would be made to counteract ambition, and the government would be made to control itself. But, in addition to the conflict and friction inherent in the institutions of American government, the Framers did not contemplate another source of friction—the problem of divided government—because they did not foresee the development of political parties.

Divided government occurs when one political party does not control both houses of Congress along with the presidency. Between 1832, when political parties became a routine part of the national political system, and 1998, this condition has occurred in 68 of 166 years, or 41 percent of the time.[63] While this frequency may seem to demonstrate that divided government has been common throughout U.S. history, the condition in the last half of the twentieth century is significantly different from the rest of U.S. history, and especially from the first half of the twentieth century. (See Figure 6–2).

In the nineteenth century, divided government resulted primarily from the loss of one or both houses of Congress in the midterm elections of a presidential term that began with one-party control of all three institutions. From 1832 to 1952, eighteen elections resulted in divided government, but only three of them (1848, 1876, and 1884) were in years of presidential elections.[64] But from 1897 to 1954, divided government occurred only in eight years (14 percent of the time). Presidents (in two-way races) had always carried the House when they were elected, and only in 1884 did the president's party not also take the Senate.[65] Divided government in the first half of the twentieth century was so unusual that when the Republicans captured both houses in the 1946 elections, Senator J. William Fullbright (D–Ark.) suggested that President Truman resign. With no vice president in office (after Roosevelt's

---

[63]Morris Fiorina, *Divided Government* (New York: Macmillan, 1992), pp. 6–14.

[64]Fiorina, *Divided Government,* p. 11.

[65]Fiorina, *Divided Government,* p. 12.

death in 1945), the next in line of succession to the presidency was Senate Majority Leader Arthur Vandenburg, thus providing a unified government. Truman, of course, rejected the proposal and began referring to its author as "Senator Halfbright."[66]

This background highlights how strikingly different recent partisan balance between the two institutions has been. In 1956, when President Eisenhower was reelected but the Democrats took both houses of Congress, it was the first time in the twentieth century that a president failed to carry both houses of Congress. Since 1956, presidents have failed to carry both houses in seven of eleven presidential election years, and from 1968 to 1998 the branches have been unified by party only one-fifth of the time. Bill Clinton's victory in 1992 ended twelve years of Republican control of the presidency and returned the government to unified Democratic control, but unified government lasted only two years, and the Republicans won control of both houses (for the first time in forty years) in 1994 and kept control in the 1996 elections.

The proximate cause of divided government in presidential election years is ticket-splitting, when voters vote for a president of one party and members of Congress from the other party. The percentage of congressional districts that have voted for a president of one party and House member of the other party has increased from a low of 3 percent in 1900 to a high of 45 percent in 1984. The percentage of individuals who split their ballots between a presidential candidate of one party and a house candidate of another increased from 12 percent in 1952 to an average of 25 percent between 1972 and 1988. the record was 36 percent in 1996, but it included the voters who voted for Ross Perot.[67]

Since majorities of respondents to public opinion polls say that they favor divided government because it keeps the government in check, some pundits argue that Americans *intend* to produce divided governments by their votes. Despite the accuracy of the polls, it is doubtful that many citizens cast their votes with the intention to divide the government between the two parties. In the 1992 National Election Survey, 78 percent of respondents reported voting for the same party for president and House, and of those who said they favored divided government, 75 percent voted a straight ticket. Of those who preferred divided government and split their votes, 15 percent voted for a Republican president and a Democrat for the House, and 10 percent voted for a Democrat for president and a Republican for the House. Thus, the outcome of divided government is highly unlikely to be caused by voters who cast their balots with the intention of producing divided government. In 1996, exit polls indicated a

[66]Clark Clifford, *Counsel to the President* (New York: Random House, 1991), p. 83.

[67]Morris Fiorina, "The Causes and Consequences of Divided Government: Lessons of 1992–94," in Peter F. Galderisi, *Divided Government* (Lanham, MD: Rowman and Littlefield, 1996), p. 38. See also Lee Sigelman, Paul J. Wahlbeck, and Emmett H. Buell, Jr., "Vote Choice and Preference for Divided Government: Lessons of 1992," *American Journal of Political Science* (July 1997) Vol. 14, no. 3, pp. 879–894. For the 1996 data see *The New York Times* exit poll, November 10, 1996.

similar situation.[68] The reason that divided government is problematic was expressed by Woodrow Wilson:

> You have an arrested Government. You have a Government that is not responding to the wishes of the people. You have a Government that is not functioning, a Government whose very energies are stayed and postponed. If you want to release the force of the American People, you have got to get possession of the Senate and the Presidency as well as the House.[69]

In his study of the American system of government, *Congressional Government,* Wilson emphasized the domination of policymaking by Congress in the nineteenth century and the difficulty presidents had getting the system to work for their own policy priorities.

The Framers designed the system to be biased against sudden change, but the addition of division by party as well as by institution exacerbates the problem of getting the system to move at all. The main theoretical problem with divided government is the problem of accountability. If, in a democracy, the electorate is to hold the government responsible for its policies, voters must be able to assign credit or blame to those in office. The doctrine of responsible party government holds that this can be done in the separation-of-powers system only if one political party controls both Congress and the presidency. If control is split between the two parties, each can try to take credit for good developments and blame the other party for any problems. This type of finger pointing has been a common characteristic of national politics in the second half of the twentieth century.

Proponents of the responsible party government model of American democracy view the occurrence of divided government with alarm. They argue that voters do not have clear bases for their votes and that coherent national policies are difficult to obtain under conditions of divided government. James Sundquist argues:

> For coherent and timely policies to be adopted and carried out—in short, for government to work effectively . . . the president, the Senate, and the House must come into agreement. When the same party controls all three of these power centers, the incentive to reach such an agreement is powerful despite the inevitable institutional rivalries and jealousies. The party *does* serve as a bridge or the web, in the metaphors of political science.[70]

Sundquist and others argue that divided control of Congress and the executive

---

[68]John Petrocik and Joseph Doherty, "The Road to Divided Government," in Galderisi, *Divided Government,* p. 94.

[69]Quoted by Lloyd N. Cutler, "The Cost of Divided Government," *The New York Times* (November 22, 1987).

[70]James Sundquist, "Needed: A Political Theory for the New Era of Coalition Government in the United States," *Political Science Quarterly* 103 (Winter 1988–89), p. 629.

branch leads to policy stalemate; that is, neither the president nor Congress can take any major action on its own and each is able to block the other from acting.[71] Sundquist argues that stalemate is more dangerous than letting one party have its way to lead the country in one direction or another, even if it is the wrong direction. At least in these circumstances voters can reject that party and replace them in the next presidential election with the other party.

Proponents of the responsible party government model argue that political parties make cooperation between the two branches more probable. They believe that the forces of fragmentation in the U.S. political system and government are so strong that the unifying factor of party is essential to coherent national policymaking. Presidents have a hard enough time gaining acceptance of their policies when their own party controls Congress; it is doubly difficult when the opposition party is in control of Congress.

If the same party controls both branches there is a common long-term interest in producing a successful record to run upon for reelection. But with opposing parties in charge of the two institutions, there is an incentive for each to frustrate the other's policy initiatives.[72] Divided government may be one of the factors that have led some recent presidents to centralize power in the White House and try to accomplish their goals through administrative means, rather than going to Congress and facing probable frustration.[73] This presidential frustration can result in overreaching, as it did when President Nixon resorted to impounding money for programs he disapproved of and his other attempts to get his way over the Democratic Congress. President Reagan's frustration with the Democratic House was one of the causes of the Iran–Contra scandal that almost brought down his presidency.[74]

Sundquist and others have proposed several constitutional changes to strengthen the party system and alleviate the consequences of divided party control of government. They have proposed constitutional amendments that include:

- Forcing voters to vote for a team ticket from one party, by not allowing them to split votes between president and members of Congress.
- Instituting four-year terms for House members and eight-year terms for Senators so that each institution could be substantially changed in election years and presidents would be allowed four full years to implement change without the usual losses by their party in off-year elections.

---

[71]See Mezey, *Congress, the President, and Public Policy,* p. 125.

[72]See the analysis in Gary W. Cox and Samuel Kernell, *The Politics of Divided Government* (Boulder, CO: Westview Press, 1991), pp. 4–8.

[73]See Cox and Kernell, *The Politics of Divided Government,* p. 7.

[74]See James P. Pfiffner, "Divided Government and the Problem of Governance," in James A. Thurber, ed., *Divided Democracy* (Washington, DC: CQ Press, 1991); and "The President and the Postreform Congress," in Roger Davidson, ed., *The Postreform Congress* (New York: St. Martin's Press, 1992).

- Providing for special elections at times of a "failed government" and constitutional deadlock.
- Allowing concurrent service in Congress and the executive branch to facilitate policymaking between the branches.

These proposed reforms are not new to American politics and have been proposed before by those who would move the U.S. system closer to a parliamentary model of government. In a parliamentary system, the executive, ministers, and prime ministers are also members of the legislature, and the institutional rivalry built into the separation-of-powers system is not present.

Other scholars, however, do not see the same problems in divided government as do proponents of the responsible party government model of U.S. democracy. They argue that divided government is merely another wrinkle on the Framers' intention to make it difficult for major change to occur in the American political system. The system will not respond with major change unless there is a consensus in the electorate that change should take place. Without this consensus, they argue, major change is not desirable. They point out that periods of divided government in the nineteenth century occurred during periods of great societal strain, such as the division over slavery, or economic divisions.[75] In this argument, the second half of the twentieth century is a period of political division, and when the major fissures have been resolved, the electorate will give control of the government to one political party again.

Some political scientists have argued that the negative consequences of divided government have been exaggerated by proponents of constitutional change. Senate confirmation of presidential nominations does not seem to be related to divided government, nor does Senate approval of treaties or the frequency of executive agreements.[76] In examining the 1948–1990 period, David Mayhew has found that there was no significant difference between periods of divided and unified party control of the government in two major dimensions of party conflict. Hostile investigations of the executive by Congress are just as likely to occur in periods of unified as divided control of the government. Similarly, significant laws are passed with similar frequency during periods of divided control and periods of unified government.[77] Mayhew argues that we should not be as concerned about presidential success as about the ability of the whole political system to produce significant legislation.

But just because significant laws are passed regardless of unified or divided government, it does not mean that divided government makes no difference. Examining the laws that are passed by Congress does not tell us about laws

---

[75]Fiorina, *Divided Government,* pp. 8–9.

[76]Fiorina, *Divided Government,* pp. 96–103.

[77]David Mayhew, *Divided We Govern* (New Haven, CT: Yale University Press, 1991).

that might have been passed but were not because of divided government. Systematic examination of potentially significant measures that were considered but not passed during the same period examined by Mayhew reveals that divided government has a considerable impact. Edwards et al. found that the presence of divided government increases the number of bills that presidents will oppose from 12 to 37 percent. They also found that the odds that potentially significant legislation will fail are increased by 45 percent. Divided government does not, however, affect the ability of presidents to block laws they oppose, which they can do more than 90 percent of the time in any case. Nor does it affect the ability of presidents to get passed measures that they endorse, since divided government is only one of several factors that affect presidential success.[78] In addition, the period 1948–1990 was characterized by internally divided political parties. There is some evidence that in the 1990s we entered into an era of relatively more cohesive and ideologically polarized parties. If so, Mayhew's argument that divided government makes little difference might be less applicable.

So divided government does make a difference, but primarily by decreasing the amount of potentially significant legislation that is passed. It is one of many factors that affect presidential legislative success and the ability of our system to produce important public policy. Those who are concerned about the seeming gridlock of American government and the seeming inability of the political system to deal with pressing public policy issues, whether by eliminating the deficit or by pursuing a consistent foreign policy, must look deeper than divided government to solve our problems.

While the problems of gridlock may be real, their ultimate cause is likely to be a genuinely divided electorate whose contradictory wishes are accurately reflected in the divided governments sent to Washington. Most citizens may want a balanced budget, but significant minorities would balance it in mutually exclusive ways. Most citizens may want universal health care, but no coalition may exist to support any one way to achieve the general goal. In general, most voters may be dissatisfied with the status quo, but significant minorities would move in opposite directions to change it.[79]

CONCLUSION

Modern presidents have had varying degrees of success with Congress. President Kennedy's liberal policies did not get enacted until the Johnson administration. After Johnson's Great Society legislative victories, he lost favor in Con-

---

[78]George C. Edwards III, Andrew Barrett, and Jeffrey Peake, "The Legislative Impact of Divided Government," *American Journal of Political Science* 41 (2) (April 1997), pp. 545–563.

[79]See Morris Fiorina, *Divided Government,* 2nd ed. (Boston: Allyn and Bacon, 1996), pp. 173–177.

gress over Vietnam and decided not to run for a second term of his own. President Nixon's confrontational actions did not accomplish most of what he attempted, and he ended up resigning in disgrace. President Ford's vetoes deflected the Democrats' policies but did not achieve his own agenda. President Carter did not achieve as much as he might have had he handled his congressional relations differently. President Reagan's initial budgetary leadership quickly dissipated, and confrontation with Congress marked most of his term. President Bush's virtually unbroken string of vetoes did not bring him a strong record on which to run in 1992. President Clinton had mixed success with Congress, and his confrontations with the Republican 104th Congress played a role in his reelection.

In evaluating how different presidents have dealt with Congress, it is important to remember that the Framers put Congress in Article I of the Constitution for a reason: they expected that Congress would dominate the national policy agenda. It is easy to lose sight of this historical reality when considering the modern presidency. Presidents now have many more resources to influence Congress, they are regularly active in doing so, and we expect them to try. But despite our expectations, and the famous legislative victories of Presidents Franklin Roosevelt, Lyndon Johnson, and Ronald Reagan, the president remains in a relatively weak position with respect to Congress.[80] Even the most successful presidents could not sustain their initial string of victories, and their legislative performance soon fell off. Public popularity of presidents can help them when it is high and undermine them when it is low, but popularity by itself cannot guarantee legislative success.

---

[80]See George C. Edwards, *At the Margins* (New Haven, CT: Yale University Press, 1989); Jon R. Bond and Richard Fleisher, *The President in the Legislative Arena* (Chicago: University of Chicago Press, 1990); Mark A. Peterson, *Legislating Together* (Cambridge, MA: Harvard University Press, 1990); and Charles O. Jones, *The Presidency in a Separated System* (Washington, DC: Brookings Institution, 1994).

Seven

THE PRESIDENT AND NATIONAL SECURITY

Of all the constitutional powers and political roles of the president, perhaps the most vital is the direction of national security policy. As John Kennedy said: "The big difference [between domestic and foreign policy] is that between a bill being defeated and the country [being] wiped out."[1] In the mid-twentieth century the pressures of the Cold War with the Soviet Union tended to make U.S. policymakers view all aspects of foreign policy, not only military policy, as aspects of national security policy. Later in the century, increasing global economic interdependence, including balance of trade issues and energy dependence, made the performance of the American economy a vital element of national security.

This chapter will consider three major aspects of the presidency with respect to national security: the constitutional powers of the president, the growth of the institutional capacity of the White House to dominate foreign policy, and the leadership styles of different presidents in crisis situations. The chapter has a dual theme: centralization of control in the presidency and the constitutional balance with Congress. The modern presidency has seen the development of a large and expert National Security Council staff, whose policy-development functions often overshadow the Departments of State and Defense. This increased control has favored the president in the struggle with Congress over the direction of U.S. foreign policy. The Congress, however, has used its own constitutional authority to assert its prerogatives. The chapter will conclude that Congress now is much more active in affecting U.S. foreign policy, but that the president continues to dominate the war power.

In formulating the Constitution the Framers were faced with the dilemma of designing a government not too weak to act, as under the Articles of Confederation, but one that was not so strong that it would abuse its power. With respect to the chief executive, the office had to be powerful enough to defend the nation and lead the government in times of emergency. But the danger was

[1]Quoted in Michael Nelson, ed., *Congressional Quarterly Guide to the Presidency* (Washington, DC: CQ Press, 1989), p. 497.

that a too-powerful president might abuse power, as had the various monarchs in European history who were fresh in the minds of the Framers. The Framers were determined that the power to take the nation to war would not be entrusted to an executive who might gather tyrannical power, and so the "power of the sword" was split between the president and Congress.

In this division the president's power was designated by the conferring of an office, the "Commander in Chief of the Army and Navy." Other foreign-policy powers included the right to "receive ambassadors from other nations" and the right to make treaties, subject to advice and consent of the Senate. In contrast, Congress was given a number of specific powers and duties: "To declare War, grant Letters of Marque and Reprisal . . . To raise and support Armies . . . ; To provide and maintain a Navy, To make Rules for the Government and Regulation of the land and naval forces . . . To provide for calling forth the militia. . . ."

This formula for sharing the foreign-policy and war-making powers between the president and Congress led the distinguished presidency scholar, Edward S. Corwin, to declare that the constitutional provisions constituted an "invitation to struggle" for the control of foreign policy.

The argument of this chapter is that the presidency has come to dominate the foreign policy of the United States, and this trend has been accelerated in the post–World War II years of the Cold War. Advances in the technology of communication and warfare have made this inevitable. After the "imperial presidencies" of Johnson and Nixon, Congress began to assert itself in many aspects of foreign policy, but the war-making power is still dominated by the president. An important aspect of this domination is the increasing centralized White House control of the formulation of foreign policy. What in the past had been the main responsibility of the executive branch Departments of State and Defense, after 1960 came to be dominated by the president's assistant for national security affairs. In the final part of the chapter, these themes will be illustrated with contrasting examples of crisis decision-making by several presidents.

THE WAR POWER

The most far-reaching power of modern chief executives is the ability to engage their nations in war, especially in the modern age when millions of lives may be lost and the destructive potential of nuclear weapons has the frightening capacity to make much of the globe uninhabitable. In deliberating over the war power, the delegates to the Constitutional Convention were concerned that one person not be able to commit the country to war. An early draft of the Constitution provided that Congress be given the power to "make war." But since Congress would not always be in session and the nation might have to respond to sudden attacks, the wording was changed to "declare" war, so that the president could respond quickly to emergency situations.

In the debate over the Constitution, James Madison wrote that the "fundamental doctrine of the Constitution" was:

> That the power to declare war is *fully* and *exclusively* vested in the legislature; that the executive has no right, in any case, to decide the question, whether there is or is not cause for declaring war; that the right of convening and informing Congress, whenever such a question seems to call for a decision, is all the right which the Constitution has deemed requisite or proper . . . [for the President].[2]

Alexander Hamilton, one of the foremost exponents of a strong executive in the constitutional debate, defined the commander in chief power in *Federalist* No. 69:

> It would amount to nothing more than the supreme command and direction of the military and naval forces, as the first general and admiral of the Confederacy; while that of the British king extends to the *declaring* of war and to the *raising* and *regulating* of fleets and armies—all which, by the Constitution under consideration, would appertain to the legislature.[3]

Hamilton defined the war power as: "when the nation is at peace, to change that state into a state of war; whether from calculations of policy or from provocations or injuries received: in other words, it belongs to Congress only, to go to war."[4] There can be little doubt that the Framers intended to give the war power to Congress.

Despite this clear intention on the part of the Framers, the exigencies of international relations, precedents set by strong presidents, and the technologies of the twentieth century have all combined to make the president the dominant decision-maker with respect to committing the nation to war. Congress has often been more hawkish than the president, and has often consciously delegated sweeping powers to the president for purposes of national security. If there is a difference of opinion over the wisdom of military action, it is most often the president who has prevailed.

While the president has committed U.S. troops to combat more than 100 times over the past two centuries, most of these actions have been relatively minor incidents intended to protect American lives or property from pirates or

---

[2]Gaillard Hunt, ed., "Letters of Helvidius, No. 1," in *The Writings of James Madison,* vol. 6 (Putnam, 1900–10), p. 174; quoted by Robert A. Katzman, "War Powers: Toward a New Accommodation," in Thomas E. Mann, ed., *A Question of Balance* (Washington, DC: Brookings Institution, 1990), p. 38.

[3]*The Federalist Papers* (New York: Mentor Books, 1961), p. 418.

[4]Quoted by Michael J. Glennon, "The Gulf War and the Constitution," *Foreign Affairs* 70 (2) (Spring 1991), p. 88.

revolutionary factions, rather than attacks on sovereign nation-states.[5] Congress has declared war only five times in the nation's history:

The War of 1812 (fought against the British)

The War against Mexico in 1846 (to acquire disputed territory)

The Spanish-American War in 1898 (over Caribbean and Pacific parts of the Spanish empire)

World War I in 1918 (to prevent Germany from dominating Europe)

World War II in 1941 (to defeat Germany and Japan)

The United States has also engaged in major undeclared wars, including the Civil War, that for various political and legal reasons were never declared by Congress.

With respect to the constitutional balance between the president and Congress, the important issue is whether the decision to go to war is shared as intended by the Constitution. It is to be expected that, in times of war, power will flow to the chief executive. There is a need for unified leadership of the country in times of threat, and the president commands the bureaucratic apparatus to wage war: the military services, intelligence-gathering agencies, and the diplomatic capacity of the State Department. In addition, Congress has been willing to delegate sweeping powers to the president during wartime as the nation rallies behind the commander in chief.

The major wars of the twentieth century have been different in kind from the military conflicts of the nation's first century. World War I involved the massive mobilizing of the nation's resources, and Congress delegated unprecedented control of the national economy to President Wilson under the Lever Food and Fuel Act and over the executive branch in the Overman Act.

World War II

World War II saw even more far-reaching power delegated to and claimed by President Franklin Roosevelt. The 1930s were a time of isolationist fervor in the United States, when the public was fearful of being drawn into the coming European war. But as Hitler began to conquer much of eastern Europe, occupied France, and threatened England, President Roosevelt became convinced that the United States would have to enter the war to save England and, ultimately, the United States. At Prime Minister Winston Churchill's desperate request as a "matter of life or death," Roosevelt traded with Britain fifty U.S. destroyers of World War I–vintage for rights to military bases in the Atlantic and Caribbean. He did not ask the Senate to ratify a treaty because he knew it would likely be defeated, but accomplished the trade through executive order after

[5]See Arthur Schlesinger, Jr., *The Imperial Presidency* (Boston: Houghton Mifflin, 1989), p. 443.

consulting with congressional leaders. In 1941 Congress passed the Lend-Lease Act, giving Roosevelt the authority to continue his economic trades and delegating unprecedented economic and military powers to him short of authorizing direct military intervention.

Roosevelt's task of convincing the nation that war was the only way to protect U.S. security was solved by the Japanese attack on Pearl Harbor, Hawaii, on December 7, 1941. Congress immediately declared war on Japan and Germany, and the United States committed its full economy and military might to defeat the Axis powers. Roosevelt's powers during the war were even more sweeping than those delegated to Wilson. He directed the economy, created executive branch agencies, and exercised wide-ranging emergency powers. He even threatened to ignore a law (concerning price controls) passed by Congress if it were not revised to meet his objections. The war ended with many emergency powers of the president still in effect, but their exercise was not seen as necessary by President Truman.

Korea

When North Korean troops invaded South Korea on June 24, 1950, President Truman, after consulting with his advisors, but not Congress, decided to commit U.S. troops to defend South Korea. Within a few days, the United Nations Security Council had met and called for a international effort to drive the North Koreans back above the thirty-eighth parallel. Truman claimed the authority to send troops under the commander in chief power and the UN resolution. On June 27 he met with a delegation from Congress that expressed support for his actions, though some complaints were made that he should have asked for formal congressional approval. With general political support from Congress, Truman decided not to ask for formal approval and to risk a split vote or a debilitating debate.

As U.S. forces under General Douglas MacArthur were successful in pushing back North Korean forces over the thirty-eighth parallel, pressure began to grow for the full defeat of North Korea and the reunification of the country under non-Communist rule. When MacArthur pushed further north toward the Yalu River, the border with Communist China, China entered the war and drove U.S. forces back to the south, beginning a protracted war of stalemate. MacArthur's public disagreement with the president over the conduct of the war provoked Truman to fire him, asserting in a very visible way the primacy of civilian control of the military under the U.S. Constitution.

Congressional support for Truman's early actions in the war gradually evaporated as the war waged on, and U.S. forces suffered heavy casualties after the entry of the Chinese. Public and congressional disenchantment with the war eventually forced the United States to disengage. After a prolonged period of negotiations, and after Eisenhower had been elected president, an armistice was signed on July 27, 1953. But an important constitutional precedent had been set by Truman's failure to consult Congress and ask for its approval to engage in war in Korea.

Vietnam

The United States had been supporting the French in Vietnam during the Eisenhower administration, though Eisenhower refused to commit U.S. forces when the French were finally defeated by nationalist forces at Dien Bien Phu in 1954. John Kennedy felt that the United States had to counter communist movements worldwide, and by the time of his death had sent more than 16,000 military advisors to support the South Vietnamese government. Lyndon Johnson had promised in the presidential campaign of 1964 to limit U.S. military involvement, but by the summer of 1965 he had begun the escalation of military actions against the communist North Vietnam and Vietcong guerillas in the South. In 1965, he changed the U.S. role from support of the South Vietnamese government to direct participation in the war by bombing North Vietnam and ordering 50,000 more U.S. troops to the South. Eventually U.S. troop strength was increased to 500,000 troops.

Johnson derived his authority to commit the United States to war in Vietnam from the Tonkin Gulf Resolution. In August 1964, two U.S. destroyers were operating off the coast of North Vietnam in the Gulf of Tonkin and engaged North Vietnamese patrol boats. Johnson reported the incidents to Congress as unprovoked attacks on U.S. military forces and asked for approval of an administration-prepared joint resolution from Congress to sanction U.S. retaliation. Congress quickly passed the resolution, which read in part: "The Congress approves and supports the determination of the President, as Commander-in-Chief, to take all necessary measures to repel any armed attack against the forces of the United States and to prevent further aggression. . . . [T]he United States is, therefore, prepared, as the President determines, to take all necessary steps, including the use of armed force, to assist any member or protocol states of the Southeast Asia Collective Defense Treaty requesting assistance in defense of its freedom."[6]

Although this was not a declaration of war, President Johnson used it as the functional equivalent when he was questioned about the appropriateness of the U.S. presence in Vietnam. In addition, he pointed out the willingness of Congress to continue to appropriate funds for military action.

As with Korea, Congress and public opinion supported the president's actions at the beginning of U.S. involvement. But as the war wore on, and the numbers of U.S. soldiers killed in action mounted, public opinion began to change and congressional dissent grew in stridency. U.S. public opinion was so split over the war that Johnson decided that he would not run for reelection in 1968.

---

[6]Nelson, *Congressional Quarterly Guide to the Presidency,* p. 542.

President Nixon came to office with promises to end the war, but when it became clear that his definition of "peace with honor" necessarily entailed years of further fighting, congressional opposition grew. Nixon's invasion of Cambodia in May 1970, and his secret bombing of Cambodia without congressional authorization, provoked the Congress to try to force the president to end the war. In an amendment to a foreign military-sales bill, the president was forbidden to expend funds on military actions in Cambodia after July 1, 1970. In a series of laws in 1973 and 1974, Congress placed restrictions on the expenditure of funds on military actions in Southeast Asia. There was no question about the authority of Congress to cut off funds for fighting.

The war in Vietnam was the second major nondeclared war after World War II, though the president had congressional approval in the Tonkin Gulf Resolution. Members of Congress, however, felt that President Johnson used the resolution to justify a much broader involvement than was contemplated when it was passed. The resolution was made in response to a minor naval incident and was used to conduct a major ground and air war. In the eyes of many in Congress, the president had used the resolution as a blank check to pursue his own policies in spite of congressional opposition.

The War Powers Resolution of 1973

In response to what it felt was the abuse of presidential military power by Presidents Johnson and Nixon, Congress passed the War Powers Resolution over President Nixon's veto. Its proponents intended it to correct the constitutional balance and restore the rightful congressional role in committing the nation to war.

The War Powers Resolution provided that the president is permitted to send U.S. forces into combat, "or into situations where imminent involvement in hostilities is clearly indicated by the circumstances," *only* pursuant to:

1. a declaration of war,
2. a specific statutory authorization, or
3. a national emergency created by attack upon the United States, its territories or possessions, or its armed forces.

It provides that the president shall consult "in every possible instance" before committing U.S. troops to hostilities. It required that the president report to Congress in writing within forty-eight hours on any commitment or substantial enlargement of U.S. combat forces abroad. If U.S. forces were committed and there was no approval by Congress, the resolution required that they be withdrawn within sixty days, with the possible extension of thirty more days if the president certifies to Congress that there is an unavoidable military necessity.

The experience with the operation of the War Powers Resolution has generally been unsatisfactory. Beginning with President Nixon's veto, presidents have felt that the law infringes on their constitutional powers as commander in chief. In most instances of the use of military forces since 1973, presidents have reported to Congress only "consistent with" the War Powers Resolution, not "pursuant to" it. This has preserved their position that the law is not constitutional, yet prevented them from being accused of violating its provisions to report to Congress.

From the perspective of Congress, the experience has not been satisfactory either. The law has not been successful in forcing presidents to consult with Congress before introducing military forces abroad, though Congress has mostly been informed immediately before or after the fact, as would have been the case even without the law. The law has not been successful in reasserting Congress' power of the sword, though some argue that it has acted as a restraining influence in how long presidents feel able to leave U.S. troops committed overseas. Senator Thomas Eagleton even argued that the War Powers Resolution provides the president with an undated blank check to use U.S. forces for ninety days without any regard to Congress. He felt that the war powers clause of the Constitution was a more reliable check on the chief executive.

President Ford reported military actions to Congress in three minor actions, as well as his unilateral decision to send troops to rescue the crew of the U.S. ship *Mayaguez* when it was captured by Cambodians in 1975. Forty-one soldiers lost their lives in the rescue mission. President Carter informed Congress after he had sent a small force to attempt to rescue the U.S. hostages in Iran in 1979. The mission was aborted when a helicopter crashed and eight soldiers lost their lives.

President Reagan resisted consulting with Congress about the military actions he initiated overseas. When he decided to increase the number of U.S. troops on a peacekeeping mission in Lebanon in 1982 and 1983, however, he felt the need to negotiate the terms of their stay with Congress. Congress agreed to an eighteen-month period that troops could stay in Lebanon, but after 241 Marines were killed in a terrorist bombing in October 1983, the president withdrew the troops. In 1983, when President Reagan sent U.S. troops to invade Grenada and oust a newly installed Marxist government without reporting to Congress under the provisions of the War Powers Resolution, Congress voted that the sixty-day clock had started when the invasion began. The troops, however, were brought home soon after they had taken control of the island, and the timing became irrelevant.[7]

But the ticking clock provision (the sixty-day period that troops are permitted to remain without congressional approval) pointed to a key weakness of the War Powers Resolution. The problem was that if presidents did not want to officially report their actions according to the provisions, Congress would have to do it for them. But Congress is then faced with the problem of seeming to oppose a presidential action that may be publicly popular. Often it has

[7]See Ellen C. Collier, "The War Powers Resolution: Eighteen Years of Experience," Library of Congress, Congressional Research Service, Report No. 92–133F (February 4, 1992).

not had the resolve to do this, as was evident in the case of U.S. reflagging of Kuwaiti tankers in the Persian Gulf in 1987.

Iran had been attacking Kuwaiti oil tankers in the Persian Gulf, and Kuwait had appealed to the United Sates and the Soviet Union for protection. President Reagan decided to preempt Russian presence in the Gulf by providing naval escorts for the Kuwaiti tankers that would be allowed to fly the U.S. flag. It was quite evident that U.S. naval forces that were deployed to the Gulf were in danger from possible hostilities by Iran, but the president refused to report the action to Congress and start the sixty-day clock ticking. A number of initiatives to begin the clock by Congress failed to gain adequate support. Members of Congress did not want to take the responsibility for undermining the president in the Gulf, but they did not want to legitimize his actions either. They wanted the option to be able to criticize the president if anything went wrong without being implicated in his actions. Luckily, in this case U.S. forces did not become involved in a military fight with Iran.

A key problem with the procedures set up by the War Powers Resolution is that Congress by its inaction can force the president to remove forces from combat. Thus, Congress does not have to take political responsibility for its actions and make tough decisions about war and peace and whether to support the president or not. It can merely wait and decide whether to back the president, if the action is successful, or blame the president, if his actions fail. Presidents naturally resent this unwillingness of Congress to take responsibility. There have been a number of proposals to revise the War Powers Resolution to make it more workable, but none have been acceptable to presidents.

Some scholars have argued that the Supreme Court Chadha decision, which invalidated the legislative veto, also invalidated the War Powers Resolution provision that requires the president to withdraw troops if Congress does not approve of a troop deployment within ninety days. This allows Congress to force presidential action without any specific law that would be subject to a presidential veto. Constitutional Law scholar Louis Fisher, however, argues that the War Powers Resolution does not delegate any congressional authority to the president and thus cannot contain a legislative veto (which, by definition, delegates congressional power to the president). Congress did pass a separate bill to allow a joint resolution (which requires a presidential signature or a veto override to take effect), but the concurrent resolution remains in the War Powers Resolution.[8]

The Persian Gulf War

When the forces of Saddam Hussein invaded and occupied Kuwait in August 1990, President Bush decided that it was imperative for the United States to respond militarily in order to protect Saudi Arabia and its oil fields from capture by Iraq. After convincing the Saudis to accept U.S. troops, he deployed

[8]See Louis Fisher, *Presidential War Power* (Lawrence: University Press of Kansas, 1995), pp. 194–197.

about 200,000 troops in defensive positions along the Saudi-Kuwait border. Though he did not consult Congress, after it was back in session each house passed resolutions of support for the president's actions. By then the president had widened U.S. goals in the Gulf to include forcing Iraq to leave Kuwait.[9]

During the fall of 1990, President Bush became convinced that the U.S. policy of economic sanctions against Iraq would not be successful in forcing Iraq out of Kuwait. When the president announced immediately after the 1990 elections that troop levels in the region would be doubled, it was clear that the administration was preparing for an offensive action against Saddam Hussein. Concerns were raised throughout the country and in Congress that the United States might engage in war prematurely, and there were questions about whether the aims of a possible war were worth the likely price in U.S. lives.

The Democratic leadership in Congress was faced with a dilemma. Memories of the 1964 Gulf of Tonkin Resolution were still in its collective memory, and Congress did not want to give the president a blank check to pursue policies over which Congress would have no control. On the other hand, members of Congress wanted to support the president's defensive actions in Saudi Arabia without endorsing an offensive to throw Saddam Hussein out of Kuwait. They did not want to appear to undermine the president or the troops, but they were not willing to endorse a war.

The president's dilemma was that it would be politically useful to get a congressional declaration of support, and it would strengthen his hand against Saddam Hussein. On the other hand, weak support or a split vote would be worse than no vote at all and would encourage Saddam Hussein in his aggression.

Finally, in early January 1991, a resolution of support for the president's actions was debated in Congress. The president won heavily in the House, 250–183, but with a closer vote of 52–47 in the Senate. The resolution that was passed authorized the president to use U.S. armed forces to implement the UN resolution to force Iraqi forces out of Kuwait. The resolution was not a formal declaration of war but, according to Speaker of the House Tom Foley, the action constituted: "the moral and constitutional equivalent of a declaration of war."[10]

The congressional action thus fulfilled the constitutional requirement that Congress participate in the decision to commit the United States to war. But President Bush maintained publicly, even after the war, that he had the constitutional right to make the decision without congressional action. "Though I felt after studying the question that I had the inherent power to commit our forces to battle after the UN resolution, I solicited congressional support before committing our forces to the Gulf war."[11]

---

[9]For an analysis of these issues, see James P. Pfiffner, "Presidential Policy Making and the Gulf War," in Marcia Whicker, Raymond Moore, and James Pfiffner, eds., *The Presidency and the Persian Gulf War* (New York: Praeger Publishers, 1993).

[10]Statement of Tom Foley at a luncheon for the 75th anniversary of the Brookings Institution, Capital Hilton, Washington, DC (May 6, 1991). The author was present.

[11]"Remarks by the President at Building Dedication of the Social Sciences Complex," Princeton University (May 10, 1991), p. 2 of White House press release.

This was an extraordinary claim on the part of President Bush to presidential war power to the exclusion of Congress. Over the history of the United States, most presidential military actions taken without congressional approval were either minor or taken in the press of needed quick military response. This is the type of action Bush took immediately after the invasion of Kuwait by Saddam Hussein. Despite the military implications of this action, there was no constitutional objection by Congress. It was only when the offensive option was considered that the issue of war powers was raised. Even President Truman's actions in Korea were taken in response to a sudden invasion, and the U.S. push into North Korea was decided in the heat of a shooting war.

But President Bush's decision to take the offensive against Saddam Hussein was prepared over a number of months. It was quite obvious to all that the United States was preparing for a major military offensive. If the president would not admit that such a situation fell under the war declaration clause of Article I of the Constitution, it is hard to see what the independent role of Congress would be in committing the nation to war.

While some might be willing to trust the goodwill of a president like George Bush for vital decisions of war and peace, the separation of powers system was designed to prevent the exercise of arbitrary powers by anyone who might occupy the office of president. As Justice David Davis argued in *Ex Parte Milligan*:

> This nation, as experience has proved, cannot always remain at peace, and has no right to expect that it will always have wise and humane rulers, sincerely attached to the principles of the constitution. Wicked men, ambitious of power, with hatred of liberty and contempt for law, may fill the place occupied by Washington and Lincoln; and if this right is conceded, and the calamities of war again befall us, the dangers of liberty are frightful to contemplate.[12]

OTHER CONSTITUTIONAL POWERS

Besides the commander-in-chief power, the most important constitutional power of the president in foreign affairs is the authority to negotiate and sign treaties. Article II gives the president the authority "by and with the Advice and Consent of the Senate, to make treaties, provided two-thirds of the Senators present concur." The most important international commitments of the country are made by treaties, e.g., international alliances of mutual protection, the conclusion of wars, and territorial agreements.

Early in his presidency, George Washington attempted to consult with the Senate on the provisions of a treaty he was negotiating with the Creek Indians. The Senate delayed its reply and did not satisfy Washington with its eventual action. After that time, Washington interpreted the clause "advice and consent"

---

[12]*Ex Parte Milligan 4 Wall.* (71 U.S.) 2 (1866) 246, 249.

to include merely the submission for Senate consent treaties he had negotiated and not consultation with the Senate during negotiations. The precedent has remained as constitutional practice ever since, even though political caution may convince presidents to consult with some members of the Senate during negotiations. The Senate may, however, make changes in treaties negotiated by the president and leave to him the decision whether to sign them or not. This happened when President Carter negotiated the treaty with Panama that phased out U.S. control over the Panama Canal. The Senate insisted on several changes in the understanding, and Carter was forced to accept them in order to win a close vote (68–32) for ratification of the treaty in 1978.

While virtually all treaties (about 99 percent) are approved by the Senate, ratification is not automatic, and about 15 percent are approved only after changes demanded by the Senate.[13] The most famous instance of a treaty being rejected by the Senate was the Treaty of Versailles that ended World War I. President Wilson had gone to Europe to negotiate the treaty himself, and had failed to consult or even inform the Senate of the terms he was negotiating. One of the provisions that was included, at the insistence of Wilson, was the creation of a League of Nations. When it became clear that the Senate would not approve any treaty that included the league, Wilson continued to insist on it, and the treaty went on to defeat in the Senate.

The ability of a president to end a treaty agreement was established by the Supreme Court after President Carter decided, in 1978, to establish full diplomatic relations with the People's Republic of China and terminate the Mutual Defense Treaty of 1954 with the Republic of China (Taiwan). Senator Barry Goldwater filed suit in federal court to challenge Carter's action, arguing the Senate had to approve of treaty terminations. In 1979, the Supreme Court declared that the president has the constitutional authority to terminate a treaty.

The authority to terminate a treaty does not, however, include the authority to change the accepted interpretation of one. In 1985, the Reagan administration decided that it was going to develop parts of its "Strategic Defense Initiative" that included a space-based antimissile system. Opponents of the administration in Congress objected that this would violate the 1972 Antiballistic Missile (ABM) Treaty with the Soviet Union. This new interpretation of the 1972 treaty constituted a break with the interpretation of the three previous administrations, but the Reagan administration argued that the executive branch was the sole judge of what a treaty meant. Members of the Senate argued that the president could not unilaterally change the understanding of treaty terms that had been the basis for initial Senate ratification of the treaty. After about a year of confrontation and argument, the administration abandoned its attempt to reinterpret the treaty and proceeded with development of the Strategic Defense Initiative (SDI) that fell within the previously existing interpretation of the 1972 treaty, but without conceding the principle that the president was bound by the original interpretation of treaties.

---

[13]Nelson, *Congressional Quarterly Guide to the Presidency,* p. 1100.

Presidential roles include being a statesman and director of U.S. foreign policy. Here, President Clinton hosts Middle East leaders for peace talks at the White House on October 1, 1996. *(Left to right)* Palestine Liberation Organization (PLO) leader Yasser Arafat, King Hussein of Jordon, President Clinton, and Israeli Prime Minister Benjamin Netanyahu. (AP/Wide World Photos/Wilfredo Lee)

Of course all agreements between nations are not weighty enough to create a formal treaty for each agreement, so for issues of a minor or routine nature the president relies on executive agreements. There is no clear distinction between the two types of agreement except the label and whether it has to be submitted to the Senate for ratification. But the lack of need for Senate approval constitutes a temptation for presidents to accomplish their aims that might not get through the Senate by the use of an executive agreement. The use of executive agreements has proliferated since World War II, with over 10,000 agreements having been made that constitute about 95 percent of all U.S. international agreements.[14] (See Table 7–1.)

When the Senate discovered that the Nixon administration had made a number of secret executive agreements with significant policy implications in its first two years in office, the Congress passed the Case Act of 1972, requiring the ex-

---

[14]Cecil Crabb, *Presidents and Foreign Policy Making* (Baton Rouge: Louisiana State University Press), p. 27. Lock Johnson and James M. McCormick, "Foreign Policy by Executive Fiat," *Foreign Policy,* 28 (Fall 1977), p. 117.

TABLE 7-1
Treaties and Executive Agreements Approved by the United States, 1789-1996

Year	Number of Treaties	Number of Executive Agreements
1789–1839	60	27
1839–1889	215	238
1889–1929	382	763
1930–1932	49	41
1933–1944 (F. Roosevelt)	131	369
1945–1952 (Truman)	132	1,324
1953–1960 (Eisenhower)	89	1,834
1961–1963 (Kennedy)	36	813
1964–1968 (Johnson)	67	1,083
1969–1974 (Nixon)	93	1,317
1975–1976 (Ford)	26	666
1977–1980 (Carter)	79	1,476
1981–1988 (Reagan)	125	2,840
1989–1992 (Bush)	67	1,371
1993–1996 (Clinton, first term)	97	1,137

Note: Varying definitions of what compromises an executive agreement and its entry-into-force date make the above numbers approximate.

Source: 1989–1992 Harold W. Stanley and Richard G. Niemi, *Vital Statistics on American Politics,* 4th ed. (Washington, D.C., CQ Press, 1994), p. 280. Reprinted by permission of Congressional Quarterly Books. Data from 1993–1996 provided to the author by the Office of Treaty Affairs, Department of State.

ecutive branch to report all executive agreements to Congress within sixty days. When it became clear that not all agreements were being reported, legislation was passed in 1977 requiring that Congress be informed of any agreement, written or oral, that might constitute a commitment on the part of the United States.[15]

The president also has the authority to decide which foreign governments the United States will recognize as legitimate by virtue of the constitutional provision that the president shall "receive Ambassadors and other public Ministers." This also implies the ability to conduct the diplomacy of the United States. While the recognition power is most often routine, at times it can be an important policy-determining prerogative. Theodore Roosevelt made the decision to recognize the rebelling government of Panama, making it possible for the United States to build the Panama Canal. Franklin Roosevelt decided, over heavy opposition in the United States, to recognize the government of the Soviet Union in 1933. President Truman decided, over the objection of Secretary of State George Marshall, to recognize the newly declared state of Israel in 1948. Jimmy Carter decided to establish full diplomatic relations with the People's Republic of China in 1977.

The president's constitutional power to appoint ambassadors and other officials of the executive branch also gives the president additional control over foreign and national security policy. The Senate's right to confirm appointments does not often impinge on the president's discretion, but it occasionally provides

[15]Nelson, *Congressional Quarterly Guide to the Presidency,* p. 513.

some leverage. President Carter nominated Theodore Sorensen to be director of the Central Intelligence Agency in 1977, but when it became clear that influential members of the intelligence community would make confirmation problematical, Carter withdrew the nomination. President Bush's first nomination for secretary of defense, John Tower, was defeated in the Senate over a variety of allegations about his personal life and conflicts of interest. This was the first time that a president's choice for his initial cabinet was defeated in the Senate.

Congressional power of the purse has been used increasingly in post-World War II years to influence national security policy. The authorization for defense programs had been on a standing basis, but between 1961 and 1983 Congress increased the percentage of required annual authorizations from 2 percent to 100 percent.[16] Actual appropriations requests from the executive branch have been increasingly altered after the president's budget gets to Congress. In 1970, 180 programs were changed in the authorization process and 650 in appropriations. By 1988, the changes were 1,184 in authorization and 1,579 in appropriations.[17] Congress has also been deeply involved in decisions over procurement and acquisition of weapons systems. At times disagreements with the executive branch stem from policy differences about the desirability and effectiveness of different systems, but at other times they reflect traditional pork-barrel politics, with members of Congress taking care of their own districts.

These congressional actions, among others, have been seen by the executive branch as "micromanagement" of the implementation of national security policy. While this close control of some aspects of national security management by the Congress is frustrating to the president, some of it is a legitimate response to abuses of power and some is encouraged by factions within the executive branch.[18]

The irony of congressional involvement in the management and implementation of national security policy at the end of the twentieth century is that Congress has greater control over more and more details of policy management. In contrast, Congress has less control over the major issues of war and peace.

THE NATIONAL SECURITY COUNCIL DOMINATES THE EXECUTIVE BRANCH

The president has always been in charge of U.S. foreign policy and of the executive branch departments charged with the formulation and implementation of national security policy. During the first 150 years of the Republic, presidents have most often used their secretaries of state and war as their principle advisors in foreign and national security policy.

---

[16]Barry Blechman, *The Politics of National Defense* (New York: Oxford University Press, 1990), p. 31.

[17]Blechman, *The Politics of National Defense,* p. 41.

[18]See James P. Pfiffner, "Congressional Oversight of Defense Management," George Mason University, The Institute of Public Policy, Working Paper 92:12 (April 1992); "The President and the Postreform Congress," in Roger Davidson, ed., *The Postreform Congress* (New York: St. Martin's Press, 1992).

But after World War II a new institutional apparatus was created to deal with national security policy. The National Security Act of 1947 (amended in 1949) created the Department of Defense to give unitary leadership to the military services, the Central Intelligence Agency to replace the Office of Strategic Services, and the National Security Council (NSC) to advise the president.

Ironically, the purpose of early proposals for an NSC, and part of the reason for its creation, was to force the president to consult with military experts in order to ensure more coherent strategic policy and to give a greater role to the military. President Truman soon ensured that he would have complete control of the NSC by insisting that its office be in the Old Executive Office Building (OEOB), immediately adjacent to the White House, rather than in the newly built Pentagon across the Potomac River. He also made the NSC a component of the Executive Office of the President in 1949.[19]

The purpose of the NSC was "to advise the president with respect to the integration of domestic, foreign, and military policies relating to the national security."[20] Its membership consists of the president, vice president, secretary of state, and secretary of defense. The director of central intelligence and the chairman of the joint chiefs of staff are statutory advisors to it. President Clinton in 1993 also included as "Standing Participants" at National Security Council meetings several officials not included by law: Secretary of the Treasury, U.S. Representative to the UN, Chief of Staff, Assistant to the President for Economic Policy, and the Assistant to the President for National Security Affairs (who has always been a participant).[21] In contemporary usage, the term NSC refers to the staff of the council that is directed by the assistant to the president for national security affairs.

Fully aware that support for creation of the NSC in the Republican Congress stemmed from a desire to limit exclusive control of security policy by the president, Harry Truman insisted that its offices be located in the OEOB and purposely downplayed its importance by attending only about one-forth of its meetings before mid-1950. But after the beginning of the Korean War in June 1950, NSC meetings were held weekly and the president presided at them most of the time.[22]

President Truman presided over the creation of the NSC and ensured that it would be a tool of the president, but President Eisenhower institutionalized it. From his experience in World War II he valued thorough staff work and an orderly policy process, so he established a highly regularized process of policy development in the NSC. Within the NSC system, major roles were played by the Planning Board (at the assistant secretary level), which developed policy-planning papers, and by the Operations Coordinating Board (at the undersecretary level), which ensured implementation of policy decisions by the pres-

---

[19]See the analysis of John Hart, *The Presidential Branch* (New York: Pergamon Press, 1987), p. 65.

[20]Hart, *The Presidential Branch*, p. 65.

[21]*United States Government Manual 1996/1997* (Washington, DC: Government Printing Office, 1996.

[22]Hart, *The Presidential Branch*, p. 67.

ident. Ideas would have to be walked up a "policy hill" in their development, through the committees to the top where they would be considered by the NSC. When the president had made a decision, they would be walked down the other side of the hill to ensure proper implementation.[23]

Eisenhower used his NSC as he used his cabinet: as a deliberating body where policy options would be fully discussed and any difference among advisors or the different departments and agencies would be ironed out. There was never any doubt that final decisions belonged to the president, and as they were made, they were duly recorded and followed up by the OCB. Eisenhower upgraded the role of executive secretary of the NSC by creating the position of special assistant for national security affairs to manage the NSC staff. Eisenhower's first special assistant, Robert Cutler, firmly believed that his role was to coordinate the national security policy process. He felt that he was in charge of the National Security Council staff rather than national security policy, a distinction that would be lost on some future national security assistants.[24]

While the processes of the NSC were orderly and ensured presidential control and follow-through, the system was criticized in Congress as being too cumbersome and bureaucratic. Senator Henry Jackson held hearings, which reported that "The root causes of difficulty are found in overcrowded agenda, overly elaborate and stylized procedures, excessive reliance on subordinate interdepartmental mechanisms," and his committee recommended that the process be "deinstitutionalized."[25]

When John Kennedy came to office he intended to do precisely that. He disbanded the interagency committees of the NSC and replaced the regular meetings with a more ad hoc approach to dealing with discrete issues one at a time. Kennedy preferred smaller and more informal meetings to larger, formal ones. Kennedy increased the influence of the special assistant when he moved McGeorge Bundy into a west wing office after the Bay of Pigs disaster. His choice of Bundy was also significant because Bundy was a substantive expert on foreign policy, who played an active role in policymaking, not merely a process manager, as were previous special assistants. Bundy stayed on in the beginning of Lyndon Johnson's presidency and was later replaced by Walt Rostow.

The role and relationship to the president that Bundy had initiated with JFK was enlarged and brought to its peak by Henry Kissinger. From the beginning, Kissinger intended to dominate national security policymaking, and he engineered the return to a more formalized process in order to do it. Pursuant to a plan that President Nixon signed the day of his inauguration, he established interdepartmental groups (IGs), at the assistant secretary level, and the Senior Review Group (SRG). The IGs were chaired by State Department of-

---

[23]See John Prados, *Keepers of the Keys* (New York: William Morrow, 1991), pp. 57–96.

[24]See Anna Kasten Nelson, "National Security I: Inventing a Process 1945–1960," in Hugh Heclo and Lester Salamon, eds., *The Illusion of Presidential Government* (Boulder, CO: Westview Press, 1981), p. 250.

[25]Hart, *The Presidential Branch,* p. 70.

ficials, but the SRG was chaired by Kissinger, and no policy proposal could get to the president until it had passed through Kissinger's hands.

While Kissinger's control of the process was virtually complete, this was possible only because Richard Nixon wanted it that way and had full confidence in Kissinger. Nixon intended to be his own secretary of state because he distrusted the State Department as too tied to the eastern establishment and felt that his own foreign policy experience was sufficient for the conduct of foreign policy.

Kissinger recruited a first-rate staff from throughout the government and academia. In effect, he created a counterbureaucracy in the White House to give him an independent policy-formulation capacity. He could use the Departments of State and Defense, but he was not dependent on them. He had his own staff and policy-development capability. Soon after the inauguration, Kissinger began to establish "backchannels" of communication in which key communications from his agents throughout the world could be directed directly to the White House and bypass the State Department.

In addition to his control of the policymaking process, Kissinger changed the traditional role of NSC advisor by becoming the public spokesperson for administration policy and completely overshadowing Secretary of State William Rogers. So complete was Kissinger's domination that he personally conducted the diplomacy for Nixon's highest priority foreign policy initiatives: the opening to China, peace talks with the Vietnamese, and strategic arms limitations talks (SALT) with the Russians. Finally, Kissinger was made secretary of state in fact as well as function. His deputy at the NSC, Brent Scowcroft, became assistant to the president for national security affairs and remained in that position during the Ford administration.

Jimmy Carter came to office determined to restore the traditional role of secretary of state as the primary foreign policy spokesperson for the president, and made that promise to Cyrus Vance when he nominated him. But his appointment of Zbigniew Brzezinski to be assistant to the president for national security affairs made the fulfillment of his promise impossible. Brzezinski had an aggressive personality and strong preferences in foreign policy. By the second year of the administration there were open disputes between the two highest foreign policy appointees of Carter. Their disputes extended to the substance of policy (with Brzezinski taking a much harder line than Vance), as well as to who would speak for the administration short of the president. Predictably, this led to incoherence in the Carter administration's foreign policy and ended in the resignation of Vance after the failed hostage rescue attempt.

Ronald Reagan, in his 1980 campaign, decried this disarray in the nation's foreign policy, and declared that if he were elected he would restore the primacy of the secretary of state.

> The present administration has been unable to speak with one voice in foreign policy. This must change. My administration will restore leadership to U.S. foreign policy by organizing it in a more coherent way. An early pri-

> ority will be to make structural changes in the foreign policy-making machinery so that the secretary of state will be the president's principal spokesman and adviser. The National Security Council will once again be the coordinator of the policy process. . . .[26]

Accordingly, he appointed the formidable Alexander Haig to be secretary of state and the self-effacing Richard Allen to be his adviser for national security affairs. While Haig declared his intention to be the president's "vicar" in foreign affairs, Allen was relegated to reporting to the president through Edwin Meese. Allen was soon eased out of his position, and Haig's deputy, Judge William T. Clark, came to head the NSC staff, with Robert C. McFarlane as his deputy. Despite the naming of George Shultz to be secretary of state, this marked the beginning of the takeover of the nation's foreign policy by the NSC staff.

Under NSC advisers McFarlane and John Poindexter, the NSC staff undertook the sale of missiles to Iran in exchange for U.S. hostages and the diversion of funds from the sales to the Contra rebels in Nicaragua. The arms-for-hostages deal was inconsistent with several U.S. laws and directly contradicted official U.S. policies, though much of it was carried out with the explicit approval of the president. The diversion of funds to the Contras violated U.S. law, and President Reagan denied any knowledge of the illegal activities. In these activities, the NSC staff, which candidate Reagan had promised to make subordinate to the State Department, took control of U.S. foreign policy in the vital areas of the Middle East and Central America.

In the Iran case, it did so with presidential approval but against the strong objections of the secretaries of state and defense. In the Contra case, it acted without the knowledge of the secretaries of state and defense and also without the president's explicit authority. After the Report of the President's Special Review Board (the Tower Commission) was given to the president, the NSC policy process was overhauled in order to ensure that the lack of accountability did not lead to similar incidents in the future.

The development of the national security policy process since 1947 has led to the centralization of control of policy in the White House. While the control of executive branch foreign policy by presidents is one of their constitutional responsibilities, much of the expertise and organizational machinery for policy development and implementation lies with the Departments of State and Defense. The temptation is to try to run everything out of the White House, but significant assets are lost when the cabinet departments are ignored. They contain the institutional memory and professional expertise that is essential to a sound foreign policy. To ignore these assets can very well lead to disaster, as it did in the Iran–Contra scandal.

---

[26]Quoted in I. M. Destler, "National Security II: the Rise of the Assistant," in Heclo and Salamon, *The Illusion of Presidential Government,* pp. 263–264.

PRESIDENTIAL LEADERSHIP AND CRISIS DECISION-MAKING

We will now examine three sets of presidential national security decisions:

Eisenhower and Johnson on Vietnam

Kennedy on Cuba in 1961 and 1963

Carter and Reagan on Iran

The purpose is to show different presidents reacting to crisis situations. The cases will highlight different aspects of presidential leadership, advisory structures, and approaches to decision-making.

Two Decisions on Vietnam: Eisenhower and Johnson

VIETNAM I: EISENHOWER IN 1954 The United States had been involved with Vietnam since the end of World War II, and it had been supporting French interests, which had resulted from their colonial control of Vietnam in the nineteenth century. Vietnamese nationalists fought the Japanese occupation during World War II and shifted their opposition to the French after the war. By 1954, the Vietnamese resistance had taken on a communist ideology and the French were faced with a military defeat at Dien Bien Phu. The United States had been giving the French military aid, but U.S. forces were not directly involved in fighting the Vietnamese. In the early months of 1954, President Eisenhower was faced with the decision of whether to commit U.S. forces to support the French against the communist rebellion.

Eisenhower held weekly meetings of the National Security Council during the crisis period where the issues of U.S. intervention were discussed. The United States did not want to abandon its long-time ally, France, and it particularly did not want Vietnam to fall under the control of a communist government that might be allied with Russia and China and that might aid the subversion of other countries in Southeast Asia. On the other hand, the communist nationalists had wide support in Vietnam, and it was not clear how much of a military commitment would be necessary to keep the communist insurgency from taking control of the country.

In considering the French request for military aid and U.S. interests in the region, the president and his advisers made a thorough analysis of the implications and consequences of a U.S. commitment. The NSC meetings were marked by spirited debate and vigorous give-and-take. The process was designed to highlight any differences of opinion and force proponents to defend their positions. Participants were willing to disagree with the president. The role of Robert Cutler, Eisenhower's special assistant for national security affairs, was to ensure that no differences among the group were ignored and that all alternatives were thoroughly explored.[27]

---

[27]See Fred I. Greenstein and John P. Burke, "Dynamics of Presidential Reality Testing: Evidence from Two Vietnam Decisions," *Political Science Quarterly* (Winter 1989–1990), pp. 557–580.

Eisenhower's NSC process, which had been criticized for being too formal, had the advantage of ensuring that all points of view were examined. Part of this was due to Eisenhower's personality and leadership style. According to Eisenhower, "I know of only one way in which you can be sure that you've done your best to make a wise decision. That is to get all of the people who have partial and definable responsibility in this particular field . . . in front of you and listen to them debate."[28] Eisenhower's final decision was that he would not commit U.S. forces directly in order to aid the French, because if the United States did "the Vietnamese could be expected to transfer their hatred of the French to us," and "This war in Indochina would absorb our troops by divisions!"[29]

VIETNAM II: JOHNSON IN 1965 Eleven years later, President Lyndon Johnson was faced with the decision of whether to commit U.S. combat forces to Vietnam. When the French left Vietnam, President Kennedy decided that it was in the U.S. interest to continue to try to keep Vietnam from being controlled by a communist government, and he sent 16,000 U.S. military personnel to act as advisers to the government of South Vietnam, who were fighting Vietcong guerillas and forces from North Vietnam. Lyndon Johnson felt that U.S. interests demanded continued support for the government of South Vietnam, but he was unwilling to make a public commitment until after the 1964 election, which he won in a landslide over Barry Goldwater.

The key decisions to escalate the U.S. military commitment were made by Johnson and his advisers in early 1965. When communist forces attacked an American air base at Pleiku, Johnson ordered retaliatory air strikes against the North. Soon after that the decision was made to undertake sustained bombing of the North, and not only in response to specific incidents. Without fanfare, ground and support troops were sent to protect U.S. air bases. By July 1965, U.S. troops in Vietnam had increased to 180,000 and President Johnson had committed the United States to large-scale military action in South Vietnam.

One of the striking aspects of the series of decisions that resulted in the open-ended commitment of U.S. troops to Vietnam, with a peak of 500,000 troops in the country and 58,000 U.S. deaths, was the lack of rigorous analysis of the full implications of the 1965 decisions. The meetings called by the president during the early spring took place in a crisis atmosphere, and the discussions were "singularly devoid of analysis."[30] There was little exploration of the differences of opinion among his advisors, and there was no analysis of the long-term implications of the commitment of combat forces.

Johnson dominated the NSC meetings and did not encourage the presenta-

---

[28]Quoted by John P. Burke and Fred I. Greenstein, *How Presidents Test Reality* (New York: Russell Sage Foundation, 1990), p. 54.

[29]Greenstein and Burke, "Dynamics of Presidential Reality Testing," p. 564.

[30]Greenstein and Burke, "Dynamics of Presidential Reality Testing," p. 565.

tion of differing views, as Eisenhower had.[31] There were significant differences of opinion about the wisdom of escalating the war. General Maxwell Taylor, Senator Mike Mansfield, and George Ball all expressed reservations, but their objections were never thoroughly explored and defended at a full meeting of Johnson's advisors. When Mansfield expressed disagreement with the decision for a U.S. air strike, Johnson reacted so emotionally against him that Mansfield communicated his future disagreements with Johnson by way of private memo rather than by speaking up at meetings. McGeorge Bundy laid out differences among his advisors in a memorandum on July 1, 1965, but the memo was not taken up at the next-day NSC meeting.[32] The meetings often ended with an unwarranted feeling of unanimity about the direction of U.S. policy in Vietnam.

While it is not obvious that Johnson's final decisions about Vietnam would have been any different had his NSC process been more systematic, scholars Fred Greenstein and John Burke describe the process as an "organizational shambles." "It was marked by the absence of regular meetings and routinized procedures, shifts in the membership of advisory and other decision-making groups, a reliance on out-of-channel advocacy, and other impediments to rigorous policy analysis."[33] Had Johnson insisted that his advice be more systematically organized, at least the broader implications would have been more fully explored and the decisions would have been better informed. The system also suffered because Bundy took the role of advocate rather than the role of neutral broker or process manager, whose job it was to ensure that all points of view were forcefully expressed and fully explored.[34]

These two cases on Vietnam illustrate important differences between the two presidents. Eisenhower was an experienced military leader, and his White House national security decision-making structure was designed to explore the full implications of important decisions in a deliberative manner. Lyndon Johnson's main strength was domestic politics, and his approach to decision making was much less formal than Eisenhower's. Johnson's personal style led to his domination of meetings and the unwillingness of subordinates to voice their doubts about the wisdom of LBJ's inclinations.

It is also striking that Eisenhower, the military leader of the victorious allies in World War II, was skeptical of the efficacy of U.S. military action in

---

[31]Chester Cooper described the atmosphere of NSC meetings: "During the process I would frequently fall into a Walter Mitty-like fantasy: when my turn came I would rise to my feet slowly, look around the room and then directly look at the president and say, very quietly and emphatically, 'Mr. President, gentlemen, I most definitely do *not* agree.' But I was removed from my trance when I heard the president's voice saying, 'Mr. Cooper, do you agree?' And out would come a 'Yes, Mr. President, I agree.'" Quoted in Larry Berman, *Planning a Tragedy: the Americanization of the War in Vietnam* (New York: Norton, 1982), p. 3.

[32]Greenstein and Burke, "Dynamics of Presidential Reality Testing," p. 571.

[33]Greenstein and Burke, "Dynamics of Presidential Reality Testing," p. 575.

[34]See Alexander L. George, *Presidential Decisionmaking in Foreign Policy* (Boulder, CO: Westview Press, 1980).

Southeast Asia, while Johnson was much more optimistic. Of course, the historical context of the two decisions was different, with the Cold War hotter in the 1960s than the 1950s. But in retrospect, Eisenhower's reticence was more farsighted than Johnson's optimism about the role of U.S. military forces in the political and military context of Vietnam.

Two Decisions on Cuba: Kennedy's Lessons

CUBA I: BAY OF PIGS, 1961 In 1959, Fidel Castro led a revolution in Cuba that overthrew the discredited Batista regime and drew Cuba into the communist camp. The Eisenhower administration saw this as a threat to U.S. interests, and after urging by Vice President Nixon, the CIA began in the spring of 1960 to plan to overthrow the Castro regime. Anti-Castro exiles were organized into a military force and trained in Guatemala, with the hope of invading the island to wrest control from Castro.

When President Kennedy came to office, he was briefed on the plans and gave his approval for further planning. In March 1961, the fully developed plan was presented to the president. It called for an invasion of the island at Trinidad, with the invading brigade of Cuban exiles being supported by U.S. air cover. The invasion was expected to precipitate a popular uprising against Castro and lead to his overthrow. The fallback, in case the invading forces were not victorious, was for the surviving exiles to retreat into the adjoining mountains and organize guerilla resistance to the Castro regime.

Kennedy was reluctant to provoke a confrontation with Russia, which was supporting Castro, and decided that no U.S. forces would be allowed to participate and that the "noise" level should be kept down by moving the invasion away from the major city to the Bay of Pigs. But he was also reluctant to stop the plan. During the 1960 presidential campaign he had criticized the Eisenhower administration for not moving more vigorously against Castro, and he did not want to be accused of being soft on communism. It would have been difficult to keep secret a decision not to move forward because the disappointed exile brigade would have talked to the press, and he would have been accused of passing up a chance to get rid of Castro.

So the modified plan for the invasion was approved and in April 1961 the invasion took place, but not according to plan. Kennedy relented and allowed one U.S. supporting air mission to take out Castro's air force, but the attack was not fully successful. He did not provide further air cover or allow any other U.S. participation. Castro's air force took control of the skies and defeated the hapless invading force. The switch of the location of the invasion meant there was a swamp between the invaders and the mountains, closing off any means of escape.

The whole incident was a disaster. Kennedy was criticized from the right for not providing sufficient support to ensure a U.S. military victory and the throwing out of Castro. He was attacked from the left for the U.S. backing of an invasion of a sovereign nation. Kennedy took full public responsibility, but his private reaction was "How could we have been so stupid?"[35]

The answer was that the president had not explored fully enough all of the implications of his decision. Because of secrecy concerns he did not allow full staffing-out of the decision, even by experts in the CIA. He asked the Joint Chiefs of Staff for an analysis of the CIA invasion plans, but did not allow them to staff it out fully. Their assessment was the chance for success of the operation was "fair," which Kennedy took to mean reasonably good. But the military assessment meant "fair," as opposed to good or excellent, and the analyst said that his judgment was three to one against success.[36] The CIA incorrectly expected that when the chips were down, and the invading exiles got in trouble, that Kennedy would allow U.S. military support. The expectation that there would be a popular uprising against Castro was unrealistic.

Part of this can be explained by the pressures of transition. The administration was a new team of people who did not yet know each other. They were involved with so many other pressing actions in taking control of the government that they were unable to devote sustained attention to this case. They were reluctant to challenge the expertise of the CIA, who had been working on the plan for a year. They did not want to seem weak by being afraid to take strong military action, and they did not want to be accused of blowing a chance to dethrone Castro. They were also affected by a hubris that often comes with new administrations that gives them the confidence that they are on a roll and can do nothing wrong.

The decision-making process was marked by a number of flaws. Experts who should have been heard from were not apprised of the plans. There was not a full military analysis. The same people who developed the plan in the CIA were trusted to evaluate it objectively. The assumptions underlying the plan were not fully explored and the planners were not pushed.

Kennedy let the CIA advocates of the plan dominate NSC meetings. The Kennedy advisors also suffered from what Irving Janis calls "groupthink." When a small group meets under high pressure there is a tendency for them to develop a defensive attitude about their rectitude and wisdom. They tend to stereotype their adversaries as immoral and stupid and suffer from the illusion of invulnerability. They develop a shared illusion of unanimity because any differences of opinion are not pursued and are seen as a threat to the good of the group.[37]

The implications of the Bay of Pigs invasion were far-reaching. Castro was pushed into further dependence on the Soviets and felt very insecure about a possible future invasion. Khrushchev saw the invasion simultaneously as a sign of weakness, because Kennedy did not ensure a U.S. victory, and as a sign of

[35]Irving Janis, *Victims of Groupthink* (Boston: Houghton Mifflin, 1982), p. 139.

[36]Richard Neustadt and Ernest May, *Thinking in Time* (New York: The Free Press, 1986), p. 142.

[37]Janis, *Groupthink*.

the reckless adventurism of an aggressive U.S. policy against communism. But Kennedy also learned lessons in crisis management that may have saved the world from nuclear war the next year.

CUBA II: MISSILE CRISIS, 1962 On October 16, 1962, President Kennedy was shown reconnaissance photographs of Soviet ballistic missiles that might have contained nuclear warheads being assembled in Cuba. This was the kind of a Russian threat that the U.S. political system would not accept, and Kennedy decided immediately that he had to act. He called together a group of advisors as an Executive Committee (ExCom) of the National Security Council to consider the U.S. response.

The immediate consensus of the group, and Kennedy's first inclination, was that the U.S. should take out the missiles with a quick air strike.[38] But before acting, Kennedy led the group through a series of high-tension meetings over the next thirteen days to decide what to do. The debate considered a range of options, from ignoring the action to a full-scale invasion. In contrast to the earlier Cuban crisis, Kennedy and his civilian advisers did not hesitate to press the military people on recommended options. They discovered that a "surgical air strike" would not do the job. Even a full air attack that would kill many Cubans and Russians, and perhaps provoke Russian retaliation, would not ensure the full destruction of the missiles, and it might leave some with nuclear warheads that could still be launched against the United States.

Kennedy finally decided that a naval blockade would be a way to confront Khrushchev, yet not close off as many options as an air attack would. It would also give Khrushchev time to reconsider his actions and possibly withdraw the missiles. Kennedy was careful not to fall into the groupthink syndrome this time. He deliberately did not attend some sessions of the ExCom so that his presence would not inhibit some of the junior members from speaking their minds. His brother Robert, the attorney general, played the role of inquisitor by carefully questioning the assumptions behind each proposal. Kennedy tried to put himself psychologically into Khrushchev's position and to understand the situation from his perspective. While he thought Khrushchev was duplicitous, he did not think that he was stupid. Despite the need for secrecy in the beginning, outside experts on the Soviet Union were brought into meetings to get their best advice. Weaknesses of each proposed course of action were carefully plumbed and contingency plans were carefully formulated. The group was not forced into an early and false consensus, which was sometimes frustrating, but instead kept open minds, demonstrated by the fact that each member changed his mind at least once during the course of the deliberations.[39]

Kennedy was sensitive to Khrushchev's political and psychological need to save face and not appear to be backing down. So communications were care-

---

[38]Janis, *Groupthink*, p. 143.

[39]Janis, *Groupthink*, p. 152.

fully worded, and Kennedy deliberately refrained from attacking Khrushchev personally. He tried not to back Khrushchev into any corner that would make him feel so trapped that his only option would be to launch a nuclear strike against the United States.

After thirteen days of tension, the crisis ended when Russian ships carrying more missiles turned around rather than confront the American blockade. Khrushchev announced that he would disassemble the missiles already in place in return for a U.S. promise not to invade Cuba. Robert Kennedy also made secret assurances to the Soviet ambassador that U.S. missiles in Turkey would be withdrawn, but this was not acknowledged as part of the deal.

These contrasting cases from the Kennedy administration illustrate several dimensions of presidential decision-making. From Cuba I, we learn the importance of presidential advisory structures. In 1961, the Kennedy administration was new in office, the White House team was not yet fully seasoned, and the president accepted uncritically the advice of the CIA, which was both planner and evaluator of the proposed invasion. The possible consequences of the invasion were not realistically evaluated or fully explored.

In 1963, a more experienced Kennedy paid much more attention to structuring the decision-making process, and he took pains to ensure that a range of options was fully explored. The United States was sensitive to the psychological dimensions of the Soviet leader and was careful not to close off his options prematurely. The failure at the Bay of Pigs had clearly taught Kennedy lessons that led to the peaceful resolution of the 1962 Cuban missile crisis.

Two Decisions on Iran: Carter and Reagan

IRAN I: CARTER AND HOSTAGES TAKEN Both the Carter and Reagan administrations had serious problems with U.S. hostages held by Iran or its agents. The fate of Jimmy Carter's presidency became tangled with Iran when rioting Iranian "students" surrounded and occupied the U.S. embassy in Tehran in November 1979. It had been U.S. policy since the 1950s to support the regime of the Shah, and the U.S. continued to supply him with arms into the 1970s. Thus, when the revolutionary forces led by the Ayatollah Khomeini drove the Shah from the country and took over, they saw the United States as their enemy. While U.S. diplomats were trying to establish relations with the new regime, the embassy was taken over and fifty-three U.S. diplomatic personnel were captured as hostages.

Carter's reaction was to put the White House in a crisis mode to deal with the situation. The problem was that, given the intransigence of the Iranian government and its claimed inability to control the "students" occupying the U.S. embassy and holding the U.S. diplomats hostage, there was not much that Carter could do.

Iranian assets in the United States were frozen and diplomatic pressures were applied, but to no avail. Carter made the release of the hostages his highest priority and cut back on public appearances to work on their release. The news media helped focus public attention on the hostage crisis and the nightly TV news shows reminded viewers how many days had elapsed since the hostages were captured.

Although Carter's public-approval ratings initially went up when the hostages were captured, the longer-term effect of the situation was corrosive. The situation seemed to symbolize the helplessness of the U.S. superpower in the face of a small band of terrorists. Carter's personal political popularity declined and left him vulnerable to a challenge in his own party in the 1980 Democratic primaries and to defeat by Ronald Reagan later in the year.

Though the hostages were Carter's highest priority during his last year in office, there was little he could realistically do to solve the problem. While a military attack would initially have been a popular move with the American public, the hostages would probably have been killed. So Carter seemed helpless in the situation. In April 1980, after months of frustration, Carter ordered a commando raid to attempt to rescue the hostages. The mission was launched by ninety U.S. military personnel. But in a nighttime rendezvous in the desert a helicopter collided with a plane, killing eight men, and the mission had to be aborted. The probability for success of the mission was always minimal since the rescuers would have had to travel to urban Tehran undetected, neutralize all of the guards at the embassy, and extract more than fifty hostages safely.

After the rescue-mission failure, Carter continued to use diplomatic means to try to free the hostages. During the 1980 presidential campaign, the hostage situation made Carter seem weak and ineffectual and was a major factor in his defeat by Ronald Reagan. Although progress in obtaining the release of the hostages was made in the fall of 1980, final agreement was not reached until the last hours of the Carter administration. The hostages were finally released minutes after Ronald Reagan was sworn in as president.[40]

Iran II: Reagan Hostage Release Attempts The fate of the Reagan administration was also to become entwined with hostages in the Middle East. In 1984 and 1985, seven Americans were kidnapped in Lebanon by Shiite Muslims closely connected to the Iranian leadership. Iran and Iraq were at war, and Iran had a desperate need for military equipment and spare parts to fix its weapons, many of which came from the United States during the period it supported the Shah. Several intermediaries proposed a deal that would include the release of the hostages in exchange for the United States supplying spare airplane parts and missiles to Iran.

Through news accounts and appeals from families of the hostages, President Reagan had become extremely concerned with the plight of the hostages, one of whom was a CIA station chief. His concern was reflected by NSC staffers,

[40]For a compelling personal account of the hostage crisis, see the book by Ambassador L. Bruce Laingen, charge' d'affaires of the U.S. embassy in Tehran, when he was taken with the rest of the hostages: *Yellow Ribbon* (Washington, DC: Brassey's, 1992).

who made arrangements to exchange U.S. arms and spare parts for Iranian intervention to have the hostages in Lebanon released. NSC staffers also argued that it was important to try to reestablish U.S. ties to Iran, so that when the Ayatollah Khomeini died, the United States would have some influence in Iran. Iran had been a Cold-War ally of the United States, and the Reagan White House did not want it to fall under Soviet influence. Thus, the hostages deal was intended to strengthen U.S. ties to "moderates" in Iran. Israel also wanted to open ties to Iran and to support it in its war with Iraq. So Israel agreed to ship arms to Iran, which would then be replaced by the United States. Later, the United States shipped arms directly to Iran.[41]

Reagan's decision to trade arms for hostages can be questioned on several grounds, from its wisdom to its legality. First of all, although the NSC staffers believed they were negotiating with "moderates" in the Iranian government, there is some doubt that there were any "moderates" in positions of influence in Iran at the time. Khomeini held tight control of the government, and it is doubtful that he would have allowed any officials not controlled by him to negotiate U.S. arms shipments or the release of the hostages held in Lebanon.

Second, the United States had a firm policy of not negotiating with terrorists for the sound reason that it would merely encourage them to continue their terrorist tactics. President Reagan called Iran part of "Murder Inc." and promised never to make concessions to terrorists. The Carter administration had imposed an embargo on arms shipments to Iran, and the Reagan administration initiated "Operation Staunch," a diplomatic effort to stop U.S. allies from sending arms to Iran. For these reasons, in meetings on the hostage deal, Secretary of State George Shultz and Secretary of Defense Caspar Weinberger vigorously opposed sending arms to Iran. Trading arms in hopes of freeing hostages contradicted long-standing U.S. policies and public statements of President Reagan.

In addition, there was the legal problem of the Arms Export Control Act of 1976, which prohibited the sale of U.S. arms to nations designated as sponsors of terrorism. Iran had been so designated since 1984. Presidential approval of the transfer of U.S. arms from Israel and, later, direct U.S. sales of arms to Iran, appeared to violate this law. In addition, the National Security Act governing covert actions specified that they were to be taken only after an official "finding" by the president that the covert action is important to national security. National Security Adviser John Poindexter testified before Congress that President Reagan had signed such a finding for the earlier approaches to Iran, but that Poindexter had later destroyed it to save the president from possible embarrassment. President Reagan also signed a finding on January 17, 1986, authorizing U.S. direct arms sales to Iran. Public law provides that Congress is to

---

[41]For a vivid account of the futile attempts of Secretary of State George Shultz to stop President Reagan from continuing to try to trade arms for hostages (and even to admit that he was in fact doing so), see George Shultz, *Turmoil and Triumph: My Years as Secretary of State* (New York: Charles Scribner's Sons, 1993).

be notified before covert actions are undertaken, or if that is impossible, "in a timely fashion."[42] Congress did not learn of the arms-for-hostages initiatives until they were disclosed by a Mideast newspaper months later.

The Reagan administration's actions to gain the release of the hostages over the course of several shipments of arms turned out to be futile. Three hostages were released, but three more hostages were captured shortly thereafter. The courting of "moderates" in Iran was also not successful because some of the missiles were inferior equipment, and the Iranians were overcharged for the missiles. How would inferior goods at artificially high prices induce the Iranian "moderates" to undertake a rapprochement with the United States?

These problems deepened when it was disclosed that Oliver North, a Marine Lieutenant Colonel on the National Security Council staff who had done much of the negotiating with Iran, undertook to use the surplus funds from the sales of arms to Iran to support the Contras in Nicaragua during a period when such support was prohibited by law. The constitutional crisis provoked by North's actions will be analyzed in the next chapter.

The two episodes with Iran illustrate several aspects of the presidency, one international and one personal. Presidents must now deal with a modern world where the United States is vulnerable to terrorism of several types for which the U.S. military cannot be effectively used. Despite the most powerful military establishment in the world, the United States could not use that power to save a relatively small number of U.S. citizens held hostage.

The second insight is that U.S. presidents are personally vulnerable to emotional pleas from the families of U.S. citizens in trouble in foreign lands. The plight of the hostages in Iran led President Carter to undertake a highrisk military operation that failed to save the hostages. The plight of the hostages in Lebanon led President Reagan to act contrary to his own principles, counter to declared U.S. policy, and against the advice of his secretaries of state and defense, in a futile attempt to gain the release of the hostages.

CONCLUSION

This chapter has examined some of the most far-reaching and important powers that U.S. presidents wield. The struggle between the president and Congress over the war powers, divided in the Constitution between the two branches, has tilted toward the president in the twentieth century. On the other hand, since the "imperial presidencies" of Johnson and Nixon, Congress has played a more active role in the details of national security and foreign policy.

---

[42]See the discussion in William S. Cohen and George J. Mitchell, *Men of Zeal* (New York: Viking, 1988), pp. 12–13.

Executive branch national security policy development has been centralized and institutionalized in the White House since 1960, as national security issues have become more complex. Presidential crisis decision-making, however, is still highly dependent on personality and context.

An understandable irony of American politics is that presidents who deal successfully with crises—especially via military confrontations—are treated as heroes by the American public. Danger and the possibility for disaster is high, and Americans rightly give credit to leaders who save us from disaster. But the irony of leadership is that the same adulation is not given to those who *prevent* situations from becoming crises in the first place.

For instance, John Kennedy is justly given credit for his effective leadership in the Cuban missile crisis of 1962. His restraint and sensitivity in confronting Khrushchev brought the world back from the brink of nuclear war. Yet, some historians argue that if Kennedy had sent clear early signals to Khrushchev that Soviet missiles in Cuba would be seen as a direct threat by the United States, Khrushchev might not have put the missiles there in the first place.[43]

Similarly, George Bush is justly praised for his leadership as commander in chief of U.S. forces during the Persian Gulf war of 1991. But it is also clear that U.S. policies toward Iraq during the 1980s—to build up its military power as a counterbalance to Iran—encouraged Saddam Hussein and made possible his formidable military capacity and the development of his nuclear weapons program. U.S. actions up to the months before the war continued to support and encourage Saddam Hussein.

Both of these observations are made with the benefit of hindsight, which President Eisenhower used to say is usually more accurate, but much less useful, than foresight. The principle still holds, however, that military leadership is an important dimension of our evaluation of presidents.

[43]See Michael Beschloss, *The Crisis Years* (New York: HarperCollins, 1991), p. 564.

Eight

ABUSE OF POWER AND PRESIDENTIAL REPUTATION

The previous chapters have explored the growing capacity and resources of the presidency. The modern presidency has seen the presidential staff grow in numbers, organizational resources, and power. The need for managerial oversight and limits to that staff power is one of the lessons of the modern presidency. Chapters 1 and 2 explored the relationship of the president with the American public. Chapters 3, 4, and 5 analyzed the growth in importance of the White House staff vis-à-vis the rest of the executive branch, the departments and agencies. Much of this centralization of control and concentration of power has been inevitable, and parts of it are desirable.

Insofar as centralization enables the president to direct the executive branch and be held accountable for his actions it is justified. But the executive branch is far too vast and complex to be run from the White House. To be effective, presidential interventions at the programmatic level must be selective. The theme of Chapters 3, 4, and 5 is that central direction from the White House should be balanced with policy advice and implementation in the departments. Presidents should use, and not let atrophy, the talents of the line officers they appoint and the career executives who run the programs of the government.

Chapters 6 and 7 emphasized the role that Congress plays in the making of public policy and the struggle between the president and Congress over the national agenda. This chapter will take up these themes again. First we will analyze the two most serious and dangerous cases of corruption in the presidency—Watergate and Iran–Contra—most serious because they were carried out at high levels in the White House, and most dangerous because the goals of the actions were the subversion of the legal and constitutional order in the polity. These two scandals were made possible by a large and highly centralized White House staff.

But the danger of these scandals was mitigated by the operation of the constitutionally designed separation of powers system. According to scholar Hugh Heclo:

> [T]he first and, historically speaking, most astonishing answer to the question of what has happened to the separation of powers system is, it has survived. . . . The Founders' mixed view of human nature seems to have gotten it about right: people are bad enough not to be trusted with power

but virtuous enough to govern themselves within properly designed constitutional institutions for allocating power.[1]

Despite the frustrations of modern presidents, the Framers never intended that presidents would be able to dominate the political system. Congress has, at times, overstepped its bounds and interfered with legitimate executive functions. More often, it has abdicated its right and duty to take a clear stand on public-policy issues. It has not asserted itself in confronting budget deficits or presenting coherent foreign policy alternatives to the nation. But whatever the faults and weaknesses of Congress as an institution, we ought not to ignore Article I of the Constitution, as some executivists would have us do. Congress may not always be wise but it is an essential balance and check on the executive. This theme of balance is illustrated in the role that Congress played in the Watergate and Iran–Contra scandals.

In evaluating the presidency in the constitutional system the few cases of corruption and abuse of power raise broad, normative issues. So, also, do questions of the historical reputations of presidents. Presidents sometimes take on mythic qualities after sufficient time has passed, and modern presidents always seem to suffer in comparison to great presidents of the past. This chapter will examine some of the vagaries of presidential reputation and the relationship between short-term popularity and longer-term reputations of modern presidents. Finally, the problem of unrealistic expectations we have of our presidents will be examined.

CORRUPTION AND ABUSE OF POWER

Corruption is no stranger to the American political system, and the presidency is no exception. There are plenty of examples of presidential advisors and cabinet secretaries who have succumbed to temptations to enrich themselves at the public's expense. Some of the larger scandals have involved bribery and illegal gain by presidential aides, and even vice presidents. The Credit Mobilier scandal of the 1870s involved the acceptance by public officials of stock in the Transcontinental Railroad Building Company in order to stop an investigation of profit skimming. President Ulysses S. Grant's vice president, Schuyler Colfax, had accepted some of the railroad stock when he was a member of Congress. Grant's second-term vice president, Henry Wilson, was also implicated in the scheme, and other Grant administration officials were involved in corruption, although Grant himself was cleared of any wrongdoing.[2]

The Teapot Dome scandal during Warren Harding's administration involved the bribery of Secretary of the Interior Albert B. Fall to lease valuable U.S. oil reserves. Fall was paid about $400,000 by two oil companies for granting them leases

[1]Hugh Heclo, "What Has Happened to the Separation of Powers?" in James P. Pfiffner, ed., *Governance and American Politics* (Fort Worth, TX: Harcourt Brace, 1995), p. 297.

[2]Michael Nelson, ed., *Congressional Quarterly Guide to the Presidency* (Washington, DC: CQ Press, 1989), p. 1280.

for the two oil reserves. Fall was eventually sentenced to a year in jail and a $100,000 fine.[3] Several White House aides in the Truman administration were convicted of taking bribes and other unethical advantage of their official positions.[4] Sherman Adams was forced to resign after accepting a vicuña coat and other favors from a businessman who was under regulatory investigation. In the 1960s, Democratic campaign contributor Billy Sol Estes engaged in fraud concerning federal subsidy programs and used his influence in the Department of Agriculture to help his business. Lyndon Johnson protégé Bobby Baker, secretary to the Senate majority, used his influence to obtain a government contract for a friend and was involved in questionable campaign contributions to the Democratic party.[5]

Financial corruption reached the vice-presidential level again when President Nixon's vice president, Spiro Agnew, was forced to resign in October 1973. In a plea bargain, Agnew was allowed to plead nolo contendere to one count of income-tax evasion and was fined $10,000 and given three years of unsupervised probation. If he had not made the deal with prosecutors, the Justice Department was ready to charge him with accepting payoffs from engineering firms that had received contracts when Agnew was county executive of Baltimore County and governor of Maryland. Even as vice president, Agnew continued to receive money (from the firms) from men who came into his office and residence with envelopes containing thousands of dollars in cash. Agnew also received payments for a contract by the General Services Administration when he was vice president.[6]

All of these examples, and there are more of them, involve money and the pursuit of personal gain by government officials. While these are illegal, morally wrong, reprehensible, and undermining of the public trust in government, they are also mundane forms of petty corruption, in the sense that the primary motivation was *personal* greed. When such instances of corruption are discovered, the guilty can be punished and their actions condemned. As bad as these types of crimes are, they are not as corrupting of the public trust as some broader political crimes of abuse of power. These crimes undermine the very fabric of limited and constitutional government by using the power of government not merely for personal gain, but for the more insidious ends of staying in power or undermining the political process.

The Clinton Scandals

During President Clinton's first term a number of ethical issues were raised that suggested potential ethical problems, though no charge of illegality was proved through 1996.

---

[3]Nelson, *Congressional Quarterly Guide to the Presidency,* p. 108.

[4]Richard T. Johnson, *Managing the White House* (New York: Harper & Row, 1974), p. 58.

[5]For details on these and other aspects of political corruption, see Suzanne Garment, *Scandal: The Culture of Mistrust in American Politics* (New York: Times Books, 1991).

[6]Nelson, *Congressional Quarterly Guide to the Presidency,* pp. 1386–1387.

WHITEWATER When he was governor of Arkansas Governor Clinton and his wife, Hillary Rodham Clinton, invested in a vacation development property known as Whitewater with James and Susan McDougal. The McDougals also acquired Madison Guarantee Savings and Loan and mingled the funds between the two enterprises, contributed to Clinton's campaigns, and took over some of the mortgage payments for the Clintons. If any of the funds from Whitewater were illegally diverted from the Whitewater account to Clinton's gubernatorial campaign and Clinton knew about it, he would be subject to prosecution. Or if Clinton, while he was governor (as some charged), had put pressure on David Hale to obtain a government small business loan illegally for Susan McDougal, it would also have made him liable to prosecution.

SEXUAL HARASSMENT A state government employee, Paula Jones, charged that Bill Clinton, when he was Governor of Arkansas, had propositioned her in a hotel room. She said that she rejected the advances but felt intimidated because she worked for the state, and Clinton as governor might have had her fired because of her refusal. The issue was raised to the Supreme Court to decide whether a president could be subject to a civil suit while in office for actions before he was elected, or whether the case could be delayed at the request of the president until the end of the administration. The Court decided that the case could proceed and go to trial, with due consideration for the president's official duties.

WHITE HOUSE TRAVEL OFFICE In May 1993 it was discovered that the head of the White House travel office, who had stayed over from the Bush administration, had deposited more than $50,000 in his personal bank account. He was subsequently fired, along with his subordinates. But in the process of firing them, the White House brought in the FBI to investigate and implied publicly that the financial discrepancies were broader than the evidence warranted. Insofar as White House officials used the FBI to provide an excuse to fire people for political reasons, it was a potential abuse of power.

FBI FILES During Clinton's first term, workers in the White House asked the FBI for the files of people who held White House passes. The FBI sent over about 700 files, but some of the files were on people who had worked for the Bush administration and who did not have current passes to the White House. This raised the possibility that the White House was using the results of FBI investigations for information on prominent Republicans. Insofar as the information might have been used for partisan purposes, it would have been an abuse of power on the part of the Clinton administration.

CAMPAIGN FUND-RAISING After the 1994 midterm elections in which the Republicans regained control of Congress, President Clinton felt great pressure to raise sufficient money for his reelection campaign to preclude a Democratic challenger in the primaries and to mount a credible campaign against the Republicans. While Clinton was successful in raising a record amount of money for the Democratic Party, he was still outspent by the Republicans, and a number of his fund-raising techniques were potentially unethical or illegal. The president was involved in inviting his political supporters to the White House for social events and sometimes to spend the night. His fund-raisers made it clear to campaign contributors that large donations could lead to invitations to the White House. Other administrations had engaged in similar practices, and the line between entertaining friends and selling access to the president is a very fine one. If campaign funds were solicited on federal property, it was illegal, and certainly if any governmental action was promised in exchange for a donation, it would have constituted bribery. In addition, large sums of money were donated to the Democratic National Committee by people who had close connections with foreign countries (the Democratic National Committee returned more than $3 million because of the doubtful provenance of the contributions); it is illegal to accept campaign contributions from foreign citizens or businesses.

These fund-raising practices by the Democratic National Committee and the Clinton White House certainly looked bad, whether or not they were illegal. While other administrations and members of Congress of both parties had engaged in the same or similar practices, the Clinton White House seems to have been more systematic about it. Clinton evidently felt that in the race for funds with the Republicans he had to use every advantage he had; access to himself and the White House was one of those advantages. The defense that others had done similar things was true, but other presidents had not used access to the White House quite so systematically or so brazenly as had the Clinton administration.

While some of these practices and alleged activities fall into the category of personal morality and ethical conduct, there are some potential abuses of power. Using public office improperly to raise money to help stay in office would be a political abuse of power. Insofar as campaign funds were solicited on government property or from banned foreign sources, there were potential violations of the law. If the investigatory power of the FBI had been used for partisan political purposes, it would have constituted a serious abuse of power. If President Clinton had used his power as president to cover up any breaches of the law, it would have been illegal, and he might have been subject to prosecution or impeachment.

The Watergate and Iran–Contra scandals stand out in American history as being in a category by themselves. Watergate involved, among other things, the use of the power of the presidency to illegally undermine political opposition, obstruct justice, and avoid accountability. The term "Watergate," in a narrow sense, refers to the break-in at the Democratic National Headquarters in the Watergate Building in 1972 and the subsequent White House cover-up of the crime. But more loosely the term is used to also include a number of other abuses of power and campaign "dirty tricks" engaged in by the Nixon White House. Iran–Contra involved the concerted effort by White House staffers to avoid the constitutional limits of public law by carrying out, in secret, a policy that the Reagan administration had not been able to accomplish through constitutional political and legislative processes.

Watergate

The seeds of Watergate were contained in the character of Richard Nixon. He was a tragic figure, in the classical sense of the term, because he was capable of greatness, which he showed in some of his foreign-affairs actions. But Nixon felt that his political enemies were out to get him and that he had to use every means at his disposal to fight them. He felt that his election in 1968 gave him a mandate to accomplish his policy goals regardless of the checks and balances in the constitutional system. Three aspects of Nixon's actions will be examined: (1) the pursuit of personal gain, (2) undermining his political opponents, and (3) the Watergate coverup.

Nixon, as president, was not immune from the first type of petty corruption for personal gain. He had his personal residences at San Clemente, California, and Key Biscayne, Florida, improved at taxpayer expense. These included not merely legitimate security measures but also clearly personal improvements, such as a shuffleboard court and a gazebo.[7] Nixon also made unallowable claims concerning the donation of his vice-presidential papers to the National Archives. The Internal Revenue Service ruled that the claimed deductions were not allowed, and forced him to pay back-taxes plus interest for the illegitimate claims. The most damning aspect of this set of actions was the back-dating of papers relating to the donation in order to make him eligible for the deductions that he wrongly claimed.[8]

The second and more important aspect of Nixon's abuse of power involved using the powers of his office to undermine the political opposition and stay in office. Nixon's staffers compiled lists of "enemies" that included a wide variety of persons in the media and entertainment business as well as in political life. The list included ten U.S. senators, African-American congressmen, the Brookings Institution, Common Cause, labor organizations, celebrities, businessmen and corporations, and scholars.[9] The main criterion for being on the enemies list seemed to be political opposition to some aspect of Nixon's political preferences. A constitutional, democratic polity depends, in essence, on the ability of the people to change rulers. This implies the toleration of political opposition and treating them as the "loyal opposition." That is, political opponents are considered loyal to the country and the Constitution even though they want to replace the current rulers by means of democratic elections. The distinction between a loyal opposition and enemies of the state was often lost on the Nixon White House.

The administration attempted to use the IRS to harass some of their "enemies" by having their tax returns audited, and intended to use other govern-

---

[7]Stanley Kutler, *The Wars of Watergate* (New York: Knopf, 1990), p. 433.

[8]Michael Genovese, *The Nixon Presidency* (New York: Greenwood Press, 1990), p. 223.

[9]The list is reproduced in Larry Berman, *The New American Presidency* (Boston: Houghton Mifflin, 1987), p. 279.

mental power to, as John Dean put it, "screw our political enemies."[10] Part of the attempt to ensure Nixon's reelection involved "dirty tricks" to undermine the opposition political-party candidates. Donald Segretti, the person in charge of dirty tricks, drew a $50,000 salary from Nixon's lawyer, Herbert Kalmbach. These tricks were sometimes petty and humorous, as when Segretti once dropped white mice on the floor at a Muskie press conference. The mice had blue ribbons tied to their tails that had "Muskie is a rat fink" printed on them.[11]

The intent of these systematic efforts was to undermine the democratic process by not giving voters a chance to vote for candidates on the merits of their positions, but to undermine their standing with the voters by sabotaging their campaigns. The most important and effective of these dirty tricks was the sabotage of Edmund Muskie's primary campaign for president in 1972. The Nixon White House considered Muskie the most serious potential Democratic presidential nominee, and so they set out to undermine his campaign. In addition to a number of minor harassments, the Nixon operatives stole Muskie for President campaign stationery from his headquarters and sent a letter to Democrats, supposedly from Muskie, accusing his Democratic primary opponents of scurrilous behavior.[12] But the final blow came when the ultraconservative New Hampshire newspaper, *The Manchester Union-Leader,* printed a letter accusing Muskie of insulting Canadian-Americans (calling them "Canucks") and accusing his wife of being an alcoholic. The author of the letter could never be found. In defending his wife at a press conference, Muskie shed some tears, and his candidacy was essentially finished because of the implication that he was not "tough enough" to be president. Muskie's withdrawal set the stage for George McGovern's nomination, the preferred outcome of the Nixon White House.

The Nixon campaign operation, The Committee to Reelect the President (CREEP), raised record amounts of campaign contributions for the reelection effort. The problem was that not all of it was legal. Some of the contributions were not reported as required by law; some of the money was collected illegally from corporations; and some of the funds were illegally "laundered," that is, shifted among various bank accounts to hide the origin of the funds.[13] The administration also raised money by the "selling" of ambassadorships. While many presidents have rewarded big contributors to their campaigns with ambassadorial appointments, the reward is usually not part of an explicit quid pro quo. In the Nixon administration, among other ambassadorial appointments, Nixon fund-raiser Herb Kalmback pled guilty to a charge of promising a federal job in exchange for a campaign contribution.[14]

---

[10]On August 16, 1971, John Dean sent a memo to H. R. Haldeman entitled: "How We Can Use the Available Political Machinery to Screw Our Political Enemies," Berman, *The New American Presidency,* p. 174.

[11]Berman, *The New American Presidency,* p. 276.

[12]See the analysis in Genovese, *The Nixon Presidency,* p. 182.

[13]For details see Genovese, *The Nixon Presidency,* pp. 178–180.

[14]Genovese, *The Nixon Presidency,* p. 180.

These actions were part of a pattern of the Nixon administration to undermine the democratic process by using the power of the government to undermine the political opposition and stay in power, not giving voters a fair choice in the election. As Nixon said in September 1972: "I want the most comprehensive notes on all those who tried to do us in. . . . We have not used the power for this first four years. . . . We have never used it. We haven't used the Bureau and we haven't used the Justice Department, but things are going to change now. . . . They're going to get it right."[15]

White House operatives organized a secret team of "plumbers" in order to plug "leaks" of inside information from the White House. Among other things, the plumbers broke into the office of Daniel Elsberg's psychiatrist. Elsberg had given a copy of the Pentagon Papers—an internal Department of Defense account of the decision-making about the Vietnam War—to the *New York Times,* which published the account. Although the Supreme Court decided that the analysis of past decision-making did not threaten U.S. security, the Nixon administration evidently felt that discrediting Elsberg would affect the public's perception of the account in the Pentagon Papers.[16]

The third category of corruption was the series of actions to cover up the Watergate break-in, that is, using the powers of office to impede a criminal investigation. The initial incident from which this whole series of scandals received its name was the break-in by the plumbers into Democratic National Headquarters, which was located in the Watergate complex on the Potomac River in Washington. The break-in by burglars, who had been paid by campaign funds controlled by White House officials, was for the purpose of fixing a bug (listening device) that had been placed on Democratic National Committee Chairman Larry O'Brien's phone.

The break-in on June 17, 1972, was part of a larger plan formulated by G. Gordon Liddy and presented to John Mitchell, close friend of President Nixon and attorney general of the United States. The illegal entry was discovered when the burglars were caught breaking into the building, and the whole scheme began to unravel when it was discovered that the jailed burglars had connections to the Committee to Reelect the President and the White House. But for the remainder of 1972 the connection of the burglars to the White House was successfully covered up, and Nixon was reelected by a landslide. After congressional hearings and a criminal investigation by a special prosecutor were begun in 1973, the extent of White House involvement was gradually disclosed.

Although Richard Nixon denied that he had any knowledge of the White House connection to the Watergate break-in, he was in fact closely involved with the coverup from the beginning. Five days after the burglars were caught, H. R. Haldeman told the president that FBI investigators were tracing the money carried by the Watergate burglars and were about to discover that it had come from

[15]From the White House transcripts, quoted in Berman, *The New American Presidency,* p. 286.

[16]Berman, *The New American Presidency,* p. 285.

CREEP and White House safes. On June 23, 1972, Haldeman suggested that the way to stop the FBI investigation would be to have the CIA tell the FBI that further investigations would jeopardize CIA operations and that they should drop the money trail: "That the way to handle this now is for us to have Walters [of the CIA] call Pat Gray [Director of the FBI] and just say, 'Stay the hell out of this . . . this is ah, business here we don't want you to go any further on it,' That's not an unusual development, . . ." After this suggestion, Nixon told Haldeman to tell CIA director Richard Helms that: "the president believes that it is going to open the whole Bay of Pigs thing up again. And . . . that they [the CIA] should call the FBI in and [unintelligible] don't go any further into this case period!"[17] This exchange was the "smoking gun" that convinced the House Judiciary Committee, in 1974, to vote articles of impeachment. It clearly showed incontrovertible evidence in the president's own words that he wanted to use his powers as president to interfere with a criminal investigation. This was an obstruction of justice and a felony.

Nixon tried to impede the investigation in other criminal ways. The burglars who broke into the Watergate were in jail and threatened to disclose their connections to the White House unless they were paid money. Under threat of this blackmail and with the approval of the president, the burglars were given more than $500,000.[18] The president also urged his aides to commit perjury before the grand jury that was investigating the Watergate crimes in order to maintain the coverup. On March 21, 1973, Nixon told John Dean and Haldeman: "Perjury is a tough rap to prove. . . . just be damned sure you say, 'I don't remember, I can't recall.'"[19] Suborning of perjury is also a criminal felony.

When it was disclosed in congressional hearings that Nixon had a taping system in the Oval Office, the special prosecutor who was investigating the Watergate case subpoenaed them as evidence. Nixon refused to give up the tapes on the grounds of executive privilege—that such records were confidential to the executive branch. Under pressure, Nixon agreed to release transcripts of the tapes. But at the appeal of the special prosecutor, the Supreme Court decided unanimously to compel the release of the original tapes, and it was discovered that some of the transcripts had been altered in key places to cover up presidential involvement. It was also discovered that there was an eighteen-and-one-half-minute gap in the recording of a meeting on June 20, 1972, between Nixon and his top aides about the Watergate break-in. Experts concluded that the tape had been erased.

The release of the tapes and their damning evidence provided the final impetus for the House Judiciary Committee to vote on articles of impeachment. Once passed by the committee, the articles would go to the full House for a vote, and if passed, then go to the Senate, which would try the case and decide whether to convict the president on the charges and remove him from office. Im-

[17]White House Transcripts quoted in Berman, *The New American Presidency,* p. 287; and in Genovese, *The Nixon Presidency,* p. 189.

[18]Genovese, *The Nixon Presidency,* p. 190.

[19]Quoted in Berman, *The New American Presidency,* p. 287.

peachment Article I charged the president with failure to fulfill his oath of office and obstruction of justice. It mentioned specifically the break-in of Elsberg's psychiatrist's office, misuse of the CIA to obstruct the Justice Department investigation, withholding evidence, and counseling perjury, among other things. Article II charged the president with failing to faithfully execute the laws by using the IRS to harass his political opponents, by using the FBI to place unlawful wiretaps on citizens, by maintaining a secret investigative unit in the White House paid for by campaign funds, and by impeding criminal investigations, among other things. Article III charged the president with refusing to honor congressional subpoenas lawfully issued by the House Judiciary Committee and impeding the Congress from constitutionally exercising its impeachment powers.[20]

Two other articles were debated by the committee but rejected. One of the articles would have charged the president with the secret bombing of Cambodia during the Vietnam War, undermining the constitutional powers of Congress. But it was decided that though this may have been a political crime, it was not an indictable offense, and thus not appropriate for impeachment. The other article would have charged the president with income-tax evasion. But while this was clearly an indictable crime, it was not a political offense, and thus not appropriate for impeachment. The three articles that were adopted were both political and indictable crimes.[21] But before the articles could be presented to the full House for action, President Nixon resigned and left office on August 9, 1974.

Former-President Nixon and others have minimized Watergate as a "third rate burglary" and merely one in a series of a long line of presidential abuses of power. But as William Ruckelshaus, deputy attorney general for Nixon, said: "the break-in was trivial but what happened afterwards was not trivial. It was profound."[22]

The argument made by Nixon that "everybody does it" is also not convincing. In the first place, other crimes do not justify further crimes. But in the second place, the Watergate crimes were in important ways unprecedented in American history. According to historian C. Vann Woodward:

> Heretofore, no president has been proved to be the chief coordinator of the crime and misdemeanor charged against his own administration as a deliberate course of conduct or plan. Heretofore, no president has been held to be the chief personal beneficiary of misconduct in his administration or of measures taken to destroy or cover-up evidence of it. Heretofore, the malfeasance and misdemeanor have had no confessed ideological purpose, no constitutionally subversive ends. Heretofore, no president has been accused of extensively subverting and secretly using established government agencies to defame or discredit political opponents and critics, to obstruct justice, to conceal misconduct and protect criminals, or to deprive citizens of their rights and liberties. Heretofore, no president has

---

[20]The full texts of the impeachment articles are reprinted in Nelson, *Congressional Quarterly Guide to the Presidency,* pp. 1387–1388.

[21]See the analysis in Nelson, *Congressional Quarterly Guide to the Presidency,* p. 376.

[22]Quoted in Kutler, *The Wars of Watergate,* p. 226.

President Richard M. Nixon waves goodbye at the White House on August 9, 1974, the day that he resigned the presidency. (AP/Wide World Photos)

> been accused of creating secret investigative units to engage in covert and unlawful activities against private citizens and their rights.[23]

Regardless of the domestic and foreign policy accomplishments of the Nixon administration, Watergate must stand as a cautionary lesson in American constitutional history.

Iran-Contra

The Iran part of the Iran–Contra scandal, as described in the previous chapter, involved the sale of U.S. arms to Iran in hopes of freeing U.S. hostages held in Lebanon. The violation of declared U.S. policy and the reversal of U.S. posture toward Iran over the objections of the secretaries of state and defense may have been unwise, but they were not illegal. On the other hand, the possible violations of the Arms Export Control Act and the refusal of the administration to inform Congress of the covert operations are more serious matters. But these in-

[23]C. Vann Woodward, "The Conscience of the White House," in Woodward, ed., *Responses of the President to Charges of Misconduct* (New York: Dell, 1974), p. xxvi; quoted in Genovese, *The Nixon Presidency*, p. 226.

fractions, serious as they were, do not approach in constitutional magnitude the diversion of funds from the Iran arms sales to support the Contras in Nicaragua.

From the beginning of the 1980s, the Reagan administration felt the leftist Sandinista government of Nicaragua posed a serious threat to the United States. The administration therefore helped to create a rebel armed-military opposition to the regime called the Contras. Support of the Contras was a high priority throughout the Reagan administration. Financial and operational aid were provided to the Contras by the administration, but military aid was subject to a series of limitations written into public law between 1982 and 1986. Despite the best arguments of the Reagan administration, Congress was dubious of the wisdom and efficacy of continuing to arm the Contras. In November 1984, Congress passed, and President Reagan signed, a law providing continuing appropriations for fiscal year 1985. The law contained language, known as the Boland Amendment, prohibiting the United States from giving aid to the Contras during fiscal year 1985:

> During fiscal year 1985, no funds available to the Central Intelligence Agency, the Department of Defense, or any other agency or entity of the United States involved in intelligence activities may be obligated or expended for the purpose or which would have the effect of supporting, directly or indirectly, military or paramilitary operations in Nicaragua by any nation, group, organization, movement, or individual. [Public Law 98–473, 98 STAT 1935–37, sec. 8066][24]

Despite the law, the administration was committed to continuing support of the Contras. It was at this time that National Security staffer Lt. Col. Oliver North had the "neat idea" to use money received from the sale of arms to Iran to support the Contras. To carry this out, North and his colleagues set up secret accounts in Switzerland and funneled the money through them.

In addition to the funds obtained from selling U.S. arms to Iran (and thus the legal property of the U.S. government), the administration also raised funds by requesting money from Middle East nations. Some of these nations were the recipients of U.S. military aid. North and other White House aides also solicited donations from private U.S. citizens for the purpose of aiding the Contras. North later testified that CIA Director William Casey hoped to set up an entirely independent capacity (the "Enterprise") to conduct covert operations entirely independent of congressional appropriations.

This secret attempt to fund the Contras was in direct violation of public law and a serious threat to the Constitution. The president's aides decided that what they could not achieve through the public constitutional process (continuing aid to the Contras) they would accomplish through secret means. There was no doubt about what the law prohibited; there had been a high-level public debate over aid to the Contras throughout the 1980s, and the administration had not been able

---

[24]Quoted in Robert J. Spitzer, *President and Congress* (Philadelphia: Temple University Press, 1993), p. 223.

to convince a majority of the Congress that continued military aid to the Contras in 1985 was essential to U.S. security. But the White House aides decided that aid to the Contras ought to continue, and some argued that the White House was not covered by language in the Boland Amendment. There is no doubt that President Reagan strongly supported aid to the Contras and that he communicated this directly to his staff. Reagan, however, denied any knowledge of the diversion of funds to the Contras, a denial that was later disputed by Oliver North.

It was fairly clear that a majority of the U.S. public did not favor U.S. military action in Nicaragua. Public opinion polls demonstrated this, and the refusal of the Reagan reelection campaign in 1984 to highlight the issue, in hopes of getting a mandate to support the Contras during a second term, also attests to public attitudes. But public opinion is beside the constitutional point—the way authoritative public policy is determined is through the constitutional process. The results of that process seemed clear to many in 1985: no funds for the Contras.

Some members of the administration thought that raising funds from other nations and private citizens could get around the legal and constitutional problems. But others pointed out that with a public law prohibiting the United States from giving funds to the Contras, the funds were solicited from third-world nations who were dependent on the U.S. for military aid, and who had reasonable expectations (explicit or not) that, in the future, the U.S. would make up for any funds they sent to the Contras. From the perspective of critics of the administration, the power and authority of the presidency were being used to raise money for purposes forbidden by public law. Similarly, according to this interpretation, funds were solicited from wealthy individuals, not by private-citizen Oliver North, but by an official of the U.S. government, a Lt. Colonel in the Marines, who clearly represented the president and who intended to handle the funds through the White House. North brought President Reagan in to thank groups of people who donated money for their patriotism. These donors were giving money because they were assured by government officials that their money was being used to counter a threat to the United States.

Defenders of the Reagan administration and the signers of the minority report of the congressional investigating committees argued that the administration was guilty only of "mistakes in judgment, and nothing more." The minority report continued: "We grant that the diversion does raise some legal questions. . . ." But that the fundamental issues had to do "with the policy decisions themselves, and with the political judgments. . . ." and that treating the issues as legal questions was a sign of "interbranch intimidation."[25]

To critics of the diversion of funds, however, accountability is the key concept. The president and Congress are accountable to voters, and executive branch officials are accountable to the law. In the terms of the Constitution: "The President shall take care that the Laws be faithfully executed." The ma-

[25]Report of the Congressional Committees Investigating the Iran–Contra Affair, S. Rept. No. 100–216, H. Rept. No. 100–433 (November 1987), pp. 18–21.

jority report of the congressional committee investigating the Iran–Contra affair concluded:

> In the Iran–Contra Affair, officials viewed the law not as setting boundaries for their actions, but raising impediments to their goals. When the goals and the law collided, the law gave way. . . . [T]he ultimate responsibility for the events in the Iran–Contra Affair must rest with the President. If the President did not know what his National Security Advisers were doing, he should have. . . . It was the President's policy—not an isolated decision by North or Poindexter—to sell arms secretly to Iran and to maintain the Contras "body and soul," the Boland Amendment notwithstanding. To the NSC staff, implementation of these policies became the overriding concern.[26]

At the bottom of both the Watergate and the Iran–Contra scandals is the principle that the United States is a constitutional republic of limited government. U.S. constitutional principle rejects Nixon's justification: "When the president does it, that means it is not illegal."[27] In the United States, even the president is not above the law. As Supreme Court Justice Louis Brandeis put it: "Crime is contagious. If the Government becomes a lawbreaker, it breeds contempt for law, it invites every man to become a law unto himself, it invites anarchy."[28]

Both scandals also displayed a marked lack of respect for the balance between the two branches established in the Constitution. Members of both administrations sometimes failed to distinguish disagreement with the policy preferences of the members of the opposition party in Congress and contempt for the Congress itself. President Nixon decided to accomplish by administrative means what he could not get Congress to agree to by impounding funds, keeping secret his bombing of Cambodia, and refusing to release evidence vital to the Watergate investigation. The Reagan administration refused to comply with laws in continuing to send aid to the Contras. Some members of each administration interpreted the opposition of political opponents as disloyalty to the United States of America.

Both scandals are marked by ironies. The scandals that forced Nixon to resign and constituted the greatest threat to Reagan's presidency were not due to attacks by their political enemies but to actions by White House loyalists. The lessons of each scandal are that presidents must pay attention to White House management and ensure that their lower-level subordinates are kept on a tight leash. In the Watergate case, Liddy, Colson, and others should not have been allowed to go forward with their illegal and unethical attacks on Nixon's political opponents. In the Iran–Contra affair, the chief of staff and the president should have been aware of what White House staffers were doing in the president's name.

---

[26] *Iran–Contra Affair,* Report of the Congressional Committees (S. Rept. No. 100–216, H. Rept. 100–433, 1987), pp. 437, 442.

[27] Quoted in Kutler, *Wars of Watergate,* p. 614.

[28] Quoted in the Congressional Iran–Contra Affair Report, p. 22.

After disclosures of corruption in his administration, President Harding is quoted as having said to journalist William A. White: "My God, this is a hell of a job! I have no trouble with my enemies. . . . But my damned friends, my God-damned friends, White, they're the ones that keep me walking the floor nights."[29] But in each case the atmosphere engendered by the two presidents discouraged any dissent and tended to view it as disloyalty.

The final irony is that neither set of actions accomplished what it was supposed to accomplish. Richard Nixon did not need all the extra money and extralegal help in the 1972 campaign. He would have won the election in any case. If he had acknowledged the initial Watergate break-in and denounced the aides who perpetrated it, there would have been a brief scandal, but the obstruction of justice would not have happened, and Nixon would probably have served out his full second term. In Reagan's case, only a small percentage of the funds ($3.8 of $16.1 million) that were diverted to the Contras actually got to their alleged destination; the bulk of the money went to pay middlemen and into secret Swiss bank accounts for those involved.[30]

Both of these incidents demonstrate that the constitutional system in the United States is vulnerable to those who do not respect the rule of law and feel that their own policy ends justify extralegal and extraconstitutional means to achieve them. According to Justice Brandeis, "The greatest dangers to liberty lurk in insidious encroachment by men of zeal, well-meaning but without understanding."[31] In Watergate, the "men of zeal" felt that the reelection of the president was more important than the law. In Iran–Contra, the "men of zeal" felt they could judge the national security interests of the country better than the constitutional process.[32]

The Framers were right: power must be checked, and ambition must be made to counteract ambition. The balance among the branches is crucial to liberty and constitutional government. Justice Brandeis wrote:

> The doctrine of the separation of powers was adopted by the Convention of 1787, not to promote efficiency but to preclude the exercise of arbitrary power. The purpose was, not to avoid friction, but, by means of the inevitable friction incident to the distribution of the governmental powers among three departments, to save the people from autocracy.[33]

Watergate and Iran–Contra, insofar as the country treats them as aberrations to be deplored, will not be basic threats to the Republic. The system of checks and balances will have worked. But insofar as they are treated as precedents to justify

---

[29]Quoted in Nelson, *Congressional Quarterly Guide to the Presidency,* p. 108.

[30]Congressional Report on the Iran–Contra Affair, p. 274.

[31]Dissenting opinion in *Olmstead v. U.S.,* 277 U.S. 438 (1928), p. 479.

[32]See William S. Cohen and George J. Mitchell, *Men of Zeal* (New York: Viking, 1988).

[33]Quoted in Theodore Draper, *A Very Thin Line* (New York: Hill and Wang, 1991), p. 598.

further abuses, or to justify toleration of further abuses (everybody does it), they will have contributed to the undermining of the American system of government.

PRESIDENTIAL POPULARITY AND REPUTATION

Presidential reputations fluctuate over the years depending on current political issues, differing perspectives on historical eras, and historical scholarship. Historical reputation should not be confused with presidential popularity as measured by current public opinion polls because the two can often diverge dramatically.

Franklin Roosevelt is consistently seen as one of the great presidents, primarily because of his moral leadership and vision in leading the country through the traumas of the Great Depression and World War II. When he was in office, however, he was opposed by a significant portion of the political system because his policies were seen as hostile to business interests and as giving too much economic power to the federal government. His conviction that the United States had to enter World War II on the side of the allies encountered serious opposition in the Congress and in isolationist attitudes in the population. Only the Japanese attack on Pearl Harbor galvanized the country for war. In the negotiations at the end of World War II many felt that Roosevelt conceded too much influence to the Soviet Union.

Yet, in retrospect, there is a consensus across the political spectrum that FDR was a great president. The consensus is so widespread that even Ronald Reagan, the most conservative president since the 1920s, would invoke FDR in his speeches and champion the Social Security System that conservatives of the 1930s denounced as creeping socialism. With Reagan's blessing, FDR is firmly set in the pantheon of great presidents for the indefinite future.

Harry Truman inherited the presidency quite unprepared for it. At the end of the war, he said that he thought a million men were more qualified for the office than he was. During his years as president, many politicians on both sides of the political spectrum agreed with that assessment. The Republican Speaker of the House said that Truman was "the worst president in history," and liberals felt that he was such an unworthy heir to their hero FDR that they tried to draft Eisenhower to run as the Democratic nominee in 1948.[34] Yet, in 1948, Truman became the patron saint of presidents who are down in the polls and running for reelection when he came back from what was assumed to be Thomas Dewey's insurmountable lead to win election in his own right.[35] (See Table 8–1.)

Truman's approval rating in the public opinion polls dropped from a high

[34]Alan Brinkley, "Work Hard, Trust in God, Have No Fear," *New York Times Book Review* (June 21, 1992), p. 1.

[35]Harry Truman's daughter, Margaret, wrote an article taking exception to George Bush's invocation of her father's name in his acceptance speech at the Republican National Convention in 1992. She felt that New Dealer Truman would feel uncomfortable being referred to by conservative Republican Bush. *Washington Post* (August 27, 1992), p. A31.

TABLE 8–1
Public Approval Ratings, FDR to Clinton

President	Average Approval	At End of Term	1990 Approval
Roosevelt	75%	66%	75%
Truman	41	31	68
Eisenhower	65	59	70
Kennedy	71	58	84
Johnson	56	49	40
Nixon	48	24	32
Ford	47	53	55
Carter	47	34	50
Reagan	52	63	48
Bush	61	56	N/A
Clinton (1993–1996)	50 (first term)	N/A	N/A

Source: The Gallup Poll as reported in the *New York Times* (January 24, 1993), p. E3, updated from Gallup data.

of nearly 90 percent at the close of World War II to a low of 23 percent in November 1951, tying him with Richard Nixon in the midst of Watergate in January 1974.[36] Truman's attempt to extend the New Deal with his own liberal legislative program, known as the Fair Deal, was generally unsuccessful. He proposed national medical insurance and civil rights legislation, but was unable to win passage of the proposals in Congress. Many of his proposals were not to become public policy until the Johnson presidency.

The reversal of Truman's reputation from incompetent and unpopular arose out of a broad consensus that Truman "grew into the office" and provided firm leadership in the early years of the Cold War with the Soviet Union. Truman brought World War II in Europe and the Pacific to a close. He began the rebuilding of Europe with the Marshall Plan and helped to create the North Atlantic Treaty Organization. He committed the United States to countering aggression in Korea, but when General Douglas MacArthur maneuvered to extend the war north into China, Truman fired the war hero for insubordination. Since the early 1960s, Truman has consistently ranked in the top eight presidents in the estimation of presidency scholars.[37] (See Table 8–2.)

In contrast to Truman, President Eisenhower was quite popular during his eight years in office. His public-approval rating ranged from a high in the high-seventies to a low in the high-forties, with the average at the higher end of this range. The opinion of scholars and historians in the first decade after his presidency, however, did not coincide with public opinion in the 1950s. In a 1970 ranking of presidents, Eisenhower was placed at number twenty, right behind Herbert Hoover. In popular presidency textbooks he was often faulted for

[36] *Washington Post* (August 17, 1992), p. A11.

[37] See Arthur B. Murphy, "Evaluating the Presidents of the United States," in David C. Kozak and Kenneth N. Ciboski, eds., *The American Presidency* (Chicago: Nelson-Hall, 1985), pp. 437–448.

TABLE 8–2
Presidential Reputation

Schlesinger Poll 1948*	Schlesinger Poll 1962†	Maranell Accomplishment Poll 1970‡
Great	*Great*	*Accomplishments of*
1) Lincoln	1) Lincoln	*Administrations*
2) Washington	2) Washington	1) Lincoln
3) F. Roosevelt	3) F. Roosevelt	2) F. Roosevelt
4) Wilson	4) Wilson	3) Washington
5) Jefferson	5) Jefferson	4) Jefferson
6) Jackson		5) T. Roosevelt
	Near Great	6) Truman
Near Great	6) Jackson	7) Wilson
7) T. Roosevelt	7) T. Roosevelt	8) Jackson
8) Cleveland	8) Polk	9) L. Johnson
9) J. Adams	8) Truman	10) Polk
10) Polk	9) J. Adams	11) J. Adams
	10) Cleveland	12) Kennedy
Average		13) Monroe
11) J. Q. Adams	*Average*	14) Cleveland
12) Monroe	11) Madison	15) Madison
13) Hayes	12) J. Q. Adams	16) Taft
14) Madison	13) Hayes	17) McKinley
15) VanBuren	14) McKinley	18) J. Q. Adams
16) Taft	15) Taft	19) Hoover
17) Arthur	16) VanBuren	20) Eisenhower
18) McKinley	17) Monroe	21) A. Johnson
19) A. Johnson	18) Hoover	22) VanBuren
20) Hoover	19) B. Harrison	23) Arthur
21) B. Harrison	20) Arthur	24) Hayes
	20) Eisenhower	25) Tyler
Below Average	21) A. Johnson	26) B. Harrison
22) Tyler		27) Taylor
23) Coolidge	*Below Average*	28) Buchanan
24) Fillmore	22) Taylor	29) Fillmore
25) Taylor	23) Tyler	30) Coolidge
26) Buchanan	24) Fillmore	31) Pierce
27) Pierce	25) Coolidge	32) Grant
	26) Pierce	33) Harding
Failure	27) Buchanan	
28) Grant		
29) Harding	*Failure*	
	28) Grant	
	29) Harding	

No polls rate either W. Harrison or Garfield due to their short tenures in office.

*Arthur Schlesinger, Sr., "The U.S. Presidents," *Life* 65; 55 scholars polled.

†Arthur Schlesinger, Sr., "Our Presidents: A Rating by 75 Scholars," *New York Times Magazine* (July 29, 1962), 12ff.

‡A poll of 571 historians, the results published by Gary Maranell and Richard Dodder, "Political Orientation and Evaluation of Presidential Prestige," *Social Science Quarterly* 51 (September 1970), p. 418.

TABLE 8-2
(continued)

U.S. Historical Society Poll 1977[§]	*Chicago Tribune* Poll 1982[‖]	Murray Poll 1982[¶]	Schlesinger, Jr., Poll 1996[**]
Ten Greatest	*Ten Best*	*Presidential*	
Presidents	*Presidents*	*Rank*	*Great*
1) Lincoln	1) Lincoln (best)	1) Lincoln	Washington
2) Washington	2) Washington	2) F. Roosevelt	Lincoln
3) F. Roosevelt	3) F. Roosevelt	3) Washington	F. Roosevelt
4) Jefferson	4) T. Roosevelt	4) Jefferson	*Near Great*
5) T. Roosevelt	5) Jefferson	5) T. Roosevelt	John Adams
6) Wilson	6) Wilson	6) Wilson	Jefferson
7) Jackson	7) Jackson	7) Jackson	Jackson
8) Truman	8) Truman	8) Truman	Polk
9) Polk	9) Eisenhower	9) J. Adams	T. Roosevelt
10) J. Adams	10) Polk (10th best)	10) L. Johnson	Wilson
		11) Eisenhower	Truman
	Ten Worst Presidents	12) Polk	*Average (high)*
	1) Harding (worst)	13) Kennedy	John Adams
	2) Nixon	14) Madison	Monroe
	3) Buchanan	15) Monroe	Cleveland
	4) Pierce	16) J. Q. Adams	McKinley
	5) Grant	17) Cleveland	Eisenhower
	6) Fillmore	18) McKinley	Kennedy
	7) A. Johnson	19) Taft	L.B. Johnson
	8) Coolidge	20) VanBuren	*Average (low)*
	9) Tyler	21) Hoover	Madison
	10) Carter (10th worst)	22) Hayes	J.Q. Adams
		23) Arthur	Van Buren
		24) Ford	Hayes
		25) Carter	Arthur
		26) B. Harrison	B. Harrison
		27) Taylor	Taft
		28) Tyler	Ford
		29) Fillmore	Carter
		30) Coolidge	Reagan
		31) Pierce	Bush
		32) A. Johnson	Clinton
		33) Buchanan	*Below Average*
		34) Nixon	Tyler
		35) Grant	Taylor
		36) Harding	Fillmore
			Coolidge
			Failure
			Pierce
			Buchanan
			A. Johnson

Table 8-2
(continued)

U.S. Historical Society Poll 1977§	*Chicago Tribune* Poll 1982‖	Murray Poll 1982¶	Schlesinger, Jr., Poll 1996**
			Grant
			Harding
			Hoover
			Nixon

§Was first published by Robert E. DiClerico in his book *The American President* (Englewood Cliffs, NJ: Prentice-Hall, 1979) 332; 93 historians were polled.

‖ A survey of 49 leading scholars conducted by the *Chicago Tribune*. The analysis is in the *US News & World Report* (January 25, 1982), p. 29.

¶ A survey conducted by Dr. Robert K. Murray, professor of history at Pennsylvania State University in which 953 historians completed a seventeen-page questionnaire containing 155 questions. Dr. Murray's study appears in *Journal of American History*, December 1983; however, he furnished the author with the survey ratings on December 15, 1982.

**Note that ranking is only by category and that the names in each category are listed in chronological order. *Source:* Arthur Schlesinger, Jr., polled 32 historians, political scientists, and public figures in this poll taken in 1996. See Schlesinger, "The Ultimate Approval Rating," *The New York Times Magazine* (December 15, 1996), pp. 46–51.

Source (except Schlesinger, Jr.): Arthur B. Murphy, "Evaluating Presidents of the United States," in David C. Kozak and Kenneth N. Ciboski, eds., *The American Presidency* (Chicago: Nelson-Hall, 1985), pp. 437–448.

seeming not engaged in his own presidency, preferring to play golf while Sherman Adams ran the government.

Scholarly opinion was no doubt affected by the dashing figure of John Kennedy, who advocated an activist presidency. But by the 1980s polls of presidential reputation placed Eisenhower in the top ten or eleven, and a number of scholarly reassessments of Eisenhower came out in the 1980s. Some of these were based on the release of documents from the Eisenhower presidency that were not available earlier, and showed a president much more engaged in the politics of his administration than had been evident at the time. Eisenhower was seen as consciously projecting an image of not being familiar with the details of policies and relying on the presidential role as symbolic chief of state rather than as political head of government. It was, in Fred Greenstein's phrase, a "hidden-hand" presidency.[38]

In later years, after Vietnam, Watergate, and Iran–Contra, the orderly and deliberative procedures of the Eisenhower administration were seen much more as assets than as the liabilities that many perceived in the 1950s, when it seemed that bureaucratic procedures were stifling the policy process. Policy development through an Eisenhower-style National Security Council system would not have allowed an Iran–Contra scandal to occur.[39] After the ensuing three decades, there is also a greater appreciation of Eisenhower's ability to keep the United States out

[38]Fred I. Greenstein, *The Hidden-Hand Presidency* (New York: Basic Books, 1982).

[39]See Philip G. Henderson, *Managing the Presidency* (Boulder, CO: Westview Press, 1988).

of any major military confrontation after his conclusion of the Korean War. Orderly cabinet deliberations led to Eisenhower's refusal to commit the United States to a land war in Indochina.[40] Eisenhower also demonstrated a respect for Congress as a coequal branch of government that was sometimes lacking in future Republican Presidents Nixon, Reagan, and Bush.

John Kennedy's popularity and reputation were strongly affected by his assassination and the perception of him as a fallen hero. He won election, however, in one of the closest races in American history and did not have a mandate to deal from a position of strength with the Congress. He won a few victories, but was not able to get Congress to enact a significant legislative program. His moral leadership, however, was buttressed by his stirring rhetoric and ability to perform well at live press conferences and in the international sphere (after the Bay of Pigs). A number of future leaders of both political parties, including President Clinton, said that they had been drawn to elected office and public service by Kennedy's inspiring leadership and the charge in his inaugural address: "Ask not what your country can do for you, but rather ask what you can do for your country."

Perhaps because of Kennedy's ability to inspire with his rhetoric and polished style, there is a disjuncture between evaluations of him by historians, who rank him twelfth or thirteenth among presidents, and his popularity with the American public in general. (See Tables 8–1 and 8–2.) In surveys by the Gallup polling organization, people rank Kennedy first when asked: "What three presidents do you regard as the greatest?" and "Of all the presidents we have ever had, who do you wish were president today?"[41]

What Kennedy would have accomplished had he lived, and whether he would have withdrawn the 16,000 troops he had sent to Vietnam, will never be known. But it seems likely that he will continue to be seen as a hero by liberals, as the respected Cold-War confronter of Khrushchev by conservatives, and that his rhetoric will continue to be quoted by politicians of both political parties in the future. Three decades after Kennedy's election several biographies were published that were as one-sidedly negative in their evaluation as early biographies were one-sidedly positive.[42]

Lyndon Johnson won by a landslide, beating the conservative Barry Goldwater in 1964. Johnson will continue to be respected for his ability to put through Congress the large liberal agenda of 1965. Many of these programs still exist and are popular with Americans. Even though Ronald Reagan denounced Great Society programs as part of the governmental problem, he included some

---

[40]See John P. Burke and Fred I. Greenstein, *How Presidents Test Reality: Decisions on Vietnam, 1954 and 1965* (New York: Russell Sage, 1989).

[41]James M. Burns, J.W. Peltason, Thomas Cronin, and David B. Magleby, *Government By the People* (Englewood Cliffs, NJ: Prentice Hall, 1993), p. 442.

[42]Positive accounts of the Kennedy administration include memoirs by Theodore Sorensen, *Kennedy* (New York: Bantam, 1965); and Arthur Schlesinger, *A Thousand Days* (New York: Fawcett Publications, 1965). The negative biographies include Nigel Hamilton, *JFK, Reckless Youth* (New York: Random House, 1992); and Thomas C. Reeves, *A Question of Character: A Life of John F. Kennedy* (New York: Free Press, 1991).

of them in his "social safety net" of programs not to be touched in the 1981 budget cuts (e.g., Medicare, Medicaid, and Head Start). Johnson's wiles as a politician have been viewed with awe but also with distaste. According to White House aide Joseph Califano, Johnson was "brave and brutal, compassionate and cruel, incredibly intelligent and infuriatingly insensitive, with a shrewd and uncanny instinct for the jugular of his allies and adversaries. He could be altruistic and petty, caring and crude, generous and petulant, bluntly honest and calculatingly devious—all within the same few minutes."[43] While most historians see Johnson from this dual perspective, one influential biography has interpreted Johnson's life virtually entirely in terms of power and greed.[44]

Regardless of future evaluations of Johnson's political style and domestic program, his historical reputation will be dominated by the war in Vietnam. The war was widely seen as the first major military defeat for the United States. Those who were against the war felt that the United States had no business trying to impose its will in a civil war in Southeast Asia. Those who favored the war felt that Johnson imposed his own tactical judgment in what should have been strictly military decisions and that Johnson did not commit the United States firmly enough to win. The unpopularity of the war led Johnson, as it did Truman before him in another Asian war, to decide not to run for reelection in the face of almost certain defeat.

Richard Nixon will always be remembered as the president who resigned his office rather than submit to probable impeachment for his Watergate offenses. In the short run Watergate dominated Nixon's reputation, but his foreign policy triumphs were significant. The opening to China was a historic opportunity that probably only Nixon, with his unimpeachable anticommunist reputation, could have accomplished, given domestic political fears of communism. Similarly, the strategic arms limitation talks and détente with the Soviet Union were trusted only because of Nixon's legendary distrust of the Soviet Union. The domestic programs enacted during the Nixon administration were also significant (National Environmental Policy Act, Clean Air Act, Water Quality Improvement Act, Occupational Safety and Health Act, Equal Employment Opportunity Act, etc.), though some of these were forced on Nixon by the Democratic Congress. But it is likely that these programs will be overshadowed by the story of Nixon's battles with Congress and Watergate.

In the two decades after his resignation Nixon undertook a determined effort to rehabilitate himself by meeting with foreign leaders, conferring with Republican presidents, and writing a series of books on political and international affairs. In his writings and public appearances, Nixon consistently played down Watergate as a minor incident and emphasized the role of his political enemies in bringing him down. In the end, however, it is doubtful if his reinterpreta-

[43]Joseph Califano, *The Triumph and Tragedy of Lyndon Johnson* (New York: Simon and Schuster, 1991), p. 10.

[44]Robert Caro, *The Path to Power* (New York: Knopf, 1982), and *Means of Ascent* (Knopf, 1990). A third volume covering the presidential years is forthcoming.

tions will dispel the ghost of Watergate, regardless of the credit he may be given for his domestic and foreign policies.[45]

Jimmy Carter was defeated in his run for reelection under the cloud of hostages in Iran and runaway inflation in the economy. While it can be argued that there was no easy solution to the hostage crisis and that OPEC had much to do with inflation in the economy, Carter was not able to escape blame. He was seen as an ineffectual president, rejected by the voters and ridiculed by the Reagan administration. His foreign policy successes with the Camp David Peace Accords and the Panama Canal Treaties stand out but do not dominate his popular image.

It is still too early to judge what historians will conclude about the Carter administration, but there is little doubt that he will be seen as an admirable ex-president. After returning to Georgia, Carter undertook a number of good works throughout the world. He set up programs to eradicate specific debilitating diseases in many third-world countries. He set up peacemaking conferences for wars that were internal to countries rather than international. He promoted and worked for "Habitat for Humanity," which built housing for poor people throughout the country. In addition, he wrote several books. In the late 1980s and early 1990s there was some reevaluation of Carter's presidency in a positive direction, but his presidency is still too close in history for a balanced view.

There is no doubt that Ronald Reagan will go down as one of the most conservative of the modern presidents. He led a major change in public opinion over the role of government in the United States. He led the country through a large tax cut, large domestic cuts in spending, and the largest peacetime military build up in history. On the other hand, he presided over unprecedented budget deficits and a tripling of the national debt. He directed his staff to trade arms with Iran, and his management style allowed funds from the arms sales to be diverted to the Contras in Nicaragua. It is too early to speculate about Reagan's place in history, but it is likely that he will be given credit for the conservative direction of the country in the 1980s and will be blamed for the Iran–Contra affair. Reagan will be given credit by conservatives for hastening the fall of the Soviet Union with his aggressive spending on defense and will be given credit by most scholars for his encouragement of Premier Gorbachev's transitionary leadership. History's judgment of Reagan's fiscal policies will probably depend on the state of the U.S. economy in the early decades of the twenty-first century.

As vice president for Reagan, George Bush will share some of the credit or blame for the 1980s. As president, Bush will be credited with firm leadership in the Persian Gulf war, though it is still too early to know how much the United States contributed to Saddam Hussein's tyranny by U.S. aid to him in the 1980s. And it is too early to gauge the longer-term effects of the war on the Middle East or world peace. Bush will be credited with presiding skillfully over the end of the Cold War, but may be criticized for his lack of a vision for the "new world

[45]See Kutler, *The Wars of Watergate.*

order" that he proclaimed. Some important domestic legislation was passed during the Bush administration and progress was made with his 1990 budget deal with Congress that cut the deficit by about $500 billion over five years. But in the short run his policy record and vision were not sufficient to overcome public uncertainty about the economy, which was in a recession, and the attractiveness of Bill Clinton as a candidate.

The public evaluation of President Bush's performance reflects the ambivalence and volatility of U.S. public opinion toward presidents. In the first year of President Bush's presidency he enjoyed approval ratings between 60 and 78 percent, and in 1990 his approval ratings dropped from the high seventies to below 50 percent as the U.S. military build-up in the Persian Gulf expanded. With the U.S. victory in the Gulf war, Bush's public approval shot up to a historic peak of 90 percent. But from that record high, his public-approval ratings dropped steadily in the longest sustained drop in history (57 percentage points) to 33 percent in August of 1992.[46] While the economy was still performing sluggishly and the president had not reacted decisively to racial disturbances in Los Angeles, there were no major blunders or changes that explained the huge drop in popularity. Bush was the same man, with all of the assets and liabilities evident throughout his presidency and public career. The precipitous drop must be explained as much by exaggerated public expectations as by presidential performance.[47]

The historical evaluation of the Clinton administration is uncertain, but his reputation is unlikely to reach the great or near-great status, based on the evidence of his first term. He made progress with the budget deficit and economy with his first budget, and the federal deficit dropped to $107 billion in Fiscal Year 1996, the lowest since 1980. He had mixed success on his domestic priorities, with a significant defeat for his health care proposal. The major policy success in his first term came with his ability to counter the Republicans in the 104th Congress in their determination to make significant cuts in domestic programs. He was able to position himself as the protector of Medicare, Medicaid, education, and the environment and refused to change his stance even at the cost of shutting down the government. The voters rewarded him with reelection in 1996.

CONCLUSION: PUBLIC EXPECTATIONS AND THE PRESIDENCY

The very rating of presidents by historical reputation is an indicator of the importance that Americans attach to their presidents, an importance usually out of proportion to the power that presidents wield or their abilities to deliver on the expectations of them. The high level of power people assume presidents have—

[46] *Washington Post* (August 17, 1992), p. A11.

[47] See the insightful article by Marjorie Williams, "What We Know About George," *Washington Post Magazine* (August 16, 1992), p. 7.

either for good or for evil—is the result of several factors. One is the combination in the United States of the roles of symbolic chief of state with the more mundane role of head of government. The combination of the two roles in one office creates the opportunity for U.S. presidents to call on their symbolic role to shore up their political standing. But the combination of the two roles also creates high expectations in the electorate that the president will be above petty politics and will always act in the best long-term interests of the country.

Public expectations of U.S. presidents are magnified by the psychological functions they perform in the lives of Americans as symbols of the nation and vehicles for patriotic feelings. Schoolchildren are taught stories about early presidents, who come to symbolize historical periods for them. And the public tends to use the image of the president to reduce the complexity of American government and public policy.[48]

Despite the hagiography of presidents from the Federalist era and Lincoln, the nineteenth century did not create the high expectations that presidents would control the political agenda and deliver the country from all of its troubles. But in the early twentieth century, the Progressives raised expectations by advocating an activist central government led by a president who represented the national interest and who would counter the legislature, which was dominated by narrow sectional interests.[49]

Public expectations were further raised by Franklin Roosevelt and the birth of the modern presidency. Roosevelt was the symbol of U.S. resolve that got us through the Great Depression and the determination that won World War II. For the rest of the twentieth century, public expectations would force presidents to live "in the shadow of FDR."[50] In national security-making, presidents would now be aided by a centralized NSC staff. In the economic sphere, presidents would henceforth be aided by a Council of Economic Advisers and the national government would be responsible for full employment and the health of the economy.

After the Eisenhower hiatus from the activist presidency, public expectations were raised by John Kennedy's promise to "get the country moving again." The image of the presidency in contemporary textbooks was that of a powerful, benevolent, and forceful leader; often a liberal pitted against the conservative and regressive forces in Congress.

Public expectations were soon dashed by race riots in the cities of the 1960s, the quagmire of Vietnam, and the horrors of Watergate. But the postimperial presidencies of Ford and Carter did not suit U.S. tastes, and Reagan's 1981 return of grandeur to the office, along with his impressive early victories,

---

[48]See Thomas Cronin, "The Textbook and Prime-Time Presidency," *The State of the Presidency* (Boston: Little, Brown, 1980).

[49]See Lester G. Seligman and Cary R. Covington, *The Coalitional Presidency* (Chicago: Dorsey Press, 1989), chap. 2.

[50]William E. Leuchtenburg, *In the Shadow of FDR* (Ithaca, NY: Cornell University Press, 1983).

eased public fears of an imperilled presidency. He seemed to end the string of truncated presidencies after Eisenhower: Kennedy assassinated, Johnson forced not to run again, Nixon resigned, and Ford and Carter each defeated as incumbents.

But the lesson of the Reagan presidency is that even large electoral victories cannot ensure sustained policy performance. After the whirlwind performance of 1981, Reagan's legislative success steadily declined and he was not able to accomplish much of the rest of his conservative agenda. His second term brought the 1986 Tax Reform Act but was marred by the Iran–Contra scandal.

Americans' high expectations of their presidents are not sensitive to the fact that presidential powers are limited in the U.S. system. The failure of presidential policy performance, the inability to deliver on promises made, stems rather from unrealistic expectations and overpromising. It is not that presidents and candidates are so small; it is that the performance that we expect is so large.[51] Social trends (such as crime, drug use, or educational performance) in a country of 250 million people cannot be controlled by any one person or agency. A $7 trillion capitalist economy cannot be controlled by any one person or agency. The U.S. government is limited and cannot control our society or economy, and the result would be disastrous if it tried. Thus, our expectation that a president in our separation of powers system can control these broad forces is unrealistic. Americans tend to attribute more credit and blame to their presidents than a realistic assessment of actual presidential power would justify.

If presidential candidates would not overpromise, and citizens would lower their policy expectations of presidents, people might become less cynical and more realistic about U.S. politics. But in the United States, high public expectations of presidents will continue to prevail and will remain both an opportunity and a danger to U.S. presidents.

[51]See Charles Krauthammer, "Why Presidents Seem So Small," *Time* (June 20, 1988), p. 90.

Appendix A

PRESIDENTS OF THE UNITED STATES

1.	George Washington (F)	(1789–1797)
2.	John Adams (F)	(1797–1801)
3.	Thomas Jefferson (DR)	(1801–1809)
4.	James Madison (DR)	(1809–1817)
5.	James Monroe (DR)	(1817–1825)
6.	John Quincy Adams (DR)	(1825–1829)
7.	Andrew Jackson (D)	(1829–1837)
8.	Martin Van Buren (D)	(1837–1841)
9.	William Henry Harrison (W)	(1841)*
10.	John Tyler (W)	(1841–1845)
11.	James K. Polk (D)	(1845–1849)
12.	Zachary Taylor (W)	(1849–1850)*
13.	Millard Fillmore (W)	(1850–1853)
14.	Franklin Pierce (D)	(1853–1857)
15.	James Buchanan (D)	(1857–1861)
16.	Abraham Lincoln (R)	(1861–1865)†
17.	Andrew Johnson (R)	(1865–1869)
18.	Ulysses S. Grant (R)	(1869–1877)
19.	Rutherford B. Hayes (R)	(1877–1881)
20.	James A. Garfield (R)	(1881)†
21.	Chester A. Arthur (R)	(1881–1885)
22.	Grover Cleveland (D)	(1885–1889)
23.	Benjamin Harrison (R)	(1889–1893)
24.	Grover Cleveland (D)	(1893–1897)
25.	William McKinley (R)	(1897–1901)†
26.	Theodore Roosevelt (R)	(1901–1909)
27.	William H. Taft (R)	(1909–1913)
28.	Woodrow Wilson (D)	(1913–1921)
29.	Warren G. Harding (R)	(1921–1923)*
30.	Calvin Coolidge (R)	(1923–1929)
31.	Herbert C. Hoover (R)	(1929–1933)
32.	Franklin D. Roosevelt (D)	(1933–1945)*
33.	Harry S Truman (D)	(1945–1953)
34.	Dwight D. Eisenhower (R)	(1953–1961)
35.	John F. Kennedy (D)	(1961–1963)†
36.	Lyndon B. Johnson (D)	(1963–1969)
37.	Richard M. Nixon (R)	(1969–1974)‡
38.	Gerald R. Ford (R)	(1974–1977)§
39.	Jimmy Carter (D)	(1977–1981)
40.	Ronald Reagan (R)	(1981–1989)
41.	George Bush (R)	(1989–1993)
42.	Bill Clinton (D)	(1993–)

F = Federalist. DR = Democratic Republican. R = Republican. D = Democratic. W = Whig.
*Died in office of natural causes.
†Assassinated.
‡Resigned August 9, 1974.
§Appointed Vice President in 1973.

Appendix B

THE CONSTITUTION OF THE UNITED STATES OF AMERICA: ARTICLES I AND II

We the People of the United States, in Order to form a more perfect Union, establish Justice, insure domestic Tranquillity, provide for the common defence, promote the general Welfare, and secure the Blessings of Liberty to ourselves and our Posterity, do ordain and establish this Constitution for the United States of America.

Article I

SECTION 1. All legislative Powers herein granted shall be vested in a Congress of the United States, which shall consist of a Senate and House of Representatives.

SECTION 2. The House of Representatives shall be composed of Members chosen every second Year by the People of the several States, and the Electors in each State shall have the Qualifications requisite for Electors of the most numerous Branch of the State Legislature.

No Person shall be a Representative who shall not have attained to the age of twenty five Years, and been seven Years a Citizen of the United States, and who shall not, when elected, be an Inhabitant of that State in which he shall be chosen.

Representatives and direct Taxes shall be apportioned among the several States which may be included within this Union, according to their respective Numbers, which shall be determined by adding to the whole Number of free Persons, including those bound to Service for a Term of Years, and excluding Indians not taxed, three fifths of all other Persons. The actual Enumeration shall be made within three Years after the first Meeting of the Congress of the United States, and within every subsequent Term of ten Years, in such Manner as they shall by Law direct. The Number of Representatives shall not exceed one for every thirty Thousand, but each State shall have at Least one Representative and until such enumeration shall be made, the State of New Hampshire shall be entitled to chuse three, Massachusetts eight, Rhode-Island and Providence Plantations one, Connecticut five, New-York six, New Jersey four, Pennsylvania eight, Delaware one, Maryland six, Virginia ten, North Carolina five, South Carolina five, and Georgia three.

When vacancies happen in the Representation from any State, the Executive Authority thereof shall issue Writs of Election to fill such Vacancies.

The House of Representatives shall chuse their Speaker and other Officers; and shall have the sole Power of Impeachment.

SECTION 3. The Senate of the United States shall be composed of two Senators from each State, chosen by the Legislature thereof, for six Years; and each Senator shall have one Vote.

Immediately after they shall be assembled in Consequence of the first Election, they shall be divided as equally as may be into three Classes. The Seats of the Senators of the first Class shall be vacated at the Expiration of the second Year, of the second Class at the Expiration of the fourth Year, and of the third Class at the Expiration of the sixth Year, so that one third may be chosen every second Year; and if Vacancies happen by Resignation, or otherwise, during the Recess of the Legislature of any State, the Executive thereof may make temporary Appointments until the next Meeting of the Legislature, which shall then fill such Vacancies.

No Person shall be a Senator who shall not have attained to the Age of thirty Years, and been nine Years a Citizen of the United States, and who shall not, when elected, be an Inhabitant of that State for which he shall be chosen.

The Vice President of the United States shall be President of the Senate, but shall have no Vote, unless they be equally divided.

The Senate shall chuse their other Officers, and also a President pro tempore, in the Absence of the Vice President, or when he shall exercise the Office of President of the United States.

The Senate shall have the sole Power to try all Impeachments. When sitting for that Purpose, they shall be on Oath or Affirmation. When the President of the United States is tried the Chief Justice shall preside: And no Person shall be convicted without the Concurrence of two thirds of the Members present.

Judgment in Cases of Impeachment shall not extend further than to removal from Office, and disqualification to hold and enjoy any Office of honor, Trust or Profit under the United States: but the Party convicted shall nevertheless be liable and subject to Indictment, Trial, Judgment and Punishment, according to Law.

SECTION 4. The Times, Places and Manner of holding Elections for Senators and Representatives, shall be prescribed in each State by the Legislature thereof; but the Congress may at any time by Law make or alter such Regulations, except as to the Places of chusing Senators.

The Congress shall assemble at least once in every Year, and such Meeting shall be on the first Monday in December, unless they shall by Law appoint a different Day.

SECTION 5. Each House shall be the Judge of the Elections, Returns and Qualifications of its own Members, and a Majority of each shall constitute a Quorum to do Business; but a smaller Number may adjourn from day to day, and may be authorized to compel the Attendance of absent Members, in such Manner, and under such Penalties as each House may provide.

Each House may determine the Rules of its Proceedings, punish its Members for disorderly Behaviour, and, with the Concurrence of two thirds, expel a Member.

Each House shall keep a Journal of its Proceedings, and from time to time publish the same, excepting such Parts as may in their Judgment require Secrecy; and the Yeas and Nays of the Members of either House on any question shall, at the Desire of one fifth of those Present, be entered on the Journal.

Neither House, during the Session of Congress, shall, without the Consent of the other, adjourn for more than three days, nor to any other Place than that in which the two Houses shall be sitting.

SECTION 6. The Senators and Representatives shall receive a Compensation for their Services, to be ascertained by Law, and paid out of the Treasury of the United States. They shall in all Cases, except Treason, Felony and Breach of the Peace, be privileged from Arrest during their Attendance at the Session of their respective Houses, and in going to and returning from the same; and for any Speech or Debate in either House, they shall not be questioned in any other Place.

No Senator or Representative shall, during the Time for which he was elected, be appointed to any civil Office under the Authority of the United States, which shall have been created, or the Emoluments whereof shall have been encreased during such time; and no Person holding any Office under the United States, shall be a Member of either House during his Continuance in Office.

SECTION 7. All Bills for raising Revenue shall originate in the House of Representatives; but the Senate may propose or concur with amendments as on other Bills.

Every Bill which shall have passed the House of Representatives and the Senate, shall, before it become a Law, be presented to the President of the United States; If he approve he shall sign it, but if not he shall return it, with his Objections to that House in which it shall have originated, who shall enter the Objections at large on their Journal, and proceed to reconsider it. If after such Reconsideration two thirds of that House shall agree to pass the Bill, it shall be sent, together with the Objections, to the other House, by which it shall likewise be reconsidered, and if approved by two thirds of that House, it shall become a Law. But in all such Cases the Votes of both Houses shall be determined by Yeas and Nays, and the Names of the Persons voting for and against the Bill shall be entered on the Journal of each House respectively. If any Bill shall not be returned by the President within ten Days (Sunday excepted) after it shall have been presented to him, the Same shall be a Law, in like Manner as if he had signed it, unless the Congress by their Adjournment prevent its Return, in which Case it shall not be a Law.

Every Order, Resolution, or Vote to which the Concurrence of the Senate and House of Representatives may be necessary (except on a question of Adjournment) shall be presented to the President of the United States; and before the Same shall take Effect, shall be approved by him, or being disapproved by him, shall be repassed by two thirds of the Senate and House of Representatives, according to the Rules and Limitations prescribed in the Case of a Bill.

SECTION 8. The Congress shall have Power To lay and collect Taxes, Duties, Imposts and Excises, to pay the Debts and provide for the common Defence and general Welfare of the United States; but all Duties, Imposts and Excises shall be uniform throughout the United States;

To borrow Money on the credit of the United States;

To regulate Commerce with foreign Nations, and among the several States, and with the Indian Tribes;

To establish an uniform Rule of Naturalization, and uniform Laws on the subject of Bankruptcies throughout the United States;

To coin Money, regulate the Value thereof, and of foreign Coin, and fix the Standard of Weights and Measures;

To provide for the Punishment of counterfeiting the Securities and current Coin of the United States;

To establish Post Offices and post Roads;

To promote the Progress of Science and useful Arts, by securing for limited Times to Authors and Inventors the exclusive Right to their respective Writings and Discoveries;

To constitute Tribunals inferior to the supreme Court;

To define and punish Piracies and Felonies committed on the high Seas, and Offences against the Law of Nations;

To declare War, grant Letters of Marque and Reprisal, and make Rules concerning Captures on Land and Water;

To raise and support Armies, but no Appropriation of Money to that Use shall be for a longer Term than two Years;

To provide and maintain a Navy;

To make Rules for the Government and Regulation of the land and naval Forces;

To provide for calling forth the Militia to execute the Laws of the Union, suppress Insurrections and repel Invasions;

To provide for organizing, arming, and disciplining, the Militia, and for governing such Part of them as may be employed in the Service of the United States, reserving to the States respectively, the Appointment of the Officers, and the Authority of training the Militia according to the discipline prescribed by Congress;

To exercise exclusive Legislation in all Cases whatsoever, over such District (not exceeding ten Miles square) as may, by Cession of Particular States, and the

Acceptance of Congress, become the Seat of the Government of the United States, and to exercise like Authority over all Places purchased by the Consent of the Legislature of the State in which the Same shall be, for the Erection of Forts, Magazines, Arsenals, dock-Yards, and other needful Buildings;—And

To make all Laws which shall be necessary and proper for carrying into Execution the foregoing Powers, and all other Powers vested by this Constitution in the Government of the United States, or in any Department or Officer thereof.

SECTION 9. The Migration or Importation of such Persons as any of the States now existing shall think proper to admit, shall not be prohibited by the Congress prior to the Year one thousand eight hundred and eight, but a Tax or duty may be imposed on such Importation, not exceeding ten dollars for each Person.

The Privilege of the Writ of Habeas Corpus shall not be suspended, unless when in Cases of Rebellion or Invasion the public Safety may require it.

No Bill of Attainder or ex post facto Law shall be passed.

No Capitation, or other direct, Tax shall be laid, unless in Proportion to the Census of Enumeration herein before directed to be taken.

No Tax or Duty shall be laid on Articles exported from any State.

No Preference shall be given by any Regulation of Commerce or Revenue to the Ports of one State over those of another; nor shall Vessels bound to, or from, one State, be obliged to enter, clear or pay Duties in another.

No Money shall be drawn from the Treasury, but in Consequence of Appropriations made by Law; and a regular Statement and Account of the Receipts and Expenditures of all public Money shall be published from time to time.

No Title of Nobility shall be granted by the United States; And no Person holding any Office of Profit or Trust under them, shall, without the Consent of the Congress, accept of any present, Emolument, Office, or Title, of any kind whatever, from any King, Prince or foreign State.

SECTION 10. No State shall enter into any Treaty, Alliance, or Confederation; grant Letters of Marque and Reprisal; coin Money; emit Bills of Credit; make any Thing but gold and silver Coin a Tender in Payment of Debts; pass any Bill of Attainder, ex post facto Law, or Law impairing the Obligation of Contracts, or grant and Title of Nobility.

No State shall, without the Consent of the Congress, lay any Imposts or Duties on Imports or Exports, except what may be absolutely necessary for executing its inspection Laws; and the net Produce of all Duties and Imposts, laid by any State on Imports or Exports, shall be for the Use of the Treasury of the United States; and all such Laws shall be subject to the Revision and Control of the Congress.

No State shall, without the Consent of Congress, lay any Duty of Tonnage, keep Troops, or Ships of War in time of Peace, enter into any Agreement or

Compact with another State, or with a foreign Power, or engage in War, unless actually invaded, or in such imminent Danger as will not admit of delay.

Article II

SECTION 1. The executive Power shall be vested in a President of the United States of America. He shall hold his Office during the Term of four Years, and, together with the Vice President, chosen for the same Term, be elected, as follows

Each State shall appoint, in such Manner as the Legislature thereof may direct, a Number of Electors, equal to the whole Number of Senators and Representatives to which the State may be entitled in the Congress; but no Senator or Representative, or Person holding an Office of Trust or Profit under the United States, shall be appointed an Elector.

The Electors shall meet in their respective States, and vote by Ballot for two Persons, of whom one at least shall not be an Inhabitant of the same State with themselves. And they shall make a List of all the Persons voted for, and of the Number of Votes for each; which List they shall sign and certify, and transmit sealed to the Seat of the Government of the United States, directed to the President of the Senate. The President of the Senate shall, in the Presence of the Senate and House of Representatives, open all the Certificates, and the Votes shall then be counted. The Person having the greatest Number of Votes shall be the President, if such Number be a Majority of the whole Number of Electors appointed; and if there be more than one who have such Majority, and have an equal Number of Votes, then the House of Representatives shall immediately chuse by Ballot one of them for President; and if no Person have a Majority, then from the five highest on the List the said House shall in like Manner chuse the President. But in chusing the President, the Votes shall be taken by States, the Representation from each State having one Vote; a quorum for this Purpose shall consist of a Member or Members from two thirds of the States, and a Majority of all the States shall be necessary to a Choice. In every Case, after the Choice of the President, the Person having the greatest Number of Votes of the Electors shall be the Vice President. But if there should remain two or more who have equal Votes, the Senate shall chuse from them by Ballot the Vice President.

The Congress may determine the Time of chusing the Electors, and the Day on which they shall give their votes; which Day shall be the same throughout the United States.

No Person except a natural born Citizen, or a Citizen of the United States, at the time of the Adoption of this Constitution, shall be eligible to the Office of President; neither shall any person be eligible to that Office who shall not have attained to the Age of thirty five Years, and been fourteen Years a Resident within the United States.

In Case of the Removal of the President from Office, or of his Death, Resignation, or Inability to discharge the Powers and Duties of the said Office, the Same shall devolve on the Vice President, and the Congress may by Law provide for the

Case of Removal, Death, Resignation or Inability, both of the President and Vice President, declaring what Officer shall then act as President, and such Officer shall act accordingly, until the Disability be removed, or a President shall be elected.

The President shall, at stated Times, receive for his Services, a Compensation, which shall neither be encreased nor diminished during the Period for which he shall have been elected, and he shall not receive within that Period any other Emolument from the United States, or any of them.

Before he enter on the Execution of his Office, he shall take the following Oath or Affirmation: "I do solemnly swear (or affirm) that I will faithfully execute the Office of President of the United States, and will to the best of my Ability, preserve, protect and defend the Constitution of the United States."

SECTION 2. The President shall be Commander in Chief of the Army and Navy of the United States, and of the Militia of the several States, when called into the actual Service of the United States; he may require the Opinion, in writing, of the principal Officer in each of the executive Departments, upon any Subject relating to the Duties of their respective Offices, and he shall have Power to grant Reprieves and Pardons for Offenses against the United States, except in Cases of Impeachment.

He shall have Power, by and with the Advice and Consent of the Senate, to make Treaties, provided two thirds of the Senators present concur; and he shall nominate, and by and with the Advice and Consent of the Senate, shall appoint Ambassadors, other public Ministers and Consuls, Judges of the supreme Court, and all other Officers of the United States, whose Appointments are not herein otherwise provided for, and which shall be established by Law; but the Congress may by Law vest the Appointment of such inferior Officers, as they think proper, in the President alone, in the Courts of Law, or in the Heads of Departments.

The President shall have Power to fill up all Vacancies that may happen during the Recess of the Senate, by granting Commissions which shall expire at the End of their next Session.

SECTION 3. He shall from time to time give to the Congress Information of the State of the Union, and recommend to their Consideration such Measures as he shall judge necessary and expedient; he may, on extraordinary Occasions, convene both Houses, or either of them, and in Case of Disagreement between them, with Respect to the Time of Adjournment, he may adjourn them to such Time as he shall think proper; he shall receive Ambassadors and other public Ministers; he shall take Care that the Laws be faithfully executed, and shall Commission all the Officers of the United States.

SECTION 4. The President, Vice President and all Civil Officers of the United States, shall be removed from Office on Impeachment for, and Conviction of, Treason, Bribery, or other high Crimes and Misdemeanors.

Appendix C

CONSTITUTIONAL AMENDMENTS THAT AFFECT THE PRESIDENCY: AMENDMENTS XII, XX, XXII, AND XXV

Amendment XII (1804)

The Electors shall meet in their respective states, and vote by ballot for Pre
ident and Vice President, one of whom, at least shall not be an inhabitant of t
same state with themselves; they shall name in their ballots the person voted
as President, and in distinct ballots the person voted for as Vice-President, a
they shall make distinct lists of all persons voted for as President, and of all p
sons voted for as Vice-President, and of the number of votes for each, which li
they shall sign and certify, and transmit sealed to the seat of the government
the United States, directed to the President of the Senate;—The President of t
Senate shall, in the presence of the Senate and House of Representatives, op
all the certificates and the votes shall then be counted;—The person having
greatest number of votes for President, shall be the President, if such number
a majority of the whole number of Electors appointed; and if no person ha
such majority, then from the persons having the highest numbers not exceedi
three on the list of those voted for as President, the House of Representati
shall choose immediately, by ballot, the President. But in choosing the Preside
the votes shall be taken by states, the representation from each state having c
vote; a quorum for this purpose shall consist of a member or members from tw
thirds of the states, and a majority of all the states shall be necessary to a choi
[And if the House of Representatives shall not choose a President whenever
right of choice shall devolve upon them, before the fourth day of March next
lowing, then the Vice-President shall act as President, as in the case of the de
or other constitutional disability of the President—] The person having the gre
est number of votes as Vice-President, shall be the Vice-President, if such nu
ber be a majority of the whole number of Electors appointed, and if no pers
have a majority, then from the two highest numbers on the list, the Senate sh
choose the Vice-President; a quorum for the purpose shall consist of two-th
of the whole number of Senators, and a majority of the whole number shall

necessary to a choice. But no person constitutionally ineligible to the office of President shall be eligible to that of Vice-President of the United States.

Amendment XX (1933)

SECTION 1. The terms of the President and Vice President shall end at noon on the 20th day of January, and the terms of Senators and Representatives at noon on the 3d day of January, of the years in which such terms would have ended if this article had not been ratified; and the terms of their successors shall then begin.

SECTION 2. The Congress shall assemble at least once every year, and such meeting shall begin at noon on the 3d day of January, unless they shall by law appoint a different day.

SECTION 3. If, at the time fixed for the beginning of the term of the President, the President elect shall have died; the Vice President elect shall become President. If a President shall not have been chosen before the time fixed for the beginning of his term, or if the President elect shall have failed to qualify, then the Vice President elect shall act as President until a President shall have qualified; and the Congress may by law provide for the case wherein neither a President elect nor a Vice President elect shall have qualified, declaring who shall then act as President, or the manner in which one who is to act shall be selected, and such person shall act accordingly until a President or Vice President shall have qualified.

SECTION 4. The Congress may by law provide for the case of the death of any of the persons from whom the House of Representatives may choose a President whenever the right of choice shall have devolved upon them, and for the case of the death of any of the persons from whom the Senate may choose a Vice President whenever the right of choice shall have devolved upon them.

SECTION 5. Sections 1 and 2 shall take effect on the 15th day of October following the ratification of this article.

SECTION 6. This article shall be inoperative unless it shall have been ratified as an amendment to the Constitution by the legislatures of three-fourths of the several States within seven years from the date of its submission.

Amendment XXII (1951)

SECTION 1. No person shall be elected to the office of the President more than twice, and no person who has held the office of President, or acted as President, for more than two years of a term to which some other person was elected President shall be elected to the office of President more than once. But this Article shall not apply to any person holding the office of President when this Article was proposed by the Congress, and shall not prevent any person who may be holding the office of President, or acting as President, during the term within which this Article becomes operative from holding the office of President or acting as President during the remainder of such term.

SECTION 2. This article shall be inoperative unless it shall have been ratified as an amendment to the Constitution by the legislatures of three-fourths of the several States within seven years from the date of its submission to the States by the Congress.

Amendment XXV (1967)

SECTION 1. In the case of the removal of the President from office or of his death or resignation, the Vice President shall become President.

SECTION 2. Whenever there is a vacancy in the office of the Vice President, the President shall nominate a Vice President who shall take office upon confirmation by a majority vote of both Houses of Congress.

SECTION 3. Whenever the President transmits to the President pro tempore of the Senate and the Speaker of the House of Representatives his written declaration that he is unable to discharge the power and duties of his office, and until he transmits to them a written declaration to the contrary, such powers and duties shall be discharged by the Vice President as Acting President.

SECTION 4. Whenever the Vice President and a majority of either the principal officers of the executive departments or of such a body as Congress may by law provide, transmit to the President pro tempore of the Senate and the Speaker of the House of Representatives their written declaration that the President is unable to discharge the powers and duties of his office, the Vice President shall immediately assume the powers and duties of the office as Acting President.

Thereafter, when the President transmits to the President pro tempore of the Senate and the Speaker of the House of Representatives his written declaration that no inability exists, he shall resume the powers and duties of his office unless the Vice President and a majority of either the principal officers of the executive department or of such other body as Congress may by law provide, transmit within four days to the President pro tempore of the Senate and the Speaker of the House of Representatives their written declaration that the President is unable to discharge the powers and duties of his office. Thereupon Congress shall decide the issue, assembling within forty-eight hours for that purpose if not in session. If the Congress, within twenty-one days after receipt of the latter written declaration, or, if Congress is not in session, within twenty-one days after Congress is required to assemble, determines by two-thirds vote of both Houses that the President is unable to discharge the powers and duties of his office, the Vice President shall continue to discharge the same as Acting President; otherwise, the President shall resume the powers and duties of his office.

Index